CISI

CHARTERED INSTITUTE FOR SECURITIES & INVESTMENT

Certificate in Global Financial Compliance

Global Financial Compliance

Edition 9, July 2021

This learning manual relates to syllabus version 9.1 and will cover exams from **1 October 2021 to 30 September 2023**

APPROVED WORKBOOK

CISI
CHARTERED INSTITUTE FOR SECURITIES & INVESTMENT

Welcome to the Chartered Institute for Securities & Investment's Global Financial Compliance study material.

This workbook has been written to prepare you for the Chartered Institute for Securities & Investment's Global Financial Compliance examination.

Published by:
Chartered Institute for Securities & Investment

20 Fenchurch Street
London
EC3M 3BY
Tel: +44 20 7645 0600
Fax: +44 20 7645 0601

Email: customersupport@cisi.org
www.cisi.org/qualifications

Author:
Dr Natalie Schoon ACSI

Reviewers:
Alwyn Li, ACCA, CIA, CCSA, CAMS, IOC+
Karl Micallef

A learning map, which contains the full syllabus, appears at the end of this workbook. The syllabus can also be viewed on cisi.org and is also available by contacting the Customer Support Centre on +44 20 7645 0777. Please note that the examination is based upon the syllabus. Candidates are reminded to check the Candidate Update area details (cisi.org/candidateupdate) on a regular basis for updates as a result of industry change(s) that could affect their examination.

The questions contained in this workbook are designed as an aid to revision of different areas of the syllabus and to help you consolidate your learning chapter by chapter.

Workbook version: 9.1 (July 2021)

Learning and Professional Development with the CISI

The Chartered Institute for Securities & Investment is the leading professional body for those who work in, or aspire to work in, the investment sector, and we are passionately committed to enhancing knowledge, skills and integrity – the three pillars of professionalism at the heart of our Chartered body.

CISI examinations are used extensively by firms to meet the requirements of government regulators. Besides the regulators in the UK, where the CISI head office is based, CISI examinations are recognised by a wide range of governments and their regulators, from Singapore to Dubai and the US. Around 50,000 examinations are taken each year, and it is compulsory for candidates to use CISI workbooks to prepare for CISI examinations so that they have the best chance of success. Our workbooks are normally revised every year by experts who themselves work in the industry and also by our Accredited Training Partners, who offer training and elearning to help prepare candidates for the examinations. Information for candidates is also posted on a special area of our website: cisi.org/candidateupdate.

This workbook not only provides a thorough preparation for the examination it refers to, it is also a valuable desktop reference for practitioners, and studying from it counts towards your Continuing Professional Development (CPD). Mock examination papers, for most of our titles, will be made available on our website, as an additional revision tool.

CISI examination candidates are automatically registered, without additional charge, as student members for one year (should they not be members of the CISI already), and this enables you to use a vast range of online resources, including CISI TV, free of any additional charge. The CISI has more than 40,000 members, and nearly half of them have already completed relevant qualifications and transferred to a core membership grade. You will find more information about the next steps for this at the end of this workbook.

CISI

CHARTERED INSTITUTE FOR SECURITIES & INVESTMENT

1 2 3 4 5

It is estimated that this manual will require approximately 75 hours of study time.

What next?

See the back of this book for details of CISI membership.

Need more support to pass your exam?

See our section on Accredited Training Partners.

Want to leave feedback?

Please email your comments to learningresources@cisi.org

CISI
CHARTERED INSTITUTE FOR SECURITIES & INVESTMENT

VOP – variation of permission

LEA – law enforcement agency

FATF – financial action task force

UNODC united nations office on drugs + crime

IMF international monetary fund

FSAP financial security assessment programme

OFC off shore financial centre

TTF tropical trust funds

World bank – International bank for reconstruction + development + international development

StAR Stolen asset recovery initiative

WGTM – working group on terrorist financing + money laundering ~~project team~~

PFPT project team on proliferation finance

UNCAC united nations against crime

FinCEN financial crimes enforcement network

OFAC office of foreign control

Shariah Supervisory board (SSB)

ISO international standards organisation

TCFD – task force climate related financial disclosures

OECD organisation for economic co operation + development

NCCU National Cyber Crime Unit

Chapter One

The International Regulatory Environment

This syllabus area will provide approximately 20 of the 100 examination questions

CISI
CHARTERED INSTITUTE FOR SECURITIES & INVESTMENT

BSBS – Basel committee banking supervision
IOSCO – International organisation of securities commission
SRO – self regulatory organisations
ISDA – international and derivatives association
AAOIFI – Accounting + Auditing organisation for Islamic financial institutions
IFSB – Islamic Financial Services Board
ICB – independent commission on banking
FDIC
SIPC – securities investor protection corporation
FSOC – Financial stability oversight council +
OFR – Office of financial research
– Bureau of consumer financial protection
PSD2 – payment services directive 2
PCAOB – Public Co Accounting Oversight Board (PCAOB)
OECD – Organisation for economic co operation + development
IRS – internal revenue service
DNFBP – Designated non financial businesses + professions
FATF / Financial action task force
CDD – customer due diligence
ESMA – European securities markets authority
SI – systematic internalizers
BIS – Bank of international settlements
IBFed – international banking federation
FSB – financial stability board
ESFS – European system of financial supervision
EIOPA – European insurance occupational pension authority
ESA – European supervisory authorities
ESRB – European systematic risk board.
SEC – Securities exchange Commission
FSOC – Financial stability oversight Council
BCBS
EBA – european banking authority
capital adequacy eg? BIS basel II + III rules FVS
solvency directive

1. Models of Regulation

1.1 Objectives and Benefits of Regulation

Learning Objective

1.1.1 Understand the objectives and benefits of regulation

Effective capital and financial markets are an essential part of the economy. They fuel economic development and aid wealth creation. Confidence and trust in these markets are vital. Loss of confidence and trust can result in the failure of financial companies and have an adverse impact on the economy. This can, among others, result in recession, loss of jobs and income, reduction of the value of investments, reduction in market capitalisation of companies, and defaults on loans. The near collapse of large financial institutions during the 2007–8 financial crisis had a global impact and the subsequent bailout of the banks, reduction in government spending and increase in taxes has had a far-reaching impact on individuals and corporations.

As the Basel Committee for Banking Supervision (BCBS) notes in their corporate governance principles, banks and, by extension financial markets, play a crucial role in the economy by intermediating funds from savers and depositors to activities that support enterprise and help drive economic growth. Their safety and soundness are key to financial stability, and therefore, corporate governance. Thus, rules and codes of conduct are of the utmost importance to protect investors and the general public. Although the development of such rules and the extent to which they are enforced still varies from country to country, the development of global financial markets depends on an agreement on standards of behaviour and mechanisms for dispute resolution. These standards, rules and codes of conduct can be established through self-regulation of the industry, or by means of a statutory approach where governments provide enabling legislation and establish statutory-based regulatory authorities. Integrity and ethical behaviour are a key part of any code of conduct. As a result of the financial crisis, integrity and ethical behaviour has experienced renewed focus from professional bodies, governments and regulators. As financial markets have become increasingly global in nature and interdependence has grown, the financial sector has moved from self-regulation to a statutory approach. This has facilitated international cooperation and the development of improved and common standards.

Regulation has also been used to restrict the ability of criminals and terrorists to use the financial system to their advantage, and to aid enforcement and intelligence agencies to identify criminal activity. Again, this has developed from purely domestic initiatives to major international efforts to reduce crime related to financial services. These crimes include **money laundering**, fraud and tax evasion.

The objectives and benefits of regulation can be summarised as follows:

- increase in confidence and trust in financial markets, systems and products
- establish an environment to encourage economic development and wealth creation
- reduce the risk of market and system failures including their economic consequences
- enhance consumer protection, giving them the reassurance they need to save and invest, and
- reduce financial crime by ensuring financial systems cannot easily be exploited.

1.2 Law and Regulation

Learning Objective

1.1.2 Know the interaction between law and regulation

The objectives and benefits of regulation are typically achieved through a combination of laws and regulations.

Law – the principles and regulations established in a community by an authority and applicable to the people. Laws can be a combination of legislation, custom, and policies recognised and enforced by judicial decision. When a person is found guilty of breaking the law, they are typically punished with a reprimand, a prison sentence and/or a penalty. Financial services legislation provides the structural framework for the sector itself as well as the products it offers. In the UK, for example, key legislation includes the Financial Services and Markets Act 2000 (FSMA), which sets out the UK's regulatory structure, and multiple Finance Acts which contain provisions related to taxes, duties, exemptions and reliefs. National and international laws regarding the prevention of money laundering (ML) and terrorist financing (TF), tax and other financial services-related crimes will be incorporated into the appropriate regulations relevant to the structuring of banking or other financial products or customer advice.

Regulation – combination of rules and standards generally covering matters such as observing proper standards of market conduct, managing conflicts of interest, treating customers fairly, ensuring the suitability of customer advice, and ensuring stability of the financial system.

Compliance laws, rules and standards have various sources including:

- primary legislation
- rules and standards issued by legislators and supervisors
- market conventions
- codes of practice promoted by industry associations or professional bodies, and
- internal codes of conduct applicable to the staff members of financial institutions.

Industry and internal codes are likely to go beyond what is legally binding and embrace broader standards of integrity and ethical conduct.

1.3 Rules-Based and Principles-Based Approaches

Learning Objective

1.1.3 Understand the main differences between rules-based and principles-based approaches to financial regulation

When drafting regulation, regulators make a choice between rules-based and principles-based regulation.

- **Rules-based** – rules-based regulations are mainly prescriptive procedures including very detailed rules. These rules specify exactly what individuals and firms must do to ensure they comply. A rules-based approach requires strict adherence to precise rules with little allowance for interpretation. It is typically inflexible and may result in a tick-box exercise.
- **Principles-based** – principle-based regulations focus on the spirit of the rules and, therefore, the types of behaviour and outcomes. Unlike the rules-based approach, it is not about blindly following the rules. A principles-based approach acts as a fundamental source of guidance on how firms and individuals are expected to act. How individuals and firms ensure they comply with the regulations, and to what extent the principles are met, is their own responsibility.

A rules-based approach must be sufficiently detailed in order to provide a reliable distinction between right and wrong. Maintaining a comprehensive rules-based model is challenging, particularly in evolving markets with an increase in the use of technology, and a wider range of products and assets. A broader and more complicated market requires a larger body of rules which take into account evolving business activities.

The challenge faced by regulators with a principles-based approach is ensuring that firms apply consistent interpretations to their implementation of the principles.

Some firms and compliance officers prefer a rules-based approach because they know exactly what is expected of them, and they cannot be challenged or criticised as long as they strictly follow the rules. Others prefer a principles-based approach because it provides scope for innovation and the freedom to develop services and business models within the framework of the principles.

The success of a principles-based approach depends on firms and individuals making the right decisions. Strong ethical standards, often set by professional bodies like the Chartered Institute for Securities & Investment (CISI), play a key role in a principles-based regulatory environment (see chapter 4, Ethics, Integrity and Fairness).

Since 2001, the UK's financial regulators have applied a combination of principles- and rules-based approaches. The **Financial Conduct Authority (FCA)** has actively reduced prescriptive rules by adopting a more principles-based approach. One of the results of the 2008–09 financial crisis is that principles-based decision-making is deemed to have failed, leading to a greater focus on the specific outcomes expected by rules-based regulation. The demand for stricter rules is a natural political reaction to a crisis, and principles-based decision making will remain important.

1.4 Models of Self-Regulation

Learning Objectives

1.1.4 Understand models of self-regulation

1.1.5 Understand the regulation of faith- and ethical-based finance and the attendant regulatory implications

Self-regulation is a situation in which groups or industries mutually agree the rules that will govern their own collective behaviours. It exists in addition to laws or regulations established by governments or regulatory bodies. In some cases, self-regulation develops because there is no regulation in place. While self-regulation measures must operate within the parameters of national laws, strong self-regulation can reduce the need for, or extent of, state regulation.

In the financial sector, self-regulation is typically a unique combination of private interests with government oversight, which has delivered an effective and efficient form of regulation for the complex and dynamic environment. As stated in a report by the International Organization of Securities Commissions (IOSCO) on Objectives and Principles of Securities Regulation: *'Self-regulatory organisations (SROs) can be a valuable component to the regulator in achieving the objectives of securities regulation'.*

The adoption of self-regulation differs from country to country, across market sectors and across developed and emerging markets. Where its role is significant, it is almost always the result of a long track record of responsible behaviour under the oversight of statutory regulators. That relationship with statutory regulators has permitted SROs to contribute to the quality of regulation and to the content of policy in the public interest.

The broad objectives of self-regulation in financial markets are the same as those identified for government regulation in the IOSCO Objectives and Principles of Securities Regulation:

- to preserve market integrity (fair, efficient and transparent markets)
- to preserve financial integrity (reduce systemic risk), and
- to protect investors.

Many different forms of self-regulation currently exist for financial markets to achieve these objectives such as:

- industry SROs
- exchange self-regulatory frameworks, and
- private associations.

All of these define and encourage adherence to standards of best practice among their participants.

Self-regulation typically focuses on oversight of the market itself, qualification standards for market intermediation and oversight of the business conduct of intermediaries. Business conduct of intermediaries includes their relationship with their **client** market-users. A single SRO may be responsible for all of these tasks or they may be divided or shared among SROs within a given country or market sector.

Some approaches may be applied purely within the organisation, such as ethical-based finance. A firm may hold strong principles that guide its investment policies (eg, avoidance of sectors such as weaponry or tobacco). A firm might also choose to market itself according to ethical positions because it meets their values, or to attract certain customers. While there may be no specific independent party overseeing such practices, a firm that publicly takes a moral position must ensure its reputation is secure.

1.4.1 Key Elements of an Effective Self-Regulatory Model

The elements which contribute to an effective self-regulatory model include:

- **Industry specialised knowledge** – important given the complexity of markets and products.
- **Industry motivation** – business incentive to operate a fair, financially sound and competitive marketplace. Reputation and competition are powerful motivating forces for sustained behaviour.
- **Contractual relationship** – this can go beyond national boundaries and require ethical standards that go beyond government regulations.
- **Transparency and accountability** – an SRO's compliance programme should be transparent and accountable to ensure that SROs follow professional standards of behaviour on matters including confidentiality and procedural fairness. Such transparency can occur in different ways, including making SRO rules accessible to the public in printed or digital form, and by publicising significant disciplinary actions taken by an SRO and through educational outreach programmes. The inclusion of both public representatives and industry professionals on an SRO's governing body and public participation in deliberations pertaining to regulatory policy and rule making can also provide the foundation for an open organisation. In some jurisdictions, SROs prepare regulatory plans that are submitted to their statutory regulator and made available to the public. These regulatory plans describe the SRO's regulatory objectives, activities for the year, and a cost forecast.
- **Flexible SRO compliance programmes** – self-regulatory bodies are generally able to modify their rules quicker than government agencies. This is due to their experience and expertise in the industry, their size, and because they are not subject to the more rigid requirements typically imposed on the rule-making process of statutory regulators.
- **Coordination and sharing information** – coordination and information sharing between markets is important to address cross-market issues. A coordinated approach is necessary to address potential **market abuse** or systemic risk concerns that may impact more than one market.

In 2000, a report by IOSCO's SRO Consultative Committee (*Model for Effective Regulation*) indicated that an SRO's common regulatory practices and objectives should include:

- enforcing rules and regulations through investigations and disciplinary action
- conducting financial/operations and sales practice examinations
- conducting fitness screening for access to marketplace
- handling customer complaints
- having surveillance programmes to detect improper conduct
- sharing information and cooperating with other SROs, and
- providing a dispute resolution forum.

An integral component of many SRO compliance programmes is the development of guidebooks and other educational materials to help their members meet their regulatory responsibilities.

An example of self-regulation is the use of the International Swaps and Derivatives Association (ISDA) Master Agreement. ISDA is a membership association established in 1985 with the aim of fostering a safe and efficient derivatives market to facilitate effective risk management for all users of derivatives products.

Members of ISDA agree to use the ISDA Master Agreement and associated documentation as a basis for derivative transactions. Members benefit from the netting provisions, which enable firms to net their exposures with each other. As a result, the transactions are legally treated as a single transaction with a single net value.

1.4.2 Islamic Finance Adoption of Self-Regulation

Some forms of self-regulation are established to reflect wider principles, for example principles associated with religious observance. An example of faith- and ethical-based regulation is the Islamic finance industry, which is regulated by a combination of self-regulatory bodies and statutory regulation in the countries in which they operate. Islamic commercial and financial ethics stem from the principles of Shariah (also referred to as Islamic law) which includes the major prohibitions of *riba* (interest), *gharar* (unnecessary uncertainty) and *maysir* (gambling). All values, standards and rules structuring Islamic commercial and financial ethics are outlined in Shariah, which is best characterised as a framework providing legal, moral and spiritual guidance aimed at achieving the goals of Islam.

Similar to other financial institutions, Islamic financial institutions are authorised and supervised by the regulatory authority in their country of incorporation. In addition, the following two self-regulating bodies have been established:

- the Accounting and Auditing Organization for Islamic Financial Institutions (AAOIFI), and
- the Islamic Financial Services Board (IFSB).

AAOIFI is an autonomous body responsible for the formulation and issuance of accountancy, auditing ethics, governance and Shariah standards for the international Islamic banking and finance industry. The standards have been developed to encourage the harmonisation of Islamic banking and finance practices, and to ensure transparency and uniformity of financial reporting by Islamic banks and financial institutions. The IFSB is an international standard-setting organisation with a mission to promote and enhance the soundness and stability of the Islamic financial sector by issuing global prudential standards and guiding principles for the industry, broadly defined to include banking, capital markets and insurance sectors. The IFSB standards are mainly based on the identification, management and disclosure of risks relevant to Islamic products and operations. Full members of the IFSB are typically **central banks** in countries where Islamic financial institutions are incorporated. These countries are invited to apply the (optional) IFSB standards in order to provide a comparable regulated environment for the Islamic financial sector. The standards are mandatory in some countries, such as Bahrain and Sudan, and are used as guidelines in others.

From the perspective of financial institutions, Shariah compliance can be achieved in various ways including by adopting national regulation, or by the voluntary adoption of Shariah-compliant standards through the directives and resolutions of the firms' internal Shariah boards.

1.5 Extra-Territorial Reach of Legislation

Learning Objective

1.1.6 Understand the purpose of the following: Data Protection (GDPR); Tax Reporting (CRS, FATCA); Banking Reform (ICB, Dodd-Frank); Market Integrity (MiFID II, MiFIR, MAR, EMIR, PSD2, Sarbanes Oxley); Financial Crime (UK Bribery Act, FCPA, AMLD)

As the financial sector is international, many regulations and laws have application beyond national borders. Compliance officers need to be aware and understand the potential impact of such legislation. Examples of these follow.

1.5.1 Data Protection (GDPR)

The EU General Data Protection Regulation (GDPR) was enforced on 25 May 2018 and replaced the Data Protection Directive. The GDPR is designed to harmonise data privacy laws across Europe to protect EU citizens from privacy and data breaches in an increasingly data-driven world that is vastly different from the time in which the 1995 directive was established. Although the key principles of data privacy still hold true to the previous directive, many changes have been proposed to the regulatory policies; the key points of the GDPR as well as information on the impacts it will have on business can be found below.

Increased Territorial Scope (Extra-Territorial Applicability)

The biggest change to the data privacy regulations due to GDPR is the extended jurisdiction. GDPR applies to all companies processing the personal data of data subjects residing in the European Union (EU), regardless of the company's location. Previously, territorial applicability of the directive was ambiguous and referred to as data processing 'in context of an establishment'. This topic has arisen in a number of high-profile court cases. The GDPR makes its applicability very clear – it will apply to the processing of personal data by controllers and processors in the EU, regardless of whether the processing takes place in the EU or not. The GDPR also applies to the processing of personal data of data subjects in the EU by a controller or processor who is not based in the EU, where the activities relate to: offering goods or services to EU citizens (irrespective of whether payment is required) and the monitoring of behaviour that takes place within the EU. Non-EU businesses processing the data of EU citizens have to appoint a representative in the EU.

Penalties

Under GDPR, organisations in breach of the GDPR can be fined up to 4% of the annual global turnover of the previous financial year or €20 million (UK – £17.5 million), whichever is greater. This is the maximum fine that can be imposed for the most serious infringements, eg, not having sufficient customer consent to process data or violating the core of privacy by design concepts. There is a tiered approach to fining, eg, a company can be fined 2% for not having their records in order (Article 28), not notifying the supervising authority and data subject about a breach or not conducting impact assessment. It is important to note that these rules apply to both controllers and processors – meaning 'clouds' are not exempt from GDPR enforcement.

Consent

The conditions for consent have been strengthened, and companies are no longer able to use long illegible terms and conditions full of legalese. The request for consent must be given in an intelligible and easily accessible form, with the purpose for data processing attached to that consent. It must be clear and separate from other matters using clear and plain language. It must be as easy to withdraw consent as it is to give it.

Data Subject Rights

Breach Notification

Under GDPR, breach notification is mandatory in all member states where a data breach is likely to *'result in a risk for the rights and freedoms of individuals'*. This must be done within 72 hours of first having become aware of the breach. Data processors are required to notify their customers, the controllers, *'without undue delay'* after first becoming aware of a data breach.

Right to Access

Part of the expanded rights of data subjects outlined by the GDPR is the right for data subjects to obtain from the data controller confirmation as to whether or not their personal data is being processed, where and for what purpose. Furthermore, the controller must provide a copy of the personal data, free of charge, in an electronic format on request.

Right to be Forgotten

Also known as 'data erasure', the right to be forgotten entitles the data subject to have the data controller erase their personal data, cease further dissemination of the data, and potentially have third parties halt processing of the data. The conditions for erasure, as outlined in Article 17, include the data no longer being relevant to the original purpose for processing, or a data subject withdrawing consent. It should also be noted that this right requires controllers to compare the subjects' rights to *'the public interest in the availability of the data'* when considering such requests.

Data Portability

The GDPR has introduced data portability – the right for a data subject to receive the personal data concerning them, which they have previously provided in a *'commonly used and machine-readable format'* and have the right to transmit that data to another controller.

Privacy by Design

Privacy by design as a concept has existed for years now, but has become part of a legal requirement with the GDPR. At its core, privacy by design calls for the inclusion of data protection from the onset of the designing of systems, rather than as an addition. More specifically:

> *'The controller shall...implement appropriate technical and organisational measures...in an effective way...in order to meet the requirements of this Regulation and protect the rights of data subjects'.*

Article 23 calls for controllers to hold and process only the data absolutely necessary for the completion of its duties (data minimisation), as well as limiting the access to personal data to those needing to act out the processing.

Data Protection Officers (DPOs)

Under GDPR, notifications/registrations no longer need to be submitted to each local Data Protection Authority (DPA) of data processing activities. It is also no longer a requirement to notify/obtain approval for transfers based on the model contract clauses (MCCs). Instead, there are internal record-keeping requirements, as further explained below, and the appointment of a DPO is mandatory only for those controllers and processors whose core activities consist of processing operations which require regular and systematic monitoring of data subjects on a large scale or of special categories of data or data relating to criminal convictions and offences. Importantly, the DPO:

- must be appointed on the basis of professional qualities and, in particular, expert knowledge on data protection law and practices
- may be a staff member or an external service provider
- contact details must be provided to the relevant DPA
- must be provided with appropriate resources to carry out their tasks and maintain their expert knowledge
- must report directly to the highest level of management
- must not carry out any other tasks that could result in a conflict of interest.

1.5.2 Banking Reform

Independent Commission on Banking (ICB)

The Independent Commission on Banking (ICB) was a UK Government inquiry set up to investigate structural and related non-structural reforms to the UK banking sector to promote financial stability and competition in the wake of the financial crisis of 2007–08. The ICB was established in June 2010 and produced their recommendations in September 2011. The consequences of their findings and recommendations are far-reaching and have resulted in UK banks ring-fencing their retail operations from the investment banks to safeguard the retail banks from the riskier activities. The ICB recommendations have been implemented as of 1 January 2019, effectively creating separate legal entities for retail and investment banking activities.

Dodd-Frank

The Dodd-Frank Act is the result of a proposal by President Obama in June 2009 for a:

> *'sweeping overhaul of the United States financial regulatory system, a transformation on a scale not seen since the reforms that followed the Great Depression'.*

The Dodd-Frank Act includes:

- consolidation of regulatory agencies, elimination of the national thrift charter, and a new oversight council to evaluate systemic risk
- comprehensive regulation of financial markets, including increased transparency of derivatives (bringing them on to exchanges)
- consumer protection reforms including a new consumer protection agency and uniform standards for 'plain vanilla' products as well as strengthened investor protection

- tools for financial crises, including a 'resolution regime' complementing the existing Federal Deposit Insurance Corporation (FDIC) authority to allow for an orderly winding-down of bankrupt firms, and including a proposal that the Federal Reserve receive authorisation from the Treasury for extensions of credit in 'unusual or exigent circumstances'
- various measures aimed at increasing international standards and cooperation – included in this section were proposals related to improved accounting and tightened regulation of credit rating agencies.

The objective of the Dodd-Frank Act is to promote the financial stability of the US by improving accountability and transparency in the financial system, to end 'too big to fail', to protect the American taxpayer by ending bailouts, to protect consumers from abusive financial services practices, and for other purposes. The Act has changed the existing regulatory structure, creating a number of new agencies, whilst merging and removing others in an effort to streamline the regulatory process, increase oversight of specific institutions regarded as a systemic risk, amend the Federal Reserve Act and promote transparency. The Act:

- established rigorous standards and supervision to protect the economy and American consumers, investors and businesses
- ended taxpayer-funded bailouts of financial institutions
- provided for an advanced warning system on the stability of the economy
- created rules on executive compensation and corporate governance, and
- eliminated the loopholes that led to the economic recession.

The new agencies are granted explicit power over a particular aspect of financial regulation which may have been transferred from an existing agency. All agencies need to report to Congress on an annual (or biannual) basis, presenting the results of current plans and to explain future goals. Prior to the passage of the Dodd-Frank Act, investment advisers were not required to register with the Securities and Exchange Commission (SEC) if they had fewer than 15 clients during the previous 12 months and did not hold themselves out generally to the public as an investment adviser. The Dodd-Frank Act has eliminated that exemption. Certain non-bank financial institutions and their subsidiaries are now supervised by the Federal Reserve in the same manner and to the same extent as if they were a bank-holding company.

To enhance the regulatory system, changes have been proposed to existing agencies, including new powers and the transfer of powers to and from them. The institutions affected by these changes include most of the regulatory agencies currently involved in monitoring the financial system (eg, the FDIC, the SEC, Comptroller of the Currency, the Federal Reserve and the Securities Investor Protection Corporation (SIPC)). The Act impacts all US federal financial regulatory agencies, has eliminated the Office of Thrift Supervision and created two new agencies: the Financial Stability Oversight Council (FSOC) and the Office of Financial Research (OFR). In addition, the Act has introduced several consumer protection agencies, including the Bureau of Consumer Financial Protection.

1.5.3 Market Integrity

Markets in Financial Instruments Directive (MiFID II) and the Markets in Financial Instruments Regulation (MiFIR)

Markets in Financial Instruments Directive (MiFID) is a **European Union (EU) directive** introduced in 2007. MiFID II, the updated version, came into force on 3 January 2018. MiFIR is the associated regulation. One of the key aims of MiFID is to provide investor protection rules across the whole **European Economic Area (EEA)**. Investor protection is ensured by the following:

- obligation to obtain the best possible result for the client
- information disclosure requirements
- client-specific rules on suitability and appropriateness of financial products, and
- rules on inducements.

As a general principle, MiFID places significant importance on the fiduciary duties of firms. It established a general obligation for firms to act in the client's best interest, placing a fiduciary duty on firms to put their client's interests ahead of the firm's interest.

Passporting

MiFID supports two key policy goals of the EU. These are:

- extending the range of investment services for which a firm can obtain an EU 'passport' (ie, obtaining authorisation in one EU state – the **home state** – enables a firm to provide investment services in another EU member state – the **host state** – without requiring any further local authorisations), and
- removing a major hurdle to cross-border business, by no longer applying 'host state' rules to incoming passported firms.

The range of investment services passportable under MiFID includes:

- receipt and transmission of orders in relation to one or more financial instruments
- execution of orders on behalf of clients
- dealing on own account
- portfolio management
- investment advice
- underwriting of financial instruments and/or placing of financial instruments on a firm commitment basis
- placing of financial instruments without a firm commitment basis, and
- operation of multilateral trading facilities (MTFs).

The directives are binding on member states in terms of the result to be achieved but provide individual countries with the flexibility to implement the rules in their own national legal systems as they see fit. In the UK, for example, when implementing EU regulations, the FCA conducts a cost/benefit analysis on the implementation to assess the most appropriate way to proceed. Areas for consideration include:

- ensuring that market innovation is not stifled
- protecting and, where possible, enhancing the international character of the UK's financial markets, and
- considering the impact of any regulation on competition.

Prior to making any changes, the FCA publishes the proposed rules and guidance in draft for consultation. Consultation papers (CPs) are the formal means by which this consultation takes place. Discussion papers (DPs) are preliminary and informal discussion-stimulating papers. These papers give the various representative industry bodies an opportunity to respond to the proposals from the perspective of their impact on the risk management and control frameworks of their member firms. Once the consultation is concluded, the FCA takes into consideration all responses and issues a policy statement (PS), which details the decided policy and contains the feedback from the formal consultation.

As EU regulatory institutions gain more power, they have produced more detailed rules to support the implementation of EU directives. As a result, the ability of national regulators to interpret the directive differently and, therefore, the scope for regulatory arbitrage is reduced. Choosing a location because of a more lenient local interpretation of the directive is no longer an option. MiFID II is an example of increased standardisation, as it is aimed at standardising areas such as product governance, suitability and appropriateness, and the disclosure of costs and charges.

Market Abuse Regulation (MAR)

The EU Market Abuse Regulation (MAR) came into force on 3 July 2016. It applies to:

a. financial instruments admitted to trading on a regulated market or for which a request for admission to trading on a regulated market has been made
b. financial instruments traded on an MTF, admitted to trading on an MTF, or for which a request for admission to trading on an MTF has been made
c. financial instruments traded on an organised trading facility (OTF)
d. financial instruments not covered by points (a), (b) or (c), the price or value of which depends on or has an effect on the price or value of a financial instrument referred to in those points, including, but not limited to, credit default swaps and contracts for difference.

MAR includes behaviour or transactions, including bids, relating to the auctioning on an auction platform authorised as a regulated market of emission allowances or other auctioned products based thereon, including when auctioned products are not financial instruments.

MAR incorporates the following **European Securities and Markets Authority (ESMA)** guidelines:

- Inside information of commodity derivatives, including that information which is reasonably expected or required to be disclosed on relevant commodity derivative and spot markets.
- Delay disclosure of inside information.
- Market soundings detailing the factors, steps and appropriate records required to be taken into consideration when information is disclosed as part of the sounding regime.

MAR includes the requirements for disclosure of emission allowances, and the need to maintain an insider list for emission allowances, market participants and parties involved in relevant auctions.

Inside information is information that would be likely to have a significant effect on the price of financial instruments or issuers if it were to be made public. Financial instruments include spot commodity contracts, emission allowances, and related auction products. The use of inside information to execute a transaction, or to amend or cancel an existing transaction constitutes insider dealing.

In addition, persons who possess inside information are prohibited from using that information to (or attempt to) deal in financial instruments or to recommend or induce another person to transact on the basis of inside information. Firms need to maintain a register of insiders. Issuers and emission allowance market participants (EAMPs) need to publicly disclose any inside information which has been (in)directly made available to them as soon as possible. Disclosure may be delayed if it is in the interest of financial stability. The appropriate financial regulator needs to be informed immediately after the decision to delay the disclosure of inside information has been made. A firm does not have to provide a written explanation of how the conditions for delayed disclosure are met but will need to keep appropriate records which will have to be made available to the regulatory authority on demand.

MAR introduces a framework to make legitimate disclosures of inside information in the course of market soundings. A market sounding is a communication or information that is disclosed to one or more investors prior to the announcement of a transaction, in order to assess the interest of potential investors in relation to the transaction, potential size, and pricing.

Market manipulation covers any activity that gives or may give false or misleading signals about the demand, supply, or price of a financial instrument, thus, impacting trading in the instrument in a way intended by the person. Market manipulation can take the following forms:

- false or misleading signals resulting from transactions, orders, trades, or any other behaviour
- using fictitious devices or other deceptions likely to affect the price
- false or misleading signals resulting from disseminating information
- collaboration to secure a dominant position over demand and supply, creating unfair trading conditions, and other similar behaviours.

Buy-back programmes and **stabilisation** measures may be exempt from the prohibitions against market abuse. Firms will have to notify their regulatory authority prior to undertaking these transactions. Persons discharging managerial responsibilities (PDMRs) within issuers or EAMPs, and persons closely associated with them, must notify their regulatory authority and the issuer or EAMP of relevant personal transactions they undertake in the issuer's shares, debt instruments, derivatives or other linked financial instruments, if the total amount of transactions per calendar year has reached €5,000. The notification must be made public within three business days. In addition, PDMRs are prohibited from conducting certain personal transactions during a closed period.

European Market Infrastructure Regulation (EMIR)

Following the financial crisis, the G20 countries committed to address risks related to the derivatives markets. In order to make that commitment effective, the European Parliament and Council have adopted EMIR, a regulation that requires over-the-counter (OTC) derivative contracts to be cleared and derivatives contracts to be reported. EMIR sets the framework to enhance the safety of central counterparties (CCPs) and trade repositories (TRs). EMIR and the regulation on OTC derivatives, CCPs and TRs, came into force on 16 August 2012.

The main obligations under EMIR are:

- central clearing for certain classes of OTC derivatives
- application of risk mitigation techniques for non-centrally cleared OTC derivatives
- reporting to TRs

- application of organisational, conduct of business and prudential requirements for CCPs
- application of requirements for TRs, including the duty to make certain data available to the public and relevant authorities.

Payment Services Directive 2 (PSD2)

The Payment Services Directive 2 (PSD2) was introduced into national law of the EU member states on 13 January 2018. In this context, payment services are defined as follows:

> *'Services enabling cash to be deposited in or withdrawn from, for example, a bank account, as well as all the operations required to operate the account. This can include transfers of funds, direct debits, credit transfers and card payments. Paper transactions are not covered by the directive.'*

The aim of the directive is to:

- provide the legal foundation for the further development of a better integrated internal market for electronic payments within the EU
- put in place comprehensive rules for payment services, with the goal of making international payments within the EU as easy, efficient, and secure as payments within a country
- open up payment markets to new entrants leading to enhanced competition, greater choice, and better prices for consumers, and
- provide the necessary legal platform for the Single Euro Payments Area (SEPA).

PSD2 improves the existing EU rules for electronic payments incorporating emerging and innovative payment services such as internet and mobile payments. To this end, it sets out rules concerning security requirements, transparency of conditions, and the rights and obligations of users and providers of payment services. PSD2 is complemented by regulation (EU) 2015/751 which caps fees charged between banks for card-based transactions. This is aimed at reducing the cost for merchants in accepting consumer debit and credit cards.

The PSD2 rules apply to existing and new providers of innovative payment services and seek to ensure that these players can compete on equal terms. This, in turn, will result in greater efficiency, choice and transparency of payment services, while strengthening consumers' trust in a harmonised payments market.

PSD2 opens up the EU payment market to companies offering the following consumer- or business-oriented payments services:

1. **account information services** – allow a payment service user to have an overview of their financial status at any time, and
2. **payment initiation services** – allow consumers to pay by means of simple credit transfer for online purchases whilst assuring the payment is initiated and goods and services can be provided without delay.

Organisations offering account information services need to have professional indemnity insurance as a condition of authorisation.

PSD2 enhances consumer rights including reduced liability for non-authorised payment to €50 (from €150), the unconditional right to refund direct debits in euros; and the removal of surcharges for the use of a consumer debit or credit card. The European Banking Authority (EBA) will develop a central register of authorised payment institutions which will be publicly accessible and maintained by national authorities. In addition, the role of the EBA is to assist in dispute resolution between national authorities; to develop regulatory technical standards on strong customer authorisation and secure communication channels; and to develop cooperation and information exchange between supervisory authorities.

Sarbanes-Oxley (SOX) Act 2002

The US government introduced the Sarbanes-Oxley (SOX) Act in 2002 following a series of financial scandals that began in 2001 with the collapse of major US corporations such as Enron and WorldCom.

SOX includes proposals to improve the financial reporting process and restore investor confidence in the US financial markets, and was passed by Congress in July 2002. At the time, President Bush characterised it as *'the most far-reaching reforms of American business practices since the time of Franklin Roosevelt'*.

The objective of SOX is *'to protect investors by improving the accuracy and reliability of corporate disclosures'*. It applies to US public companies and their global subsidiaries. In addition, it applies to foreign companies with shares listed on US stock exchanges.

What are the Implications of the Legislation?

One of the key sections is Section 404 which lays out the requirement for the management of a US public company to report annually on the operational effectiveness of the company's internal controls over financial reporting. The company's auditors must attest to and report on the management's assertion over the effectiveness of internal financial controls. This section significantly impacts the governance and behaviour of any business with a US listing, including non-US companies, and their global subsidiaries and joint ventures.

Requirements for Auditors

SOX introduced the Public Company Accounting Oversight Board (PCAOB), whose members are appointed by the SEC to oversee auditors and to establish and enforce auditing standards.

Key changes can be summarised as follows:

- The PCAOB is required to inspect large accounting firms annually (ie, those that regularly audit more than 100 companies), and to inspect smaller firms every three years. The Act authorises the PCAOB to subpoena documents, compel testimony, suspend the right of accounting firms to audit public companies and impose substantial fines.
- In order to address conflicts of interest in firms that both perform audits and provide consulting, auditors are prevented from providing certain non-audit services; and are only permitted to provide other services, such as tax advice, if this is disclosed and approved by the audit committee of the company receiving the advice.

- Auditors have to be appointed by the audit committee of a company's board of directors rather than by company management and members of the audit committee must be independent of management.
- The lead accounting firm partner on an audit has to be replaced every five years.
- An accounting firm may not audit a company where senior executives previously worked for the firm and participated in the audit within the previous year.

Breaches of the rules are subject to criminal fines and up to ten years in prison.

Reporting Requirements

SOX requires firms to meet the following internal control standards to ensure the accurate reporting of their financial position:

- The chief executive officer (CEO) and chief finance officer (CFO) are responsible for ensuring that internal controls and procedures can provide accurate financial disclosures.
- The controls must ensure that the CEO and CFO are aware of material information.
- Compliance work must be performed on a continual basis to document and attest to the effectiveness of their internal controls.

Companies, and their auditors, must also report on the effectiveness of these internal controls. The requirements for the annual internal controls report include the following:

- It should be produced as part of the annual financial accounts.
- It must acknowledge management's responsibility for establishing and maintaining adequate controls and procedures for financial reporting.
- It must contain an assessment of the effectiveness of the firm's controls and procedures for the purposes of financial reporting.

Requirements of US Listings

To achieve and maintain US exchange listings, SOX requires a significant change in both management's reporting responsibilities, and the responsibilities of the independent auditor. In addition to those provisions described above, the Act also covers a number of other corporate governance issues, such as:

- measures to prevent conflicts of interest between securities analysts and investment banks
- the requirement for the CEO and CFO to certify the accuracy of the firm's annual and quarterly SEC reports; they are then personally responsible for the information
- all off-balance sheet transactions and material relationships must be disclosed
- the company must state whether it has adopted a code of ethics for its senior financial officers
- personal loans to officers or directors are forbidden
- greater protection is given for whistleblowers, and retaliation can be punishable with up to ten years' imprisonment.

The Act also defined the following related crimes:

- **defrauding securities investors** – up to 25 years in prison
- **CEOs knowingly signing a false financial statement** – fines of up to $5 million and 20 years in prison for wilful violations
- **obstruction of justice by destroying documents** – fines and prison terms of up to 20 years.

Compliance with Section 404 requires that businesses now have to document and attest to the operational effectiveness of a wide range of processes that have an impact upon the accuracy of their annual financial performance and reporting. These include traditional financial processes such as accounts payable and receivables, but also cover those that have an indirect financial impact; for banking and financial institutions these include the processes around the movement of money and customer funds, such as direct debit, cheque clearing and the procedures for opening or closing accounts.

To comply with the Act, many businesses documented and tested a larger number of controls. As part of the SOX requirements, this compliance work must be performed on a continual basis, and firms must document and attest to the effectiveness of their internal controls on an annual basis. Section 302 of SOX sets out that the CEO and CFO are required to certify that the financial statements and other information that is included in each quarterly report are a true and accurate representation in all material respects.

1.5.4 Financial Crime

There is no internationally accepted definition of 'financial crime'. It is generally understood to include the laundering of the proceeds of any crime, terrorist financing, the financing of the proliferation of weapons of mass destruction (WMDs), breaches of financial and trade sanctions, market abuse, and tax evasion. FSMA broadly defines the term to include *'any offence involving fraud or dishonesty; misconduct in or misuse of information relating to, a financial market; or handling the proceeds of crime'*, and defines the term 'offence' as behaviour that *'includes an act or omission which would be an offence if it had taken place in the UK'*. Thus, expanding the remit of the legislation to include conduct occurring outside the UK. In the context of global financial compliance, the UK Bribery Act and the Foreign Corrupt Practices Act are of particular importance.

UK Bribery Act 2010

The Organisation for Economic Co-operation and Development (OECD) Convention on Combating Bribery of Foreign Public Officials in International Business Transactions was signed in 1997, and reaffirmed in 2009. It establishes legally binding standards to criminalise the bribery of foreign public officials in international business transactions and provides for a host of related measures to make it effective. It is the first and only international anti-corruption instrument focused on the supply side of the bribery transaction. The 35 OECD member countries and four non-member countries – Argentina, Brazil, Bulgaria, and South Africa – have adopted the Convention.

The **UK Bribery Act 2010** is an example of legislation designed to implement the OECD Convention. The Act created new offences of:

- offering or receiving a bribe (Section 1)
- bribery of foreign public officials (Section 6), and
- a failure to prevent a bribe being paid on an organisation's behalf (Section 7).

It also provides a defence to the last offence where an organisation can show that it has 'adequate procedures' in place.

Section 12 of the Act provides that the courts will have jurisdiction over offences committed in the UK, as well as offences committed outside the UK where the person committing them has a close connection with the UK by virtue of being a British national or ordinarily resident in the UK, a body incorporated in the UK, or a Scottish partnership.

In addition, in relation to Section 7 – failure to prevent a bribe – the jurisdiction of the UK courts is extended to foreign commercial organisations. Only a 'relevant commercial organisation' can commit an offence under Section 7 of the Bribery Act.

A relevant commercial organisation is defined in Section 7(5) as:

> *'a body or partnership incorporated or formed in the UK irrespective of where it carries on a business, or an incorporated body or partnership which carries on a business or part of a business in the UK irrespective of the place of incorporation or formation'.*

It is up to the courts to determine whether an organisation carries on a business in the UK, taking into account the particular facts in individual cases.

While the Act represents a stronger approach to eradicate bribery across all firms and industries, the financial sector has previously been subject to action. In 2009, the UK financial services regulator imposed a fine of £5.25 million on insurance company Aon for:

> *'failing to take reasonable care to establish and maintain effective systems and controls for countering the risks of bribery and corruption associated with making payments to 'Overseas Third Parties' who assisted Aon in winning business from overseas clients, particularly in high risk jurisdictions'.*

Case Study

Due to its extraterritorial reach, the UK Bribery Act can have significant impact on foreign companies. A foreign company which carries on any 'part of a business' in the UK could be prosecuted under the Bribery Act for failing to prevent bribery committed by any of its employees, agents or other representatives, even if the bribery takes place outside the UK and involves non-UK persons.

For example, a German construction company with a UK subsidiary appoints an intermediary to facilitate business in Africa, and the intermediary pays a bribe to a local official. In some circumstances, the German parent could be liable under the UK Bribery Act for failing to prevent bribery. The Act is engaged simply by virtue of the existence of a UK operation.

Using the same example, the UK subsidiary is itself at risk of prosecution if a person or company associated with it is involved in bribery, as are any German nationals working for the UK subsidiary and, therefore, 'ordinarily resident' in the UK, if they are found to have paid or received a bribe. 'Part of a business' is not defined in the Act, but even a UK representative office or agent may be sufficient for the purposes of the corporate offence.

Foreign Corrupt Practices Act (1977)

The US Foreign Corrupt Practices Act (FCPA) has had significant impact on the way American firms do business, both in the US and overseas. The FCPA was originally enacted by the US Congress in 1977 and has been revised since.

The provisions of the FCPA make it unlawful for a US person, and certain foreign issuers of securities, to make a corrupt payment to a foreign official for the purpose of obtaining or retaining business for or with, or directing business to, any person. The provisions also apply to foreign firms and persons who take any act in the furtherance of such a corrupt payment while in the US.

In 1977, the International Chamber of Commerce (ICC) published Rules of Conduct to Combat Extortion and Bribery. These rules set out basic measures by which companies can reduce the likelihood of corrupt practices.

The OECD Convention on Combating Bribery of Foreign Public Officials in International Business Transactions was signed by the US and 33 other OECD member countries in 1997 and reaffirmed in 2009. Since 1997, over 400 US companies have admitted to the US SEC that they had made questionable or illegal payments in excess of $300 million to foreign government officials, politicians and political parties. Several US firms have since been convicted in the criminal courts of having paid bribes to foreign officials and have suffered large fines as well as being banned from participating in US federal procurement programmes. In addition, employees and officers have gone to jail.

Firms need to have controls in place to ensure that they know who their customers are (in particular if customers are considered to be politically exposed persons (PEPs)), and the details of the management and ownership of the entities with whom they do business. Firms need to be comfortable that their business is not associated with criminals. The SOX legislation also imposes requirements on firms to disclose instances of fraud as well as reporting annually on their systems of internal control, so compliance with the FCPA helps ensure SOX compliance too.

In order to avoid criminal prosecutions and fines, many firms have implemented detailed compliance programmes to prevent and detect any improper payments by employees or agents, particularly those operating 'in the field' in tough emerging markets, where competition and general business practice often mean that rules set at head office are difficult to implement in practice and managers may attempt to circumvent regulations to achieve a sale.

Particular controls include:

- due diligence checks on third parties to establish their *bona fides* at the outset of the relationship but, very importantly, as the relationship continues
- committees with senior executive representation to oversee the risks of bribery and corruption, to receive periodic management information
- detailed training for staff, and
- general monitoring of processes and controls by independent risk, compliance or audit functions.

Any company not implementing comprehensive compliance processes and controls and, in particular, not actively examining the history of its business partners to determine past involvement in fraud or corruption, will have significant difficulties in being able to meet anti-bribery and corruption legislation and regulation. A poor approach to compliance may result in criminal investigations, regulatory fines, restriction of trade and even jail sentences. Clearly, the reputational risk is significant and it is worth ensuring compliance with anti-bribery legislation.

The Foreign Account Tax Compliance Act (FATCA) 2010

FATCA, enacted by the US in 2010 as part of the Hiring Incentives to Restore Employment (HIRE) Act, is an important development in US efforts to combat tax evasion by US persons holding investments in offshore accounts. Under FATCA, US taxpayers holding financial assets outside the US are required to report those assets to the Internal Revenue Service (IRS). In addition, FATCA requires foreign financial institutions (FFIs) to report directly to the IRS certain information about financial accounts held by US taxpayers, or by foreign entities in which US taxpayers hold a substantial ownership interest.

Reporting by FFIs

Firms outside the US are not directly subject to US legislation, and so a series of intergovernmental agreements have been entered into so that the US authorities will receive the information they require to improve tax compliance. UK FFIs will report directly to Her Majesty's Revenue & Customs (HMRC) certain information about the financial accounts held by US taxpayers, or by foreign entities in which US taxpayers hold a substantial ownership interest. An FFI in a country not party to an intergovernmental agreement is expected to register with the IRS.

UK and US Intergovernmental Agreement

The UK and the US have entered into an intergovernmental agreement to improve tax compliance. The agreement also covers the implementation of FATCA on the basis of domestic reporting and reciprocal exchange of information. As a result of the agreement, UK firms are legally bound to report information requested by the US authorities to the UK Government.

Anti-Money Laundering Directive (AMLD)

The EU **Anti-Money Laundering Directive (AMLD)** is an EU legal act and risk-based approach that requires EU-wide risk assessments in combination with national and institutional risk assessments. It covers customer due diligence (CDD) and other requirements on financial institutions and designated non-financial businesses and professions (DNFBPs), in accordance with the Financial Action Task Force (FATF) Recommendations. DNFBPs are non-financial sectors identified to be vulnerable to money laundering abuse, such as lawyers, accountants, real estate agents and some types of businesses that deal in high-value goods. The directive extends the definition of PEPs to also include those in the home country of the institution. Over time, amendments have been made to the directive to ensure it remains current. The main amendments, in the most recent version (5AMLD), are related to beneficial ownership, removing anonymity on unpaid credit cards, risks of virtual currencies, exchange of information between financial intelligence units (FIUs), additional checks on transactions with high-risk third countries and centralised account registers or retrieval systems. 5AMLD was adopted into European law in April 2018, to be implemented by member countries by October 2020. Further changes have been incorporated in 6AMLD which came into force in December 2020, for implementation by 3 June 2021.

The main changes are:

- the standardisation of predicate offences and the inclusion of two new predicate offences: cybercrime and environmental crime
- the expansion of crimes that are categorised as money laundering to include aiding and abetting

- increased prison time and financial penalties
- enhanced cooperation between member states, and
- the extension of criminal liability to businesses.

The AMLD is incorporated in law within individual member states.

1.5.5 Common Reporting Standards (CRS) for the Exchange of Financial Information

On 6 May 2014, 47 countries tentatively agreed on common reporting standards (CRSs) to share information on residents' assets and incomes automatically in conformation with the standard. Until now, the parties to most treaties that are in place for sharing information have shared information upon request, which has not proved effective in preventing tax evasion. The new system is supposed to automatically and systematically transfer all the relevant information. On 29 October 2014, 51 jurisdictions signed an agreement to automatically exchange information based on Article 6 of the Convention on Mutual Administrative Assistance in Tax Matters.

The OECD CRS is a major step towards an internationally coordinated approach to the disclosure of income earned by individuals and organisations. As a measure to counter tax evasion, it builds upon other information-sharing legislation, such as FATCA and the EU Savings Directive. However, crucially, FATCA is much narrower in scope than the OECD standard for automatic exchange of information (AEoI).

The CRS, formally referred to as the standard for the automatic exchange of financial account information is, in practical terms, a framework of an information standard for the AEoI, developed in the context of the OECD.

The aim of this framework is for jurisdictions to obtain information from their financial institutions (FIs) and automatically exchange that information with other jurisdictions on an annual basis. It sets out the financial account information to be exchanged. The FIs are required to report the different types of accounts and taxpayers covered, as well as the CDD procedures to be followed. These initiatives involve governments obtaining information from their FIs and exchanging data automatically with other nations. FIs (and other investment entities) will have significant additional reporting responsibilities, in order to disclose details of their account holders, with potential penalties for those unable or unwilling to comply fully. The legal basis for the exchange of data is the Convention on Mutual Administrative Assistance in Tax Matters and the idea is based on the FATCA implementation agreements.

The AEoI consists of two regulations or agreements:

- **OECD Competent Authority Agreement (CAA)** is the bilateral agreement between jurisdictions that have signed up to the AEoI. The agreement is what allows the competent authorities (in most cases, this is the jurisdiction's tax authority) to exchange information.
- **OECD Common Reporting Standard (CRS)** sets out the baseline regulation to be adopted in the jurisdictions that have signed up to AEoI. It sets out who will be reporting, what will be reported and to some degree the format of the reporting. This could be seen as the minimal requirements for the regulations.

Financial information to be reported includes interest, dividends, account balance, income from certain insurance products and sales proceeds from financial assets. In gathering data, residency or tax residency within a country is the decisive factor, not citizenship. The CRS relies heavily on local anti-money laundering (AML) and know your customer (KYC) requirements, and on self-certification by account holders, although it includes some documentation remediation. The intention is to eventually have a single global standard.

1.6 Exchanges, Multilateral Trading Facilities (MTFs) and Systematic Internalisers (SIs)

Learning Objectives

1.1.7 Understand how regulation operates in an exchange-traded environment

1.1.8 Understand the key benefits of regulated market structures: exchanges; trading venues (multilateral trading facilities and organised trading facilities); systematic internalisers

1.6.1 Exchanges

A large proportion of trades in financial instruments are carried out through established investment exchanges, such as the London Stock Exchange (LSE), the New York Stock Exchange (NYSE) and the Tokyo Stock Exchange (TSE).

Example

An example of an exchange-traded environment is the stock exchange in Singapore operated by Singapore Exchange ltd (SGX). The exchange is Asia-Pacific's first demutualised and integrated securities and derivatives exchange, with members including organisations that trade derivatives and securities. The SGX operates the securities and derivatives exchange and the respective clearing houses and securities depository. The SGX performs all steps in the value chain of business – order routing, trading, matching, clearing, settlement and depository functions. The SGX is responsible for:

- regulating the stock market
- approving applications for listing
- provision and administration of business and listing rules
- supervising admission of members and compliance by listed companies with the listing rules and corporate disclosure policies
- market surveillance and risk management for the clearing of securities and derivatives, and
- overseeing the capital requirements of brokers and investigating brokers as and when it deems necessary.

These responsibilities are typical to investment exchanges.

Exchanges and their operators are normally subject to regulation and supervision by monetary authorities or other regulatory authorities. In Singapore, the Monetary Authority of Singapore (MAS) is the body charged with these responsibilities, while in the UK it is the FCA.

In the UK, any body corporate or an unincorporated association may apply to the FCA for an order declaring it to be a recognised investment exchange (RIE).

The FCA will look to establish:

- whether the applicant is 'fit and proper' to operate as an exchange
- whether it has sufficient financial resources to properly carry out its activities
- that the applicant is willing and able to share information with the FCA, and to promote and maintain high standards of integrity and fair dealing, including laying down rules for activities on the exchange
- that the applicant will record, monitor and enforce compliance with the rules of the exchange.

Exchange operators are expected to take disciplinary action against members, directors, employers and trading representatives, or against any person registered by the exchange.

Disciplinary Actions under an Exchange Environment

Disciplinary action and enforcement penalties are usually determined by a disciplinary committee. The following actions may be available – either individually or in combination:

- a reprimand
- a fine (usually within limits laid down/agreed by the exchange)
- suspension of the member, or
- expulsion of the member or trading representative.

Where the matter involves a violation of the law, the matter may be referred to the relevant authorities for further action. An appeal process is normally provided so that members of the exchange may appeal to an appeals committee against the decision of the disciplinary committee.

1.6.2 Multilateral Trading Facilities (MTFs)/Systematic Internalisers (SIs)

Multilateral trading facilities (MTFs) are described by the FCA as being any system that brings together multiple parties (eg, retail investors or other investment firms) that are interested in buying and selling financial instruments and enables them to do so. These systems can be operated by an investment firm or a market operator – these allow parties to trade among themselves away from the exchanges. Instruments may include shares, bonds and derivatives. This is done within the MTF operator's system. The introduction of MTFs, under MiFID, allowed greater competition to the formalised investment exchanges to be introduced but subject to direct prudential and supervisory oversight by national regulators.

Accordingly, MiFID replaced rules in many markets that required trades to be executed at local exchanges. Instead, for example, banks are allowed to act as SIs, matching customer orders internally rather than showing these to the market.

SIs, traditionally called **market makers**, are investment firms who could match 'buy' and 'sell' orders from clients in-house, providing that they conform to certain criteria. Instead of sending orders to a central exchange such as the LSE, investment banks can match them with other orders on their own book. Examples of such firms are Credit Suisse and UBS. It should be noted that an SI may only act as an

SI for as little as one asset class under MiFID II. Furthermore, ESMA does not have any immediate plans to issue a register of SIs.

SIs are able to compete directly with stock exchanges and automated dealing systems, but they have to make such dealings transparent. They must show a price before a trade is made. After a trade is made, they have to give information about the transaction, just like conventional trading exchanges.

1.6.3 Key Benefits of Regulated Market Structures

The following table highlights the key features and benefits of the various types of trading venue:

Type of Trading Venue	Features	Benefits
Recognised investment exchange (a regulated market)	A more formal market with the highest standards of entry. Companies raising capital must subscribe to sets of listing and disclosure standards.	Demonstrates quality of business-raising capital. Encourages investor confidence. Maintains pool of capital.
Multilateral trading facility (regulatory permission required)	Described as a form of 'exchange lite'. Does not have a listing process and cannot change the regulatory status of a security. Must be pre-trade transparent, the price of existing orders must be available on market data feeds. Must be post-trade transparent, any trades must be published real-time. Prices/charges are public and applied consistently across all members.	Introduction enabled greater competition between trading venues. Higher trading speeds which are attractive to high-frequency traders. Lower cost base. Trading incentives for members relating to trade volumes.
Systematic internaliser	A firm that executes orders from its clients against its own book or against orders from other clients. Also treated as a 'mini-exchange', hence subject to pre- and post-trade price transparency.	Similar to MTFs in having lower trading costs. Speed of trade.

1.6.4 Organised Trading Facilities (OTFs)

An organised trading facility (OTF) is a new category of trading venue introduced by MiFID II. It is a multilateral trading system that is not a regulated market or an MTF. Bonds, structured finance products, emission allowances and derivatives can be traded on an OTF, but equities cannot. As a result of the introduction of OTFs, transactions previously categorised as off-venue, now fall under a multilateral trading environment which increases overall market transparency, reduces the prevalence of opaque market models and products, and increases the quality of price discovery, investor protection, and liquidity.

OTFs assist market participants in meeting MiFID II platform-trading obligations for derivatives and provide an additional trading venue for derivatives, central counterparties, and trade repositories that are sufficiently liquid for the trading obligations to apply. Instruments not subject to the trading obligation can be traded on OTFs through market making schemes.

Due to the fact that both are multilateral trading environments, the rules for OTFs and MTFs are the same. The key difference is the ability and requirements of an OTF to use discretion when matching buying and selling interests. The use of discretion must be in line with fair and orderly trading and best execution obligations to clients. OTFs must establish clear trading rules and processes, including clear and non-discriminatory access rules. OTFs need to have the ability to suspend instruments from trading and maintain resilient systems to facilitate continuity of trading under stressed conditions. OTFs are subject to the same pre- and post-trade transparency requirements as an MTF which apply to any order or transaction executed through their systems or under their rules. OTFs will have to publish the details of current bids and offers and the depth of trading interests of those prices. In addition, details of transactions have to be made public as close to real time as is technically possible. OTFs can operate under any trading protocol it is consistent with fair and orderly trading and the exercise of discretion.

Effective arrangements and procedures need to be established and maintained to enable the regular monitoring of compliance by their members. OTFs need to identify, and act upon, breaches of rules, disorderly trading conditions or conduct that may involve market abuse in relation to any transactions undertaken by their members on the OTF's systems. OTF operators must use discretion when deciding when to place or remove an order on their OTF, and whether or not to match a specific client order with orders available in the system, subject to best execution obligations. Investment firms or market operators running an OTF need to ensure client orders are not executed against the proprietary capital of:

- the firm, or
- any entity that is part of the firm's legal group.

The use of proprietary capital is only permitted for illiquid sovereign debt instruments. An OTF may only engage in matched principal trading if this has been agreed by clients. Matched principal trading is not permitted for derivatives subject to the EMIR-clearing obligation.

The same legal entity cannot operate both an OTF and an SI. OTFs are prohibited from interacting with an SI if this allows any quotes or orders in the SI to interact. This prohibition also applies to quotes and orders in another OTF where two OTFs are interacting.

1.7 Off-Market Transactions

Learning Objective

1.1.9 Understand how regulation applies to OTC derivatives transactions

OTC derivatives are transactions conducted off-market. Trading in OTC derivatives is opaque due to the fact that they are privately negotiated contracts and consequently any information concerning any one of them is usually only available to the contracting parties.

The financial crisis brought the OTC derivatives market to the forefront of regulatory attention. The near-collapse of Bear Sterns in March 2008, the default of Lehman Brothers on 15 September 2008 and the bailout of American International Group, inc (AIG) on 16 November 2008 highlighted the shortcomings in the functioning of this market. The main observations are summarised below.

Transparency

The financial crisis highlighted a lack of information on positions and exposures of individual firms in OTC derivatives. On the one hand, this lack of information prevents regulators from a timely detection of risks building up at individual institutions and in the system as a whole. It also prevents them from accurately assessing the consequences of a default of a market participant and, therefore, from responding in an appropriate manner should such a default occur (Lehman's case was a clear demonstration of this). On the other hand, it helps fuel suspicion and uncertainty among market participants during a crisis.

Counterparty Risk

OTC derivative contracts bind counterparties together for the duration of the transaction. Throughout the lifetime of a contract, counterparties build up claims against each other, as the rights and obligations contained in the contract evolve with the underlying that the contract is derived from. This gives rise to counterparty **credit risk**, ie, the risk that a counterparty may not honour its obligations under the contract when they become due. Clearing is the function by which these risks are managed over time. It can be carried out centrally, through a CCP, or bilaterally. Although both types of clearing are used in the OTC derivatives market, bilateral clearing is the most used form of the two.

The crisis highlighted that the level of counterparty credit risk related to OTC derivatives was much higher than both market participants and regulators had previously thought. To put it differently, the amount of collateral used to mitigate counterparty credit risk was insufficient. The main reason for this lies in inadequate collateralisation in the part of the market that is cleared bilaterally, either because some market participants are not required to provide collateral to secure their OTC derivatives trades or because of issues related to the risk management processes of those market participants that do provide collateral.

Operational Risk

Between the agreement and the confirmation of the transaction, an OTC derivative follows a number of processing steps. In addition, the transaction is subject to a number of events, such as collateral management and settlement of cash payments, that are inherent in the rights and obligations of the contract.

The OTC derivatives market allows for a high degree of flexibility in defining the economic and legal terms of derivatives contracts, resulting in highly bespoke and complex contracts. These contracts require significant manual intervention in many stages of the processing. This increases operational risk, may lead to legal risk, may limit transparency, and may result in an increase of counterparty credit risk.

Proposed Actions

As a result of the financial crisis, government bodies, like the EU Commission, have identified policy actions to:

- increase transparency of the derivatives market by requiring market participants to report all the necessary information on their OTC derivatives portfolios to a trade repository or, if that would not be possible, directly to regulators
- require the publication of aggregate position information
- reduce counterparty credit risk and operational risk in trading through the use of CCP clearing for OTC derivatives that meet predefined eligibility criteria and by the setting of specific targets for legal and process standardisation, and
- enhance market integrity and oversight, through the use of a post-trading market infrastructure.

1.8 Fintech

Learning Objective

1.1.10 Understand how regulators approach Fintech products: distributed ledger technology (DLT); cryptoassets; robo-advice

---

In general terms, Fintech (financial technology) is defined as the use of technology to boost competitive advantage in the financial services sector. Fintech is disruptive in that it allows newcomers in the market to provide financial services in new and innovative ways. Fintech includes innovative mobile solutions, cryptocurrency, and artificial intelligence (AI). New ways of working come with new challenges and require additional governance and regulations to ensure continuing stability of the financial infrastructure.

1.8.1 Distributed Ledger Technology (DLT) and Cryptoassets

Distributed ledger technology (DLT) is the technological infrastructure that allows simultaneous access, validation, and updating across a network spread out over multiple entities or locations. It is commonly referred to as blockchain technology and was first introduced by Bitcoin in 2009. Bitcoin is a cryptocurrency that can be transferred between users without an intermediary.

The change in the technological environment is fast paced and requires a new approach to regulations. Most regulators have set up a regulatory sandbox in which new technology can be trialled. This is a technology neutral approach, aimed at assessing the regulatory requirements for business models and client outcomes arising from the use of the new technologies.

Regulations do not focus on the technical details but on implementation. The regulatory sandbox allows the regulator to review the implementation and assess whether new regulations are required or whether existing rules contain sufficient flexibility for firms to use the new technology. Regulators are catching up with these developments and have been introducing new regulations such as the EU rules on cryptomarkets.

1.8.2 Robo-Advice

Robo-advice or robo-advisors are digital platforms that provide automated financial planning services with little or no human intervention. A robo-advisor collects information from customers concerning their financial situation, future goals, and risk appetite by means of online surveys. This information is then used as input into an algorithm to provide investment advice.

There is a wide range of robo-advisors in the market, with the quality and customer take-up depending on a number of key characteristics:

- ease of account setup
- robust goal planning
- account services
- portfolio management
- security features
- customer services
- level of education, and
- fees.

Robo-advisors mostly use passive indexing strategies, are typically inexpensive and only require a small opening balance.

As a result, they are open to a wide range of customers. The industry is expected to grow by 20.11% per year from $987 billion in 2020 to $2,845 billion in 2025.

From a regulatory perspective, robo-advice falls under the same category of services as other financial advice and regulations such as know your customer, fair treatment of clients, and suitability of advice. Most global regulators have opted for a sandbox approach providing an environment where new developments can be tested and tried without immediately having to comply with all regulations. This approach is beneficial for both developers and regulators. It provides the opportunity for developers to understand the regulations and what they need to do to comply, and it is beneficial for regulators to have early sight of any new developments so that they can ensure the regulations are fit for purpose.

Robo-advisors generally have to follow the same rules and regulations as human advisors including a requirement to be authorised by the appropriate regulatory authority. In the US, robo-advisors must be registered with the SEC and are subject to the same securities laws and regulations as other broker-dealers. In addition, most are registered with the Financial Industry Regulatory Authority (FINRA), a self-regulation organisation.

2. The International Approach to Regulation

2.1 Jurisdiction of Different Regulators

Learning Objective

1.2.1 Know the jurisdiction of different types of regulator

The responsibilities of international regulatory organisations range from coordination and guidance through to setting cross-border principles and detailed rules.

The following summarises the typical jurisdiction of different types of regulator:

Type of Regulator	Jurisdiction
Recognised investment exchanges	Members of the exchange and listed securities, contracts or relevant financial instruments. Many stock exchanges have a national remit, but increasingly as global markets develop, they are becoming more international in nature. Membership is often international, subject to the exchange rules and terms of membership.
Other SROs	Typically cover insurance markets and investment services, such as financial advice, investment management, and mortgages. Members are usually national and, accordingly, the focus of the SRO is essentially national in nature.
Government-appointed national regulatory bodies, such as central banks and other statutory-based regulatory authorities	Broad jurisdiction covering most financial markets, participants and products. Includes banking, insurance, and investment-related activities, both retail and wholesale. Although national in focus, increasingly forced to coordinate approaches because of the global interdependent nature of financial markets.
International regulatory authorities and national authorities with international reach	Regional jurisdiction covering a number of states with a broad coverage of banking, insurance and investment. Cross-border and international in nature with extraterritorial reach. Establish principles of regulation and develop detailed rules.
International regulatory organisations	International focus, established to coordinate at the international level the work of national financial authorities and international standard-setting bodies in order to develop and promote the implementation of effective regulatory, supervisory and other financial sector policies.

2.2 International Regulatory Organisations and Standard Setting

Learning Objectives

1.2.2 Understand the role of international regulatory organisations: Bank for International Settlements (BIS); Financial Stability Board (FSB); The International Organization of Securities Commissions (IOSCO); European regulatory bodies: The European System of Financial Supervision (ESFS)/ European Supervisory Authorities (ESAs)/The European Systemic Risk Board (ESRB); US Securities and Exchange Commission (SEC)

1.2.3 Know the role that professional bodies play in relation to regulatory requirements

1.2.4 Understand how international regulatory organisations aid the implementation of regulation in developing countries

1.2.5 Know the three objectives of securities regulation as defined by IOSCO

2.2.1 Bank for International Settlements (BIS)

Established in 1930, the Bank for International Settlements (BIS) serves as a central bank for central banks, and fosters international monetary and financial cooperation. Its customers are central banks and international organisations. The BIS does not accept deposits from, or provide financial services to, private individuals or corporate entities. The BIS is headquartered in Basel, Switzerland.

The regulatory guidelines produced by the BIS do not automatically have any force in national or international law. Countries around the world that choose to implement them do so by making changes to their own legal and regulatory processes. The International Banking Federation (IBFed), incorporated in 2004, facilitates this effort.

IBFed's members are drawn from the banking associations of Australia, Canada, China, Europe, India, Japan and the US. These countries represent 700 of the world's top 1,000 banks, and every major financial centre. Their global reach enables IBFed to function as the key international forum for addressing legislative, regulatory and other issues of interest to the global banking industry. For countries that are required to implement international laws through membership of a trading bloc or political union, an extra layer of complexity exists when implementing the BIS regulation since the union or bloc's laws may not be the same as the BIS requirements.

The Basel Committee on Banking Supervision (BCBS) is part of the BIS and provides a forum for international cooperation on bank regulation. It was established in 1974 and has 28 members, each of which is represented by their central bank or the country's authority responsible for banking supervision. The BCBS's objective is to enhance financial stability by improving supervisory know-how and the quality of banking supervision worldwide. This is achieved by exchanging information on national supervisory issues and techniques, with a view to promoting common understanding between national supervisors.

The BCBS best practice standards can be used by individual regulatory authorities when designing their local arrangements. These publications include the following high-level guidelines and supervisory standards:

- International Standards on Capital Adequacy
- Core Principles for Effective Banking Supervision
- Core Principles Methodology
- Concordat on cross-border banking supervision.

The BCBS is supported by five working groups:

- Policy Development
- Supervision and Implementation
- Basel Consultative Group
- Macroprudential Supervision
- Accounting Experts.

The Basel Consultative Group provides a forum for deepening the Committee's engagement with supervisors around the world on banking supervisory issues. It facilitates broad supervisory dialogue with non-member countries on new BCBS initiatives early in the process by gathering senior representatives from various countries, international institutions and regional groups of banking supervisors that are not members of the BCBS.

The BCBS is responsible for producing the Basel Accords, which provide recommendations on banking laws and regulations. A key focus of these accords is to define global standards on the levels of capital adequacy and liquidity that banks should maintain. Such measures should enable the banking sector to survive periods of financial and economic stress – and so improve the resilience of the financial system as a whole. The Basel Accords also include measures to improve risk management, governance, transparency and disclosures within the banking sector.

2.2.2 Financial Stability Board (FSB)

The Financial Stability Board (FSB) has been established to coordinate at the international level, the work of national financial authorities and international standard-setting bodies and to develop and promote the implementation of effective regulatory, supervisory and other financial sector policies.

It brings together national authorities responsible for financial stability in significant international financial centres, international financial institutions, sector-specific international groupings of regulators and supervisors, and committees of central bank experts.

The FSB Secretariat is located in Basel, Switzerland, and hosted by the BIS. The membership consists of organisations from 24 different countries from across the world and other international organisations including the EU and standard-setting bodies such as IOSCO (see below). The mandate of the FSB is to:

- assess vulnerabilities affecting the financial system and identify and oversee action needed to address them
- promote coordination and information exchange among authorities responsible for financial stability

- monitor and advise on market developments and their implications for regulatory policy
- advise on and monitor best practice in meeting regulatory standards
- undertake joint strategic reviews of the policy development work of the international standard-setting bodies to ensure their work is timely, coordinated, focused on priorities, and addressing gaps
- set guidelines for and support the establishment of supervisory colleges
- manage contingency planning for cross-border crisis management, particularly with respect to systemically important firms, and
- collaborate with the IMF to conduct early warning exercises.

Members of the FSB must commit to pursuing the maintenance of financial stability, maintain the openness and transparency of the financial sector, implement international financial standards (including the 12 key International Standards and Codes), and agree to undergo periodic peer reviews, using among other evidence, IMF/World Bank Financial Sector Assessment Program reports.

The FSB, working through its members, seeks to give momentum to a broad-based multilateral agenda for strengthening financial systems and the stability of international financial markets. The necessary changes are enacted by the relevant national financial authorities.

The FSB Plenary meets face to face twice a year and conducts meetings by telephone if required. To broaden the circle of countries engaged in work to promote international financial stability, the FSB also holds regional outreach meetings with non-member financial authorities.

The FSB supports the development and implementation of internationally accepted economic, financial and statistical standards that can help promote sound domestic financial systems and international financial stability. While a broad range of political, social, legal and institutional factors impinge on financial stability, the focus of the FSB is on economic and financial standards which are generally accepted by the international community as being objective and relatively free of national biases.

The development, adoption, and successful implementation of international standards yield both national and international benefits. It helps to:

- strengthen domestic financial systems by encouraging sound regulation and supervision, greater transparency, and more efficient and robust institutions, markets, and infrastructure, and
- promote international financial stability by facilitating better-informed lending and investment decisions, improving market integrity, and reducing the risks of financial distress and contagion.

It is worth noting, however, that the implementation of standards in itself is not sufficient to ensure financial stability. Standards are not an end in themselves but a means for promoting sound financial systems and sustained economic growth. They need to be continually reviewed in order to remain relevant in the face of changing circumstances. The relative importance of different standards to individual economies depends on their financial structure and other domestic circumstances. Their implementation must fit into a country's overall strategy for economic and financial sector development, taking account of its stage of development, level of institutional capacity, and other domestic factors. Successful implementation of standards involves a process of interpretation, application, assessment and enforcement. It is critical that economies have in place an effective legal framework and infrastructure for enforcement.

2.2.3 International Organization of Securities Commissions (IOSCO)

The IOSCO is an international association of securities regulators created in 1983 and, as of April 2021, has 129 ordinary members. This category is open to a securities commission, or a similar government or statutory regulatory body that has primary responsibility for securities regulation in its jurisdiction. If there is no governmental, or statutory regulatory body in a jurisdiction then a self-regulatory body, such as a stock exchange, is eligible for ordinary membership of IOSCO. However, the ordinary membership of a self-regulatory body admitted to IOSCO stops if a governmental regulatory body from the same jurisdiction becomes the ordinary member for that jurisdiction. The member agencies currently assembled together in IOSCO have resolved, through its permanent structures:

- to cooperate in developing, implementing and promoting adherence to internationally recognised and consistent standards of regulation, oversight and enforcement, in order to protect investors, maintain fair, efficient and transparent markets, and seek to address systemic risks
- to enhance investor protection and promote investor confidence in the integrity of securities markets, through strengthened information exchange and cooperation in enforcement against misconduct and in supervision of markets and market intermediaries, and
- to exchange information at both global and regional levels on their respective experiences in order to assist the development of markets, strengthen market infrastructure and implement appropriate regulation.

Although IOSCO was created in 1983, the financial crisis has served to bring new focus to international regulatory standards and cooperation. IOSCO's 38 principles of securities regulation have received support from the G20 group of countries and the FSB. These principles are based on three objectives of securities regulation which are:

- the protection of investors
- ensuring that markets are fair, efficient and transparent, and
- the reduction of systemic risk.

The 38 principles do not have any legal force themselves but need to be practically implemented under the relevant legal framework in member countries, in order to achieve the objective of regulation described above. The principles are grouped into ten categories as follows:

1	Relating to the Regulator	6	Auditors, Credit Rating Agencies, and other information providers
2	Self-Regulation	7	Collective Investment Schemes
3	Enforcement of Securities Regulation	8	Market Intermediaries
4	Cooperation in Regulation	9	Secondary Market
5	Issuers	10	Clearing and Settlement

IOSCO, the BIS and the FSB are all involved in setting standards that are intended to be adopted as broadly as possible. Their membership, particularly that of IOSCO, is drawn from a wide range of countries and by sharing information and analysis and organising collaborative events they all seek to aid both developed and developing countries.

2.2.4 European Regulatory Bodies

The European System of Financial Supervision (ESFS)

The ESFS is the institutional architecture of the EU's framework of financial supervision created in response to the financial crisis. First proposed by the European Commission in 2010, it replaced three existing Committees of Supervisors with three new authorities, the EBA, ESMA and the European Insurance and Occupational Pensions Authority (EIOPA). To complement this framework, there is also a European Systemic Risk Board (ESRB) under the responsibility of the European Central Bank.

European Supervisory Authorities (ESAs)

Since January 2011, the regulation of financial services across Europe is now overseen by three **European Supervisory Authorities (ESAs)**:

- EBA
- ESMA, and
- EIOPA.

The ESAs work with the ESRB to ensure financial stability and to strengthen and enhance the EU supervisory framework. They will work to improve coordination between national supervisory authorities and raise standards of national supervision across the EU.

They replace the level 3 (otherwise known as Lamfalussy) committees: Committee of European Banking Supervisors (CEBS), Committee of European Securities Regulators (CESR) and Committee of European Insurance and Occupational Pensions Supervisors (CEIOPS).

What is the ESAs' Role?

- The ESAs aim to create a single EU rulebook. They will do this by developing draft technical standards, which will then be adopted by the European Commission as EU law. The ESAs will also issue guidance and recommendations with which national supervisors and firms must make every effort to comply.
- Where the ESAs believe that a national supervisory authority is failing to apply EU law, or is doing so in a way which appears to be in breach of EU law, they have the power to investigate. Their investigation may lead to the Authority issuing a recommendation to the national supervisor, followed by a formal opinion from the European Commission (if the recommendation is not acted upon). If the supervisor does not comply with the Commission's formal opinion, the ESAs may then take decisions binding on firms or market participants to ensure they are complying with EU law.
- They can temporarily ban certain financial activities. Legislation will set out what they can ban and in what circumstances. Where an emergency has been called by the Council, they have wide-ranging powers to ban financial activities.
- In a crisis, the ESAs will provide EU-wide coordination. If an emergency is declared, the ESAs may make decisions that are binding on national supervisors and on firms. However, these would be subject to certain conditions and would be limited to ensuring compliance with EU law.
- The ESAs will mediate in certain situations where national supervisory authorities disagree. If necessary, they will be able to resolve disputes by making a decision that is binding on both parties to ensure compliance with EU law.

- They have a role in EU supervisory colleges to ensure that they function efficiently and that consistent approaches and practices are followed.
- The ESAs will conduct regular peer reviews of national supervisory authorities to improve the consistency of supervision across the EU.
- They will be able to collect information from national supervisors to allow them to fulfil their role. This information will be used for analysing market developments, coordinating EU-wide stress tests and the macroprudential analysis undertaken by the ESRB.
- They also have a remit to consider consumer protection issues.
- ESMA has direct supervisory responsibility for credit rating agencies.

European Systemic Risk Board (ESRB)

The ESRB was established on 1 January 2011 in response to the global financial crisis and is the new body with responsibility for the macroprudential oversight of the financial system within the EU. As such, it is a key part of the new European System of Financial Supervision (ESFS).

The operation of the board has, at least initially, been entrusted to the ECB. In order to take advantage of existing and compatible structures, and to minimise any delay to the commencement of its operations, the ECB provides analytical, statistical, administrative and logistical support to the ESRB, and technical advice is also drawn from national central banks and supervisors.

2.2.5 US Securities and Exchange Commission (SEC)

The US **Securities and Exchange Commission (SEC)**, established in 1934, is an independent agency of the US federal government. The SEC's main responsibility is to enforce federal securities laws, propose securities rules, and to regulate the securities industry. The mission of the SEC is to protect investors; to maintain fair, orderly, and efficient markets; and to facilitate capital formation. They strive to promote a market environment worthy of the public's trust.

The laws and rules governing the US securities industry derive from the concept that all investors should have access to certain basic facts about an investment before buying it, and as long as they hold it. Therefore, public companies are required to openly disclose meaningful financial and other relevant information in a timely manner.

The SEC supervises key market participants including securities exchanges, securities brokers and dealers, investment advisors, and mutual funds. Although it is the primary overseer and regulator of the US securities markets, the SEC works closely with many other institutions, including Congress, other federal departments and agencies, self-regulatory organisations (eg, the stock exchanges), state securities regulators, and various private sector organisations. In addition, the Chairman of the SEC represents the agency as a member of the Financial Stability Oversight Council (FSOC).

2.2.6 Professional Bodies

Most industries and professions maintain structures to look after the overall well-being of that market and its participants. Similarly, the professional bodies within financial services markets perform a range of important functions.

These include:

- They uphold the standards of conduct of their members.
- They deliver training and other support mechanisms.
- They provide a forum for industry developments – whether self-initiated or in respect of proposed regulatory/legislative change.
- They provide a public face for agreed industry positions to be publicised, whether for public information or as part of specific lobbying efforts.

Professional bodies will often have discussions with regulators to discuss the approach to areas of concern and will provide their members with guidance on how regulatory requirements might be satisfied.

2.3 Implementing Regulatory Objectives and the Approach to Supervision

Learning Objectives

1.2.6 Understand how regulators implement their regulatory objectives

1.2.7 Understand the different regulatory approaches: risk-based; rules-based; principles-based; thematic; relationship-based

Section 1.1 described a typical set of objectives and benefits of regulation. Section 1.3 explored the differences between the rules-based and principles-based approaches to regulation. In this section, we will look at how regulators typically implement their objectives, whether they are set by a statutory body or an SRO.

Financial institutions that want to establish themselves in a certain jurisdiction typically need to apply for a licence. Regulators will ensure that minimum entry standards are applied and approve those applications where it is certain that the firm will be prudently managed with a viable business model (in relation to all its activities) and effective controls for risk mitigation. This could lead to a regulator imposing limitations and requirements on any part of the business model or even refusing to authorise a firm and grant permission for it to undertake **regulated activities**.

The methods used by regulators will typically involve the following:

- the setting of prudential requirements to ensure that an authorised firm or person maintains sufficient capital resources commensurate with the level of risk they are running
- establishing business conduct rules, evidential provisions and guidance that will govern an authorised firm's relationship with its customers or counterparties
- providing detailed product regulations, often in the areas of packaged retail products, such as collective investment schemes and pensions, which set minimum standards aimed at the protection of retail investors and establish dispute resolution and compensation arrangements
- the setting of requirements and processes for investigation, supervision and enforcement of the rules.

Regulators will seek to maintain arrangements to supervise compliance with the requirements imposed on authorised persons. These arrangements may include:

- requiring regular and potentially detailed reporting to the regulator covering, for example, the financial position of the firm, transactions undertaken, risk assessments undertaken by the firm itself and any relevant changes to its business

considering the extent to which a firm represents a risk to the regulator's objectives, ie, adopting a risk-based approach in allocating the regulator's resources and focusing more on those risks which pose a threat to its objectives.

There are a number of approaches to regulation and supervision, each of which is detailed in the sections below. Regulators typically adopt one of the approaches, although some elements of other approaches may also be used.

2.3.1 The Risk-Based Approach

The risk-based approach to regulations means that countries' competent authorities and financial institutions, are expected to identify, assess and understand the risks to which they are exposed and take the appropriate measures commensurate to those risks in order to mitigate them effectively. Regulators assess individual firms concerning the risk they present to the regulator's objectives which assists them in assessing the level of supervisory attention required for each firm.

When assessing risk, it is necessary for countries, competent authorities, and financial institutions to analyse and seek to understand how the risks they identify affect them. The risk assessment, therefore, provides the basis for the risk-sensitive application of measures and, therefore, compliance with the regulations.

The risk-based approach is not a 'zero failure' approach; there may be occasions where an institution has taken all reasonable measures to identify and mitigate risks, but it is still subject to losses. It also does not exempt countries, competent authorities and financial institutions from mitigating risks which are assessed as low.

The impact of a risk posed by an individual firm is assessed using a range of factors established by reference to the regulator's objectives. They may include:

- the degree to which the risks related to the firm would **damage confidence and trust in the markets** if they were to materialise
- the possibility of the risks if they materialise leading to **market or system failure**
- the extent to which the firm may pose risks to achieving the objective of **promoting public understanding**
- the extent to which **consumers may be adversely affected** by the firm's actions or failures
- the incidence or materiality of any **financial crime** that may be perpetrated through, or by, the firm
- the degree to which the firm may pose a risk to the country's **financial stability**.

The probability of a firm posing a risk to the regulator's objectives depends on a number of discrete sources of risk (sometimes referred to as 'risk to objectives (RTO) groups'), and on the firm's internal controls for negotiating those risks.

The RTO groups may include elements such as:

- the firm's strategy
- the firm's **business risk** (those risks that are inherent in the business, such as credit, market and operational risk)
- the financial soundness of the firm
- the nature of the firm's customers and the products and services it offers
- the internal systems and controls and the compliance culture of the firm
- the organisation of the firm and the role played by its governing body, management and staff in mitigating risk.

So, in short, such risk assessments are designed to tie in the regulator's activity with the meeting of its objectives by:

- identifying the main risks to the regulator's objectives as they arise
- measuring how important they are (impact, probability)
- mitigating them if their size justifies it (the proportionate, cost-benefit approach), and
- monitoring and reporting on the progress of the process in terms of risk management.

The regulator may also compare risks across different sectors, using its cross-sectoral experience to produce benchmark assessments and guidance, so that an appropriate baseline can be established. This may also involve detailed communication between the regulator and firms in terms of feedback on their risk assessment – focusing on the key risks identified, and the response the regulator expects from firms. This develops a greater capacity for the regulator to gain a better understanding of emerging trends and risks, through improved sector intelligence.

2.3.2 The Rules-Based Approach

Rules-based regulation provides a set of detailed rules that govern firms' behaviour. Such rules enable firms to 'tick the box' to guarantee compliance with laws and regulations. In practice, very few regulatory regimes apply pure rules-based systems, with most involving a mixture of rules and principles. Even the US, considered by many in the past to have been solely rules-based, has laws and regulations which use a combination of rules and principles.

Following the financial crisis, many international organisations have considered improvements to supervisory approaches which involve more intensive and intrusive styles of supervision and a move to a stronger outcomes-focused model. This shift requires a significant enhanced analysis and risk identification capacity which will focus on business model risk and interact with macroprudential analysis. However, increasing the focus on outcome-testing, over matters such as ensuring firms have the appropriate systems and controls, also requires capacity and structures for early, and more direct, regulatory intervention.

This may require the development of new rules on, for example, the suitability of products and services for consumers. For example, requiring firms to complete appropriate reviews and testing; and greater powers for regulators to affect a more intensive and intrusive style of supervision which may also include product intervention at an early stage. The latter means that regulators will have to devote more resources to analysis and risk assessments and be prepared to take decisions where they believe the (potential) risks require them to act to protect consumers and markets.

The risks may not have materialised at this stage and one of the possible outcomes could be to reduce consumer choice and innovation, though governments may well regard this as an acceptable trade-off for a safer financial environment.

2.3.3 Principles-Based Approach

The principles-based approach applies a broad set of principles of conduct which are then implemented by regulated institutions in the way they see fits best with their organisation. Supervision is based on how the principles are implemented and the outcomes achieved. This is contrary to the rules-based approach to supervision, in which firms are required to follow a precise set of rules. This approach provides firms with the flexibility to meet regulatory requirements in a way that best fits their business models.

2.3.4 Thematic Approach

A thematic approach allows the regulator to look at specific issues using a specialised team and helps it focus its resources and information efficiently.

Regulators have a range of tools they can use to aid their supervision of regulated firms. Typically, these are:

- **Diagnostic tools** – designed to identify, assess and measure risk.
- **Monitoring tools** – to track the development of identified risk, wherever it arises.
- **Preventative tools** – to limit or reduce identified risks and so prevent them from crystallising or increasing.
- **Remedial tools** – to respond to risks when they have crystallised.

According to its website, the Dubai Financial Services Authority (DFSA):

> *'...has a range of supervisory tools available to diagnose and monitor risks, and to prevent them from occurring. It chooses appropriate tools for each situation, with a view to cost-effective regulation for the DFSA and the firm, and to preserve and enhance the marketplace. Increasingly, the DFSA uses thematic reviews as a key tool to assess risk in the marketplace'.*

The UK's financial regulators also use thematic supervision. Analysis of a particular product, market, or practice can enable the regulator to identify a wide-scale issue that requires attention. This thematic effort is performed separately from the regulator's ongoing processes to monitor firms, though the two approaches are mutually supportive. The regulator's discussions with individual firms enable behaviours to be monitored (which may identify a new issue for thematic attention), while also enabling the regulator to observe changes made by individual firms in the light of previous thematic reviews.

By considering the activity taken by different firms across a particular sector in a consistent way, the regulators can identify good and bad practice. The results are then usually published to help firms improve their practices and reduce the risk of bad practice. The FCA and PRA expect firms to take note of such published material, as implementing the good practices identified is a way for firms to demonstrate a proactive approach to compliance and reducing risks.

2.3.5 Relationship-Based Supervision

Due to the number of firms for which a regulator may be responsible, the regulator must consider how to align its resources with the risks each firm may pose to market stability. Where its risk assessments indicate that a firm may pose a risk to the regulator's objectives, the regulator may assign particular staff members to have an ongoing direct relationship with the firm. Such an approach is normally supported by periodic visits and meetings with the management of the firm, as well as ongoing desk-based monitoring of the firm's financial and information returns.

In a small number of cases, the intensity of relational oversight may be increased. This can, for example, occur if a significant concern has been identified by the firm or the regulator. If the firm is a large bank, this represents a substantial risk to the overall market.

Such intensive oversight is reflected in the regulator:

- paying close attention to the firm's activities
- increasing the frequency of meetings, and
- requesting additional types of data/reporting.

This approach is sometimes referred to as 'close and continuous supervision' (though each regulator will determine its own label).

This more intensive supervision is characterised by frequent dialogue with the firm on the full range of supervisory issues, through ad hoc meetings, regular telephone conversations and emails. The regulator's activity may include:

- reviewing strategic and business developments through discussions with the firm
- reviewing updates from the firm regarding resolution of specific known issues
- attending results presentations
- monitoring the market in which it operates
- assessing the ongoing validity of the regulator's risk assessment
- monitoring financial data, supervisory returns and management information
- reacting to specific requests from the firm, such as around capital requirements
- undertaking the formal review process which sets the capital requirements of the firm on the basis of the risks identified by the firm, and
- selecting the firm to be included in thematic reviews where they relate to a specific area of its business.

2.4 IOSCO's Principles Relating to the Regulator

Learning Objective

1.2.8 Know IOSCO's principles 1 to 8 relating to the regulator

---

IOSCO has produced 38 principles of securities regulation; 15 apply to regulators, including those relating to self-regulation and principles for enforcement and cooperation in regulation. As noted in section 2.2.3, IOSCO has introduced 38 principles subdivided into ten categories.

The first category relates to Principles Relating to the Regulator and contains principles 1–8, which are as follows:

Principles Relating to the Regulator

1. The responsibilities of the regulator should be clear and objectively stated.
2. The regulator should be operationally independent and accountable in the exercise of its functions and powers.
3. The regulator should have adequate powers, proper resources and the capacity to perform its functions and exercise its powers.
4. The regulator should adopt clear and consistent regulatory processes.
5. The staff of the regulator should observe the highest professional standards including appropriate standards of confidentiality.
6. The regulator should have or contribute to a process to monitor, mitigate and manage systemic risk, appropriate to its mandate.
7. The regulator should have or contribute to a process to review the perimeter of regulation regularly.
8. The regulator should seek to ensure that conflicts of interest and misalignment of incentives are avoided, eliminated, disclosed or otherwise managed.

2.5 Regulator Enforcement Powers

Learning Objective

1.2.9 Know regulators' enforcement powers

IOSCO's Principles for the Enforcement of Securities Regulations (Category C, principles 10 – 12) provide an overview of the types of enforcement powers that financial services regulators may seek to use.

2.5.1 Inspection and Compliance Programmes

Supervision of market intermediaries conducted through inspection and surveillance helps to ensure the maintenance of high standards and the protection of investors. These preventative programmes are a necessary complement to investigation and enforcement programmes. The regulator should have the power to require the provision of information or to carry out inspections of business operations, whenever it believes it is necessary to ensure compliance with relevant standards. The suspicion of a breach of law should not be a necessary prerequisite to use inspection powers in respect of authorised or licensed persons.

Inspections may be carried out by the regulator itself or another competent authority. Alternatively, the regulator might consider delegating such authority to SROs or using third parties, properly supervised, to carry out some of this inspection work on its behalf. These third parties should also be subject to disclosure and confidentiality requirements. Such inspections must be carried out with adequate instruments and techniques, and these may vary between jurisdictions. In some areas, for example, the scrutiny of trading on an exchange, the use of technology will be necessary for effective regulation.

In other areas, including the inspection of broker conduct, consideration needs to be given to the balance between on-site inspection and interview and the requirement to provide information from time to time which can be reviewed off-site. Inspection visits may be rotational or driven by risk assessment or complaint. In making decisions on the efficient use of resources, the regulator must consider both the need for wide market coverage and the importance of adequate inspection in areas of high risk to investors or which threaten systemic stability.

2.5.2 Comprehensive Enforcement Powers

The complex character of securities transactions and the sophistication of fraudulent schemes require strong and rigorous enforcement of securities laws. Investors in the securities markets are particularly vulnerable to misconduct by intermediaries and others.

The regulator or other competent government authority should, therefore, be provided with comprehensive investigatory and enforcement powers including:

- regulatory and investigative powers to obtain data, information, documents, statements and records from persons involved in the relevant conduct or who may have information relevant to the inquiry
- power to seek orders and/or to take other action to ensure compliance with these regulatory, administrative and investigation powers
- power to impose administrative sanctions and/or to seek orders from courts or tribunals
- power to initiate or to refer matters for criminal prosecution
- power to order the suspension of trading in securities or to take other appropriate action
- where enforcement action is able to be taken, the power to enter into enforceable settlements and to accept binding undertakings.

These enforcement powers should, however, not compromise private rights of action.

Private persons should be able to seek their own remedies (including, for example, for compensation or specific performance of an obligation). The responsibility for all aspects of enforcement of the securities law are not necessarily given to a single body. There are several models that have been shown to be effective. These include models in which responsibilities are shared between several government or quasi-government agencies or where responsibility is shared with SROs.

The sharing of responsibility and the need for close cooperation may be particularly important in ensuring that only those who have the necessary authorisation are active participants on the markets; unlicensed persons should be prosecuted.

2.5.3 International Enforcement

Securities markets facilitate international transactions, and so matters of conduct may involve multiple jurisdictions.

Legislation and the enforcement powers of the regulator should be sufficient to ensure that it can be effective in cases of cross-border misconduct.

This means the regulator should strive to ensure that it or another authority in its jurisdiction:

- has the necessary authority to obtain information, including statements and documents, that may be relevant to investigating and prosecuting potential violations of laws and regulations relating to securities transactions, and
- that such information can be shared directly with other regulators or indirectly through authorities in their jurisdictions for use in investigations and prosecutions.

2.6 Regulated Activities and Products

Learning Objective

1.2.10 Understand what types of activities and investment products are generally required to be regulated

In the UK, regulated activities can be split into four broad categories:

- banking activities
- investment activities
- insurance activities, and
- home finance activities.

For each of the activities the firm intends to perform, it has to obtain authorisation and identify the types of specified investments it plans to offer. Also, for each proposed activity, the firm must identify the types of specified investments to which its regulated services will relate. A UK-regulated firm may, for instance, obtain permission to deal in investments as agent, in respect of **futures** and **options**, while being authorised to manage investments that are units in a collective investment scheme (CIS) or shares. Although the terminology used and the regulated activities mentioned in the remainder of this section are derived from UK regulations, they are closely aligned with other jurisdictions.

2.6.1 Banking Activities

- accepting deposits, and
- issuing e-money.

2.6.2 Investment Activities

- dealing in investments (as principal or agent)
- arranging deals in investments
- operating an MTF
- managing investments
- safeguarding and administering investments
- sending **dematerialised** instructions
- establishing CISs
- establishing stakeholder pension schemes
- providing basic advice on stakeholder products
- advising on investments

- operating an electronic system in relation to lending
- managing an Undertakings for Collective Investments in Transferable Securities (UCITS)
- acting as **trustee** or depositary of a UCITS
- managing an Alternative Investment Fund (AIF)
- acting as trustee or depositary of an AIF.

2.6.3 Insurance Activities

- effecting or carrying out contracts of insurance as principal
- assisting in the administration and performance of a contract of insurance
- Lloyd's market activities.

2.6.4 Home Finance Activities

- arranging home finance activities
- advising on home finance activities
- entering into a home finance activity
- administering a home finance activity, and
- agreeing to do most of the above activities.

2.6.5 Specified Investments

Specified investments are shown in the following list. A firm must identify the range of investment types applicable to each activity it will perform. The profiles of individual firms can, therefore, be quite dynamic in terms of the combination of activities and products. For small firms, the regulators may have standard profiles which act as guides for applicants for authorisation.

Specified Investments

- Deposits.
- Electronic money.
- Rights under a contract of insurance.
- Shares.
- Instruments creating or acknowledging indebtedness.
- Government and public securities.
- Certificates representing certain securities.
- Instruments giving entitlement to investments.
- Units in a CIS.
- Rights under a personal pension scheme.
- Rights under a stakeholder pension scheme.
- Futures.
- Options.
- Lloyd's syndicate capacity and syndicate membership.
- Contracts for differences (CFDs).
- Rights under regulated mortgage contracts.
- Rights under funeral plan contracts.

- Rights under a home purchase plan.
- Rights under a home reversion plan.
- Rights to or interests in anything that is a specified investment listed, excluding 'rights under regulated mortgage contracts', 'rights under regulated home reversion plans' and rights under regulated home purchase plans'.

2.7 Regulatory Requirements on Firms

Learning Objective

1.2.11 Understand the requirements regulation places on firms: minimum entry standards; initial and ongoing capital and other prudential requirements; requirement to establish an internal compliance function; conduct of business

The IOSCO principles 29-32 are related to Market Intermediaries, and cover, among others, entry standards and capital requirements. These provisions include the typical requirements firms are required to meet in relation to authorisation, supervision, capital adequacy and the conduct of business rules and other prudential requirements.

2.7.1 Authorisation (including Licensing and Registration) and Supervision

The regulator will set minimum standards for market participants and provide consistency of treatment for all similar firms. It should also reduce the risk to investors of loss caused by negligent or illegal behaviour or inadequate capital.

The **authorisation** process normally requires a comprehensive assessment of the applicant and all those who are in a position to control or materially influence the applicant. The regulatory authority has, in the normal course, the power to reject applications that do not meet the standards set.

The regulator also has the power to withdraw or suspend the licence or otherwise sanction the licensee, whenever the entry criteria are not fulfilled. Changes of control or material influence should be made known to the regulator or another competent authority in order to ensure that its assessment of the firm remains valid. The regulator should be empowered to withdraw a licence or authorisation where a change in control results in a failure to meet relevant requirements.

The following matters should be the subject of consideration:

- Regulation should set conditions of entry that make clear the basis of participation. The entry conditions should be consistently applied and do not need to be determined by the regulator. For example, the entry conditions could be defined by the SRO, in which case, the process should be subject to appropriate oversight by the regulator.
- Regulation should determine whether participation in the market by a firm should be based upon a demonstration of appropriate knowledge, resources, skills and ethical attitude (including a consideration of past conduct); this is sometimes referred to as the 'fit and proper' test.

- The regulator should have the authority to refuse authorisation of a firm if these requirements have not been met.
- There should be an initial capital requirement for securities firms as a condition of entry into the market. This ensures that the owners of the business have a direct financial stake in the business. The capital requirement should be maintained and should be the subject of periodic reporting to the regulator or competent SRO. The ongoing capital requirement should be directly related to the nature and amount of business undertaken by a firm. The financial position of the firm should be regularly audited by independent auditors.

To ensure that continued authorisation remains appropriate, the periodic updating of relevant information should be required as well as the reporting of material changes in circumstances affecting the conditions of authorisation.

To enable investors to better protect their own interests, the regulator should ensure that the public has access to relevant information concerning the authorised firm, such as the category of **permissions** held, the scope of its authorised activities, the identity of senior management and those authorised to act in the name of the firm.

2.7.2 Capital Adequacy

The protection of investors and stability of financial systems are increased through adequate supervision of ongoing capital standards.

Capital adequacy standards foster confidence in the financial markets and are designed to allow a firm to absorb some losses, particularly in the event of large adverse market moves, and to achieve an environment in which a firm could wind down its business over a relatively short period without loss to its customers or the customers of other firms and without disrupting the orderly functioning of the financial markets. Capital standards are designed to provide supervisory authorities with time to intervene to accomplish the objective of orderly wind down.

A firm may be required to reserve a certain level of capital as part of the authorisation process, relative to the type of activity it will be permitted to perform. Once authorised, a firm should ensure that it maintains adequate financial resources to meet its business commitments and to withstand the risks to which its business is subject. Risk may result from the activities of unauthorised and off-balance sheet affiliates and regulation should consider the need for information about the activities of these affiliates.

A capital adequacy test will be used to address the risks faced by securities firms judged by reference to the nature and amount of business undertaken by the firm.

2.7.3 The Conduct of Business Rules and Other Prudential Requirements

Firms should conduct themselves in a way that protects the interests of their clients and helps to preserve the integrity of the market. The management of a firm bears primary responsibility for ensuring the maintenance of appropriate standards of conduct and adherence to proper procedures by the whole firm. This includes the proper management of the risks associated with the business of the firm. Regulation is not expected to remove risk from the marketplace, but it should ensure that there is proper management of that risk. Periodic evaluation of risk management processes within a regulated entity is appropriate. SROs and third parties, such as external auditors, may be used to assist in this process.

Most supervisors and SROs have published guidance and rules related to the conduct of business. These rules are included, for example, in the FCA Handbook (Conduct of Business), the CFA Code of Ethics and Standards of Professional Conduct and the CISI's Code of Conduct. These rules typically address issues including acting honestly, fairly and professionally. They also apply to transparency, client communication (via any medium, and regarding any type of information provided) and assessing the suitability of the products offered given client needs. Instances of operational breach can occur despite the existence of internal procedures designed to prevent relevant misconduct or negligence.

It is not practical for the regulator to oversee adherence to those internal procedures on a day-to-day basis. That is the responsibility of the senior management of the firm. Senior management must ensure that they are able to discharge that responsibility. They must themselves understand the nature of the firm's business, its internal control procedures and its policies on the assumption of risk. They must clearly understand the extent of their own authority and responsibilities. They must have access to all relevant information about the business on a timely basis and have available to them all necessary advice on that business and on their own responsibilities. That information must also be available to the regulator upon request.

2.7.4 Internal Compliance Function

It is important that a firm maintains an independent function to ensure that the firm's activity is aligned with regulatory requirements. While the operational areas will have controls in place to ensure processes are performed as intended, this internal compliance function will also ensure that those processes remain aligned with the rules.

The internal compliance function should be a permanent and effective part of the firm's governance structures and proportionate to the scale and complexity of the firm's business. Guidance from regulators tends to reflect the following responsibilities:

1. To monitor and, on a regular basis, to assess the adequacy and effectiveness of the measures and procedures put in place and the actions taken to address any deficiencies in the firm's compliance with its obligations.
2. To advise and assist the relevant persons responsible for carrying out regulated activities to comply with the firm's obligations under the regulatory system.

In order to enable the compliance function to discharge its responsibilities properly and independently, a firm must ensure that the following conditions are satisfied:

- The compliance function must have the necessary authority, resources, expertise and access to all relevant information.
- A compliance officer is appointed and must be responsible for the compliance function and for any reporting as to compliance required by the regulator.
- The relevant persons involved in the compliance functions must not be involved in the performance of the services or activities they monitor.
- The method of determining the remuneration of the relevant persons involved in the compliance function must not compromise their objectivity and must not be likely to do so.

Where the firm's size or level of activity is at a scale that would not warrant the appointment of an independent compliance officer, the firm would be expected to allocate to a director or senior manager the function of:

a. having responsibility for oversight of the firm's compliance, and
b. reporting to the governing body in respect of that responsibility.

In some jurisdictions, the tasks performed by the compliance function may be delegated to appropriate skilled individuals but generally the regulatory responsibility will remain with the senior management of the firm and the person allocated the responsibility for oversight of compliance.

2.8 Regulation of Cross-Border Business

Learning Objectives

1.2.12 Understand how regulators facilitate and regulate cross-border business: specific legislation; memoranda of understanding between individual regulators; supervisory colleges; recognition of third countries

1.2.13 Understand what regulations apply to a firm with international branches and subsidiaries: contractual agreements between regulators; home/host

1.2.14 Understand the challenge of conducting business whilst meeting the regulatory expectations and approach of multiple regulatory bodies: international; domestic

Earlier in this chapter, we looked at the extraterritorial reach of some major pieces of legislation. In addition, we considered the IOSCO principles around regulatory cooperation and international enforcement that are aimed at the need for national regulators to share information and assist one another. This reflects the threats to domestic financial markets and financial stability resulting from the behaviour and actions of firms involved in international financial activities and the globalisation of markets.

For example, cases of fraud and money laundering that involve dealings in securities or other financial products may require close cooperation between two or more domestic regulators, including law enforcement, regulatory and judicial authorities.

Other examples where cross-border cooperation may be required is where firms may have shares listed in more than one jurisdiction, where investors invest in foreign markets, either directly or through managed funds, where financial products are traded on various markets in several countries or, as in the case of derivatives, are based on an underlying product or indices traded, produced or derived on foreign markets. Fraud, market manipulation, insider trading and other illegal conduct that crosses jurisdictional boundaries can and does occur more frequently in a world aided by modern telecommunications.

Cooperation mechanisms are, therefore, important at an international level to facilitate the detection and deterrence of cross-border misconduct and to assist in the discharge of authorisation and supervisory responsibilities.

A memorandum of understanding (MoU) is one such mechanism that may be established between two regulatory authorities. The two supervisors write the MoU to set out how they would each act where a given need for oversight straddles their respective areas of responsibility. An MoU between regulators might, therefore, include the following matters:

- defining which regulator would take the lead role in investigating certain types of issue
- the manner of support that each regulator might provide to the other
- the way in which data exchanged between the regulators would be protected, and how that data might be used.

In this way, the framework for cross-border regulation can be communicated to the market, and expectations set.

The FSB has identified three key standards in the financial regulatory and supervisory area. They are:

- IOSCO's Objectives and Principles of Securities Regulation
- the BCBS Core Principles for Effective Banking Supervision, and
- the International Association of Insurance Supervisors (IAIS) Insurance Core Principles.

The FSB, in consultation with the BCBS, IAIS and IOSCO identified, within each of these standards, principles concerning international cooperation and information exchange. A status update published by the FSB in November 2012 named 44 jurisdictions that the IMF and World Bank concluded were demonstrating sufficiently strong adherence. A range of jurisdictions were noted as taking the actions recommended by the FSB, and only one jurisdiction was currently held to be non-cooperative.

Countries not part of the EU are, for the purpose of EU regulations, considered to be third countries. Third countries could be considered as equivalent, for the purpose of regulation, if their regulatory environment is deemed to be equivalent with the regulations in the EU. In addition, third country central counterparties (CCPs) may be recognised as equivalent provided they meet the requirements.

2.8.1 Home and Host Supervisors

The Basel Committee has provided clarity and consistency in how different regulators will relate to a firm that is active in multiple jurisdictions. The approach distinguishes between the home supervisor (country of incorporation) and the host supervisor (country or countries in which the firm operates).

In general, matters relating to the firm's structure and organisation (such as regulatory capital and authorisation processes) are a matter for the home supervisor. Matters relating to customer interaction tend to be addressed by the host supervisor(s).

In the EU, this approach is seen as beneficial for consumers, who should be similarly protected regardless of the EU domicile of the firm servicing them. For firms, the combination of home and host regulations requires additional effort, and any misalignment between the rules of the different jurisdictions can add complexity to the ability to effectively perform cross-border business.

2.8.2 Supervisory Colleges

Rather than the simplistic approach of home and host state regulation, a supervisory college brings together all the EU regulators relevant to the operations of a given banking group – and may include some non-EU regulators also – to agree a model of supervision that will satisfy the needs and objectives of each regulator. The supervisory colleges are of particular importance given the size and reach of financial institutions' cross-border activity within the EU.

The college is the means by which the regulators coordinate their efforts, ensuring that all necessary aspects of oversight are achieved. Their work will consider aspects such as risk management across the banking group (including its **liquidity risk**), and ensuring that the group's recovery plans are sufficiently robust in respect of the various markets being serviced.

The aim of the supervisory college is to provide regulators with a more flexible model for cross-border supervision, enabling the approach to be tailored according to the needs of each banking group.

2.8.3 Implications for Firms

The practical application of this for firms is that expanding an existing business or service into multiple jurisdictions introduces a mix of regulatory obligations. While these regulatory mechanisms are intended to standardise the regulatory requirements, even within Europe we have not reached a point of full harmonisation.

While a firm should, therefore, have a full understanding of how to apply the rules of its domestic regulator, expanding into additional countries requires the firm to understand what cross-border supervision approach will be applied – and then understand which rules must be followed in respect of the home state and host state. The firm needs to determine whether it requires additional authorisation in either jurisdiction, in order to perform its proposed expanded business. Where an EU firm is simply expanding to perform its existing authorised business in other EU member states, it will usually be possible to avoid full authorisation through use of a 'passport' – but if the business expansion sees the firm entering non-EU jurisdictions, a formal authorisation process might be required.

When a firm first begins cross-border activity, it is, therefore, vital to gain a detailed understanding of the new jurisdiction's regulations and applicable legislation. The firm can review the regulator's website for information or make contact with a relevant trade association in the new jurisdiction in order to better understand the approach taken in that country. It is also common to obtain external legal advice, or to recruit personnel with experience of that jurisdiction.

The firm should then assess how its relationship with its domestic regulator will change. For example, which of the additional business activities will be included in domestic regulatory returns and capital adequacy calculations. At the same time, the firm needs to understand the implications of any MoU in place between the relevant regulators. A banking group operating in the EU should confirm whether a supervisory college will be assembled and understand how it should best relate with the members of that college.

There may be a need to submit certain filings to the regulators before commencing the cross-border business, and the firm might need to update its policies and procedures to ensure that the needs of all relevant regulations are satisfied. Its structures for identifying regulatory change need to have an expanded scope to ensure that regulatory change in the expanded list of jurisdictions is identified and assessed for impact.

End of Chapter Questions

Think of an answer for each question and refer to the appropriate section for confirmation.

1. State two of the objectives of regulation.
   Answer reference: Section 1.1

2. State the main differences between rules-based and principles-based approaches to regulation.
   Answer reference: Section 1.3

3. What is the mission of the Islamic Financial Services Board (IFSB)?
   Answer reference: Section 1.4.2

4. What are the penalties for breach of the General Data Protection Regulation (GDPR)?
   Answer reference: Section 1.5.1

5. List the data subject rights.
   Answer reference: Section 1.5.1

6. State the objective of the Dodd-Frank Act.
   Answer reference: Section 1.5.2

7. Name three investment services that can be subject to passporting under the Markets in Financial Instruments Directive (MiFID).
   Answer reference: Section 1.5.3

8. What does Section 404 of the Sarbanes-Oxley (SOX) Act require publicly registered US companies to do?
   Answer reference: Section 1.5.3

9. What is the definition of payment services?
   Answer reference: Section 1.5.3

10. As required in SOX, how often should a company produce an 'internal controls report'?
    Answer reference: Section 1.5.3

11. What is the punishment for defrauding securities investors?
    Answer reference: Section 1.5.3

12. What extraterritorial reach does the UK Bribery Act provide?
    Answer reference: Section 1.5.4

13. What is 6AMLD and what does it entail?
    Answer reference: Section 1.5.4

14. What are the four forms of disciplinary action that exchange operators can take against any person registered by the exchange?
Answer reference: Section 1.6.1

15. What is counterparty risk?
Answer reference: Section 1.7

16. How do regulators approach Fintech?
Answer reference: Section 1.8

17. Which types of regulator typically cover insurance markets and investment services at a national level?
Answer reference: Section 2.1

18. What does the Basel Consultative Group provide?
Answer reference: Section 2.2.1

19. What are the three objectives of securities regulation that the International Organization of Securities Commissions (IOSCO) aims to achieve?
Answer reference: Section 2.2.3

20. Describe the main responsibility of the US Securities and Exchange Commission (SEC)?
Answer reference: Section 2.2.5

21. What are diagnostic tools used in thematic-based supervision?
Answer reference: Section 2.3.4

22. State IOSCO's eight Principles Relating to the Regulator.
Answer reference: Section 2.4

23. What four categories can UK-regulated activities be split into?
Answer reference: Section 2.6

24. Why does regulation require that firms have adequate capital standards?
Answer reference: Section 2.7.2

25. Explain the difference between home and host state regulations.
Answer reference: Section 2.8.1

Chapter Two

The Compliance Function

This syllabus area will provide approximately 24 of the 100 examination questions

1. International Best Practice

1.1 Systems and Controls

Learning Objective

2.1.1 Understand the fundamental systems and controls a firm should implement in order to conduct its business in line with international regulatory standards

1.1.1 Organising Appropriate Systems and Controls to Ensure Compliance

Compliance is most effective in a corporate culture that emphasises standards of honesty and integrity and in which the board of directors and the senior management lead by example. In other words, compliance starts at the top. However, it does not stop there, and it is vital that compliance is a concern of everyone in an organisation and should be viewed as an integral part of the firm's everyday activities. This also means observing the spirit, as well as the letter, of the law.

A firm needs to establish, implement and maintain adequate policies and procedures sufficient to ensure compliance of the firm (covering its managers, employees and representatives) with its obligations under the regulatory system in which it operates, and for countering the risk that the firm might be used to further financial crime (including money laundering). Compliance risk, generally, is seen as the risk of legal or regulatory sanctions, material financial loss, or loss to reputation as a result of failure to comply with laws, regulations, rules, related self-regulatory organisation (SRO) standards, and codes of conduct applicable to the firm's business.

Compliance is not the responsibility of specialist compliance staff alone. It needs to be embedded within a firm and become part of its culture. Nevertheless, a firm will be able to manage its **compliance risk** more effectively if it has a compliance function in place, the organisation of which may vary between firms. In a small firm, it may be an individual person, it may be a separate department or it may form a discrete part of an overall risk management function. In particularly large and/or international firms, compliance staff may be located within business lines and have group and local compliance officers; separate units may also be established to deal with the prevention of money laundering and terrorist financing.

Irrespective of the organisational structure, an effective compliance function should operate independently, be sufficiently resourced, and have the following responsibilities:

1. To regularly assess and monitor the adequacy and effectiveness of the measures and procedures put in place and the actions taken to address any deficiencies in the firm's compliance with its obligations.
2. To advise and assist the relevant persons responsible for carrying out regulated activities to comply with the firm's obligations under the regulatory system.

The Basel Committee on Banking Supervision (BCBS) has issued a set of ten principles relating to compliance and the compliance function. While these principles are aimed at banks, their general approach has a much wider application for firms across the financial sector subject to regulation. The BCBS principles can be found at www.bis.org/publ/bcbs113.pdf.

1.1.2 Responsibilities of the Board

The first of the BCBS principles is that the board of directors is responsible for overseeing the management of the firm's compliance risk. The board should approve the firm's compliance policy, including a formal document establishing a permanent and effective compliance function. At least once a year, the board or a committee of the board should assess the extent to which the firm is managing its compliance risk effectively.

A firm's compliance policy will not be effective unless the board of directors promotes the values of honesty and integrity throughout the organisation. Compliance with applicable laws, rules and standards should be viewed as an essential means to this end. As is the case with other categories of risk, the board is responsible for ensuring that an appropriate policy is in place to manage the firm's compliance risk. The board should oversee the implementation of the policy, including ensuring that compliance issues are resolved effectively and expeditiously by senior management with the assistance of the compliance function. The board may, of course, delegate these tasks to an appropriate board-level committee (eg, its audit committee).

1.1.3 Responsibilities of Senior Management

The BCBS principles also set out the responsibilities of senior management who are responsible for:

- the effective management of compliance risk
- establishing and communicating a compliance policy, for ensuring that it is observed, and for reporting to the board of directors on the management of the firm's compliance risk.

Therefore, senior managers are responsible for establishing a written compliance policy that contains the basic principles to be followed by management and staff, and explains the main processes by which compliance risks are to be identified and managed through all levels of the organisation. Clarity and transparency may be promoted by making a distinction between general standards for all staff members and rules that only apply to specific groups of staff.

Senior management are also responsible for ensuring that compliance policy is observed and that appropriate remedial or disciplinary action is taken if breaches are identified. They should also identify and assess the main compliance risk issues facing the firm (with the assistance of the compliance function, at least once a year) and the plans to manage them. Such plans should:

- address any shortfalls (policy, procedures, implementation or execution) related to how effectively existing compliance risks have been managed
- address the need for any additional policies or procedures to deal with new compliance risks identified as a result of the annual compliance risk assessment.

Senior management should:

- at least once a year, report to the board of directors or a committee of the board on the firm's management of its compliance risk, in such a manner as to assist board members to make an informed judgement on whether the firm is managing its compliance risk effectively, and
- report promptly to the board of directors, or a committee of the board, on any material compliance failures (eg, failures that may attract a significant risk of legal or regulatory sanctions, material financial loss, or loss to reputation).

1.2 Adequate Resources

Learning Objective

2.1.2 Understand BIS Principle 6 and the requirement for adequate resources

Principle 6 of the BCBS principles on 'compliance and the compliance function in banks' states:

'The bank's compliance function should have the resources to carry out its responsibilities effectively'.

The resources should be both sufficient and appropriate for effective management of the firm's compliance risk.

In particular, compliance function staff should have:

- the necessary qualifications, experience and professional and personal qualities to enable them to carry out their specific duties, and
- a sound understanding of compliance laws, rules and standards and their practical impact on the firm's operations.

The professional skills of compliance function staff, especially with respect to keeping up to date with developments in compliance laws, rules and standards, should be maintained through regular and systematic education and training.

1.3 Compliance Manual and Policies

Learning Objective

2.1.3 Understand the practical applications of a formalised document of compliance policies and procedures: compliance manual

1.3.1 Purpose of the Compliance Manual

The purpose of the compliance manual is to formally document the standards to be followed by all employees in their personal conduct and in conducting business with customers and counterparties.

It also serves to expand upon compliance-related content of the company's corporate governance manual in relation to:

- the legal and regulatory obligations of employees, and contracted agents
- the policies and procedures that apply to the business and personal conduct of employees and agents to ensure that they comply with the laws, regulations, rules and codes that govern the firm's conduct of business as a regulated firm.

All managers and directors of the company are responsible for ensuring that the members of their teams read, understand and are fully conversant with the contents. It should be remembered that this manual is not a procedures manual but rather provides policy and guidance. Detailed procedures are normally produced by the various operational business areas and overseen by managers or directors who will be responsible for ensuring their staff know where to find such information.

1.3.2 Scope of the Compliance Manual

The compliance manual endeavours to give a high-level overview of the rules and regulations of the regulatory bodies governing the firm's business. For firms operating internationally, it is important to clearly document how differing or overlapping regulatory requirements will affect operations and staff. The compliance manual provides employees with the information required to comply with the rules and regulations applicable to their activities. These may include relevant laws of the countries in which the firm directly operates, or in which its clients are situated. Ignorance of the law or relevant rules and regulations will not protect the company or its employees.

Employees are urged to consult with the compliance function if problems arise. The compliance function normally seeks feedback from staff with a view to regular updating of the compliance manual. It is important that it is a 'living' document and the compliance function needs to keep everyone informed of significant developments arising from regulatory changes and experience throughout the company. Many firms now use an online compliance manual with search facilities and links to online learning modules and relevant regulatory websites.

See Appendix 1 for an example of the contents page of a compliance manual.

1.3.3 Communicating the Formal Status of the Compliance Function

The compliance function must have a formal status within the firm to give it the appropriate standing, authority and independence. This may be set out in the firm's compliance policy or in any other formal document. The document should be communicated to all staff, either electronically via an intranet site or other means. The compliance policy needs to be included in induction and other relevant training.

The compliance manual will contain the following with respect to the compliance function:

- Its role and responsibilities.
- Measures to ensure its independence.
- Its relationship with other risk management functions within the firm and with the internal audit function.
- in cases where compliance responsibilities are carried out by staff in different departments, how these responsibilities are to be allocated among the departments.

- Its right to obtain access to information necessary to carry out its responsibilities, and the corresponding duty of staff to cooperate in supplying this information.
- Its right to conduct investigations of possible breaches of the compliance policy and to appoint outside experts to perform this task if appropriate.
- Its right to be able to freely express and disclose its findings to senior management, and if necessary, the board of directors or a committee of the board.
- Its formal reporting obligations to senior management.
- Its right of direct access to the board of directors or a committee of the board.

1.4 An Effective Compliance Function

Learning Objectives

2.1.4 Understand how an effective compliance function can add value to a business

2.1.5 Know how to produce and implement an effective compliance programme

The compliance function needs to take a proactive approach to its dual responsibilities of monitoring the business and providing advice to senior management. A well-run compliance function can be a tremendous competitive advantage to a firm, helping to build a strong reputation and attract business. The key purposes are to:

- provide reassurance to the board and senior management that the business is operating in a compliant manner, through regular reports, *ad hoc* reports and other management information
- provide advice and assistance to the board directors, management and staff to help them to meet their compliance responsibilities
- identify and record good and bad practice; provide feedback on failures in controls and compliance and provide recommendations for improvements and, where necessary, remedial action
- provide analysis and early warning of regulatory change which may impact the business; and to ensure that such change is communicated to the board and the management
- build a good and open relationship with the firm's regulators to ensure they have a good understanding of the business, the risks involved and how those risks are controlled, and to facilitate business development where new permissions or licences are required and, where necessary, resolve issues
- where relevant, respond and coordinate responses to proposed legislation or regulations with a view to achieving regulations that, while meeting the objectives, take into account the practical implications for businesses; such responses may be direct with regulators or through trade associations.

An effective compliance function will add value to the business. It will keep it on a compliance path, and its involvement and advice will be sought by all levels of staff in the business. Such a function will contribute to innovation, business development and other projects. It will be seen as a business enabler rather than a stereotypical business-prevention unit.

The compliance function will provide senior management with information and advice on compliance laws, rules, and standards. It will also provide guidance and education for senior management – especially during times of substantial regulatory change or when the firm is expanding into new product areas.

While these matters can be of great value when successfully deployed, it is important that the compliance function continues to provide a thorough monitoring programme and ensure that compliance risk is understood. The compliance officer must, therefore, be able to secure the resources needed to deliver these goals.

The compliance function usually supports operational areas when preparing/reviewing their procedures and policies, to ensure that underlying regulatory requirements are correctly incorporated into the material. With this support given, the first line of defence is better equipped to prevent problems arising, and the compliance team builds valuable engagement ahead of future monitoring activity.

The compliance function may include specific statutory roles (eg, an officer fulfilling the role of money laundering reporting officer (MLRO)), and may liaise with relevant external bodies, including regulators, standard setters and external experts. They may also be responsible for ensuring that relevant regulatory returns and filings are made, for example, working with a corporate finance department and signing off the adequacy of capital calculations, or arranging for regular reporting of transactions, complaints, **client assets** and money.

Prior to new directors or senior managers taking up their responsibilities, the compliance function staff would normally coordinate the application to regulators for approval of those individuals, where required. Similarly, where there was any need for authorisations or variation in the permissions a firm has, compliance function staff would complete or advise on those applications.

1.4.1 Identification, Measurement and Assessment of Compliance Risk

The compliance function proactively identifies, documents and assesses the compliance risks associated with the firm's business activities, including the development of new products and business practices, the proposed establishment of new types of business or customer relationships, or material changes in the nature of such relationships. If the firm has, for example, a new products committee, operations committee or risk management committee, compliance function staff should be represented on such committees.

The compliance function needs to measure compliance risk (eg, by using performance indicators) and use such measurements to enhance compliance risk assessment. Technology can be used as a tool in developing performance indicators by aggregating or filtering data that may be indicative of potential compliance problems (eg, an increasing number of customer complaints, breach trends, or irregular trading or payments activity).

The compliance function must assess the appropriateness of the firm's compliance procedures and guidelines, promptly follow up any identified deficiencies, and, where necessary, formulate proposals for amendments.

1.4.2 Monitoring, Testing and Reporting

The compliance function needs to monitor and test compliance by performing sufficient and representative compliance testing. The results of the compliance testing are reported to the head of compliance in accordance with the firm's internal risk management procedures. Determining what needs to be monitored is part of developing the compliance programme.

On a regular basis, the head of compliance reports to senior management on compliance matters. The reports include the compliance risk assessment during the reporting period, including any changes in the compliance risk profile based on relevant measurements such as performance indicators; a summary of any identified breaches and/or deficiencies and the corrective measures recommended to address them; and report on corrective measures already taken. The reporting format will be commensurate with the firm's compliance risk profile and activities.

1.5 Compliance Monitoring Programme

Learning Objectives

2.2.10 Understand the purpose of a compliance monitoring programme: risk-based; reporting; planned

2.2.11 Understand the key considerations in developing a compliance monitoring programme

2.2.12 Understand how to conduct an effective compliance monitoring programme: working papers; minute meetings with senior management; management responses; risk mitigation plans

The compliance programme sets out the responsibilities of the compliance function and its planned activities such as the implementation and review of specific policies and procedures, compliance risk assessment, compliance testing, and educating staff on compliance matters. It is the responsibility of the head of compliance or equivalent, to ensure appropriate coverage across businesses and coordination among risk management functions.

The purpose of the compliance monitoring programme is to provide an independent review of the operational work performed by the firm, with a focus on two elements:

1. To confirm whether operational tasks are being performed in line with operational procedures.
2. To confirm whether operational procedures continue to reflect current regulatory requirements.

It is impractical for the compliance function to review every item of processed work – the cost of supporting such oversight would be uneconomical – and so the compliance function must establish a method for performing sufficient oversight to be confident that the underlying risks have been appropriately controlled. Hence, the compliance monitoring programme must be risk based. The programme involves the review and testing of documentation and completed work items, to identify findings and recommendations for improvements. Specific working papers are generally used, detailing the parameters of the testing to be performed, in order to ensure that the scope of each monitoring review is achieved. The completed working papers also provide a clear evidential record of the review work performed and the specific items that gave rise to findings.

While such compliance efforts should be independent of operations, it is important that senior management of the operational area concerned, understand the findings and agree on the remedial action to be taken. Formal reporting to senior managers in the business is a common step to ensure that all business areas are aware of the types of issues being identified and the actions being taken to rectify problems. In larger programmes, the compliance function produces a risk mitigation plan to provide the board with an overall view of how compliance engagement with the operational areas is improving the risk position of the business.

While firms establish their programmes in different ways, there are essentially three key stages:

Stage 1 – Information Gathering

Information is gathered on potential adverse events – such as errors that may arise in the activities undertaken by the firm in delivering its products and services. These may include:

- payments not made on time
- suspicious activity not reported
- failure to complete reconciliations (assets or money)
- late execution of client instructions
- late handling or mishandling of complaints or breaches
- unsuitable investment advice.

(The above is an illustrative rather than exhaustive list.)

Stage 2 – Scoring

The events identified as part of Stage 1 are scored for financial impact, exposure and probability. In designing the scoring method, it is necessary to decide whether each metric will be scored using discrete values (eg, a cash value in sterling or a frequency in days) or using relative values.

Financial Impact

Financial impact reflects the magnitude of financial cost were the adverse event to crystallise, and is usually a relative measure (eg, a '1' may mean an event that could threaten the company's continued existence, while a '3' may indicate significant operational disturbance but not have catastrophic potential). This has benefits because actual or estimated costs vary according to:

- the precise nature of the event (versus its high-level definition as per Stage 1)
- the particular area or element of activity that gives rise to it, and
- precise values, if the event relates to investment transactions.

Similarly, the potential financial impact of a regulatory transgression is difficult to reliably forecast. Factors to be considered should include:

- investigation costs (potentially including third-party review)
- compensation costs to affected customers
- legal costs in defending the company against regulatory action, and
- potential regulatory fines.

A final consideration is the requirement to include the future financial impact of loss of goodwill and/or reputation due to the event, but the near impossibility of attributing any particular value or amount.

Consequently, financial impact is generally scored according to a set of relative impact ratings (eg, a scale from 'high' to 'low').

The head of financial management, for example, the finance director or financial controller, will often assist by scoring individual events per area, providing experience of the level of past costs, and offering an informed assessment of likely impact were an event to occur.

Exposure Frequency Score

Exposure means how often the activity occurs that could give rise to the adverse event. This can, for example, be implemented using a conversion table that provides a value approximating to the number of occurrences expected/evidenced in a single year. Given the number of business days in a year, a value of 250 might be adopted as indicating a 'daily' event. From that starting point, you might build the following conversion table:

500	–	Real-time
250	–	Daily
50	–	Weekly
10	–	Monthly
4	–	Quarterly
2	–	Half-yearly
1	–	Annually
0.5	–	Infrequently
0.1	–	Rarely

When deciding these values, the firm should ensure that the scoring model is appropriately balanced (to prevent certain types of events being given disproportionate attention, while other types of concerns do not sufficiently emerge). For example, the 'real-time' score needs to balance the following:

- Certain activities may occur twice in the working day (eg, work item batching or the receipt of postal deliveries), matching a score of 500
- Setting a number greater than 500 increases the potential that the model could exaggerate the effect of an event.

While these scores are largely a matter of fact, care must be taken to ensure the scoring system does not incorrectly exaggerate or underplay events such as 'infrequent, with extreme financial impact' and 'real-time events having little financial impact'. Use of an 'additional probability weight field' may be appropriate, or the use of 'volume' rather than 'frequency' might be preferable for some activities.

Probability Weight

The probability of the adverse event actually occurring must then be determined, taking into account the strength of procedures and controls within the area. This may be expressed as the 'probability of the risk crystallising', known as a 'PORC' factor, which reflects the annualised likelihood of an event occurring given the management controls that are in place. For example:

Low	–	<30%
Medium	–	30% to 70%
High	–	>70%

Care must be taken when considering scores of 0% (an impossible event) or 100% (an inevitable event). Some scoring systems are designed to not recognise such scores, while others will permit them in certain circumstances. The initial assessment is based on consideration by compliance, audit and operations management of the findings from past and recent examinations or assessments, the incidence of breaches and complaints, and the extent of manual processes. Trends and proportions are more important considerations than absolute numbers, which, in any event, must be reviewed regularly.

Stage 3 – Weightings

The above variables represent the risk identified by the business. However, the compliance officer may need to use additional variables in order to determine the priority subjects for inclusion in the monitoring programme. Such weighting of priorities can be affected through variables such as:

- **Anxiety weighting** – what is currently worrying the compliance officer about industry/regulator-expressed concerns – perhaps the regulator is undertaking a thematic review on market timing or the care and protection given to client assets and money.
- **Perspective** – whereas the gathering of information has been largely based on past experience of adverse events, here it is appropriate to consider future volumes of business, propose new areas and the implications for existing operations.
- **Days since last tested** – activities may be considered low risk, perhaps because of low value impact, or because the controls are considered so strong that it is unlikely that the activity would naturally come to the top as a result of the risk factors considered so far. In such cases, using a weighting based on the time elapsed since the activity was last reviewed, ie, that increases as the time-span gets longer, means that eventually the activity will come to the top of the list and be included in the monitoring schedule.

Some firms prefer using a plan which is fixed at one point in the year, and then, following that plan for 12 months. A more dynamic approach is to aim to complete the review of all activities over, for example, an 18-month period but run the risk assessment on a quarterly basis to focus each quarter's work on the most pressing activities; this also allows for any incidents or regulator concerns to be proactively incorporated into the programme.

1.6 Integration of Regulatory Requirements

Learning Objective

2.1.6 Understand how regulatory requirements should be integrated into operating systems, policies and procedures

It is important for a firm to ensure that the operational processes and procedures it employs deliver the outcomes required by regulation. It is also important that the firm establishes controls to ensure that implementation of new processes and procedures – including changes to associated IT systems – are performed based on a sound understanding of those regulatory requirements. The regulatory requirements must be integrated within the firm's processes.

Successful integration of regulatory requirements and the maintenance of compliant systems, procedures and controls require the concerted effort of the whole business and the people who make up the board of directors, management and staff of the firm.

As with most compliance-related issues, integration starts from the top and depends heavily on the culture of the firm. The board and individual directors must consider whether they have the appropriate organisation and controls to ensure that regulatory requirements are integrated and compliance is embedded in the ethos of the firm. They should periodically review their high-level governance policies and procedures.

- **People** – the requirement is to establish an appropriate recruitment programme and hire staff with the right skills, knowledge and experience relating to the business. This includes setting out the required competencies, qualifications, experience expected and testing of candidates to ensure they have the appropriate skills and knowledge required.
- **Allocation of responsibilities** – the use of written job descriptions is a useful guide for individuals and should include, at a high level, their regulatory responsibilities. This might include a responsibility for managers to train their staff in financial crime prevention, information security and treating customers fairly.
- **Training** – comprehensive training programmes should be in place, ranging from induction courses, on-the-job training, specialist sessions on regulatory areas and a requirement to undertake continuing professional development (CPD), including appropriate professional examinations, with access to regulatory updates or bulletins produced by the compliance function and industry updates. A minimum number of CPD hours should be set. Periodic training assessments and needs analysis should be undertaken which use information from a regular appraisal of staff or personal development reviews.
- **Procedures** – written procedures need to be in place for all areas of the business which provide guidance for staff on how to perform activities and incorporate compliance processes. In some firms, they will map the procedures and processes to the relevant regulations and rulebooks. These procedures should be reviewed and signed off periodically by the local management as compliant. The compliance function will check samples of these procedures as part of their monitoring assignments to ensure the validation process is being followed. The compliance function will have procedures for its own activities.
- **Systems** – the design of operational systems should incorporate all the relevant regulatory requirements. These should be documented in business requirements, system requirement or specification documents and be included as part of a robust system and user testing scripts. While the business areas should specify their requirements, the compliance function will often be called upon to provide advice and guidance on new procedures and significant changes to regulations. Again, the regulatory effectiveness of systems and the controls will be included in the sample checks performed by compliance staff during their monitoring assignments.

1.7 Regulations, Internal Policies and Procedures

Learning Objective

2.1.7 Know the difference between regulations, internal policies and procedures

Regulations, internal policies and procedures are all important to a firm's governance, though each has a distinct purpose and origin. Regulations are provided by governments and regulatory bodies to give clear minimum rules by which businesses can operate. Regulations might be rules-based or principles-based. Internal policies are created within each firm to guide staff and management in respect of the core principles by which the firm will achieve compliance and explain the main processes to be followed. Policies go further than regulations and, for example, set internal codes of conduct with requirements that go beyond what is required by regulation. Procedures provide the detailed guidance on the action to be taken by management and staff.

Internal policies and procedures reflect the firm's interpretation of the regulations. The regulations may offer flexibility and, therefore, different firms may adopt different approaches. Once again, it is important that the compliance function is involved in reviewing policies to ensure the interpretation is valid. In some cases, an opinion from external consultants or legal experts may be beneficial.

While regulations, internal policies and procedures serve distinct purposes, conflicts between these items can arise – particularly in respect of international businesses. Conflicts may arise between the local regulations in one jurisdiction and the corporate internal policies and procedures handed down from head office. It is important to identify any such conflicts that arise, and to ensure that regulatory requirements are satisfied in the resolution.

1.8 Regulatory Implications of Business Strategies

Learning Objective

2.1.8 Understand the potential regulatory implications of business strategies: outsourcing and oversight; capital requirements; variation of permissions; control framework

1.8.1 Outsourcing and Oversight

Many firms take a strategic decision to concentrate on certain core activities and to outsource other activities and support functions to specialist suppliers. For example, a global asset manager operating collective investment funds may decide that it wants to concentrate on management of the investment portfolios but outsource all the activities to do with fund accounting, pricing and investor record-keeping.

Generally, regulations permit firms to outsource the tasks associated with regulated activities – though the firm retains regulatory responsibility for those tasks outsourced. This means that supervisory or enforcement action could be taken against the firm if the outsource service provider fails to deliver a compliant operation. Typically, when outsourcing a material task, the firm needs to advise its regulator in advance. In some countries, regulatory approval is required before outsourcing, and in some cases, outsourcing of specific tasks may not be permitted, or a geographic limitation may be applied with a view to protecting investors.

When outsourcing, a regulator will expect the firm:

- to undertake appropriate due diligence of the service provider
- to retain sufficient expertise to undertake oversight of the outsource service provider, to ensure the service is compliant and ensure access to relevant information is provided to both the firm and the regulator
- to have a written contract with the service provider together with a clear service level agreement and establish key performance indicators
- to have agreed with the service provider plans for business continuity and disaster recovery, including periodic testing of any applicable back-up facilities.

A more detailed checklist for outsourcing is provided in Appendix 2.

The European Banking Authority (EBA) has issued guidelines on outsourcing which came into force on 30 September 2019. The guidelines contain specific provisions for the governance frameworks in relation to outsourced activities of financial institutions as well as the related supervisory expectations and processes. The guidelines specifically state that the financial institution's management remains responsible for all of their activities including those that are outsourced.

The institution must have sufficient resources available to appropriately support and ensure the performance of their responsibilities including overseeing all risk and management of the outsourcing arrangements. Outsourcing must not lead to a situation in which an institution becomes an 'empty shell' that lacks the substance to remain authorised. When the service provider to which operations have been outsourced is based outside of the EU, they still need to comply with EU rules and regulations if they provide services to financial institutions based in the EU.

In the US, however, outsourcing by financial institutions is not subject to any regulations.

1.8.2 Capital Requirements

The financial crisis has led to a strengthening of capital requirements and standards by regulators in many parts of the world. Models for firms to use in calculating capital adequacy (ie, the appropriate amount of capital a firm should maintain) have become increasingly complex. Examples of international capital adequacy approaches include the Bank for International Settlements (BIS) Basel II and III Accords for banks, and the EU's Solvency II Directive aimed at harmonising capital requirements across the insurance industry in the EU.

Typically, the regulations and standards set out how to determine the appropriate levels of capital adequacy given the types of business and levels of risk the business or assets held may represent. Two approaches are commonly used:

- The use of a standard formula for calculating the minimum capital requirements. Depending on the risk-weighted assets of the firm, the minimum capital requirement may fluctuate. In simple terms, this means the higher the risk, the greater the capital requirement.
- The use of internal models to determine the risk reflecting the firm's own risk and solvency assessment. These internal models should better reflect the firm's risk profile than the adoption of a standard formula. It may be lower than the capital adequacy requirement based on a standard formula but equally, it may be higher. The models will need to be approved by the regulator, and are subject to robust governance.

It is important that the business incorporates its regulatory reporting requirements for capital within its overall strategy and operations. Retail banking will have a different risk profile to investment banking, for example. The mix of business chosen and the risk appetite of the institution as set by the board will have significant implications for capital adequacy and overall regulatory requirements.

Any plans to change the business strategy of the firm should, therefore, take into consideration any implications for the firm's capital requirements. A business expansion that might appear profitable could be undermined if it would require the firm to substantially increase its level of regulatory capital.

1.8.3 Variation of Permission (VOP)

One of the ways in which a regulator controls the risks to its objectives is to limit the regulated activities a firm may undertake. A firm must ensure it holds the relevant permissions for the business it undertakes, and will also want to ensure it does not hold excess authorisations. The broader its permissions, the greater the regulatory obligations.

Forward planning is, however, essential for business development purposes and the regulatory implications. Early involvement of the compliance function will be required if the firm plans to move into new areas of business, either in terms of an extension of current activities or to diversify into entirely new activities. In many jurisdictions, the process to amend authorisation is known as a variation of permission (VOP).

The firm typically advises the regulator at an early stage of the firm's plans and confirms the requirements for varying the firm's authorised permissions. In the event of a minor variation, the application for approval typically requires minimal documentation to be submitted. For minor variations, the approval process usually takes only a limited amount of time, and can be as little as two to eight weeks.

For major variations, such as an entirely new area of activity, more evidence will need to be provided, including a detailed overview of the firm's expertise in the new activity, the risk assessments undertaken and the detailed business plan. In such cases, the lead time for obtaining regulatory approval can be lengthy and take up to a year.

Regulators may provide a service level target for processing such applications which are designed to give the regulator ample time to consider the application.

1.8.4 Control Framework

A key part of the business strategy is understanding the key risks the business will face and how those risks will be managed. Risks can be mitigated, eliminated, or accepted. Assessment of the risks associated with any change in business strategy, together with an understanding of the need to control those risks, is vital to ensuring that the firm is prepared to expand its business activities or adopt some other change in overall strategy. While change can be positive in realising growth for a company, the compliance officer must ensure that the regulatory consequences of change have been understood and appropriate plans put in place.

1.8.5 Preparing Compliance Reports

Learning Objectives

2.1.9 Know how to prepare an effective compliance report for management

2.1.10 Know what basic information compliance officers should have access to

There is no prescribed layout for compliance reports, and firms will take differing approaches. Some firms prefer narrative styles, while others might use a recognisable corporate template to ensure consistency across the various reviews performed (such as the example shown in Appendix 3).

Regardless of the format, the following needs to be taken into consideration:

- **Initial steps:**
  - The title page and meeting corporate style/standards.
  - Designing a template that meets your needs.
  - The introduction and contents pages.

- **Report scope, parameters and people:**
  - The purpose of the (monitoring) review and report.
  - Compliance 'project' reports – summary and objectives.
  - Acknowledging key personnel.
  - Any 'points to be noted'.

- **Significant pages:**
  - Contents: subject areas considered and reviewed.
  - The executive summary.
  - Report findings and recommendations.

- **The right of reply:**
  - Incorporating management responses.

- **Issuing the report and document version control:**
  - Recording, retention and revisiting.

Access to Information and Personnel

The compliance function needs to be able to communicate with any staff member and obtain access to any records or files necessary to enable them to carry out their responsibilities. They need to be able to independently carry out their responsibilities in all departments of the firm in which compliance risk exists. They should have the right to conduct investigations of possible breaches of the compliance policy and to request assistance from specialists within the firm (eg, legal or internal audit) or engage outside specialists to perform this task if appropriate.

The compliance function should be free to report any irregularities or possible breaches disclosed by its investigations to senior management, without fear of retaliation or disfavour from management or other staff members. Although its normal reporting line should be to senior management, the compliance function needs to have direct access to the board of directors or a board committee, bypassing normal reporting lines when necessary. Further, it may be useful for the board or a committee of the board to meet with the head of compliance at least annually, as this will help the board or board committee to assess the extent to which the firm is managing its compliance risk effectively. In larger firms, the compliance function will be directly represented on the board with the appointment of a compliance director who may serve as the chief compliance officer for the company and its subsidiaries.

Examples of the types of records compliance typically access for monitoring purposes fall into three main categories:

- basic
- periodic, and
- non-essential.

Basic Records

- Customer applications/instructions.
- Suitability/appropriateness test records.
- Contract notes.
- Transaction records.
- Telephone recordings.
- Customer correspondence (written and electronic).
- Accounts – customer, bank.
- Customer asset and money reconciliations, trust letters.
- Marketing materials.
- Complaints and breach of regulation records.
- Suspicious activity reports (SARs).
- Court of Protection.
- Court orders.
- Marriage certificates.
- Probate.
- Powers of attorney.
- Death certificates.
- Anti-money laundering (AML) documents.
- Scanning.
- Tax vouchers.
- Tax-related reports/returns.
- Policies.
- Procedures.
- Distribution records.
- Cheque processing.
- Risk assessments.
- Control reports.
- Checklists.

Periodic Records

- Prospectus and instruments of constitution.
- Staff records for recruitment, fit and proper tests, references, credit checks.
- Training and CPD.
- Statements issued to customers.
- Report and accounts.
- Knowledge base.
- Websites.

Non-Essential

- Supplier invoices.
- Management accounts – forecasts/projections.
- Adviser/client agreements.

2. The Role of the Compliance Function within a Firm

2.1 Responsibilities and Accountabilities of Management and Staff

Learning Objective

2.2.1 Understand the responsibilities and accountabilities of management and staff for compliance with regulations

Regulators expect the executive management of a firm to ensure that their responsibility for the running of the firm is clear. When it comes to daily 'business as usual' activity, all staff and management of a firm must, together, ensure that it remains compliant with the regulations.

Operational processes must follow the prescribed procedures to ensure that the right outcomes are achieved. Any concerns staff might have regarding the accuracy of those procedures should be escalated for consideration by management. Staff and management must ensure that the training provided to each person remains current and suited to their role, and that any regulatory training obligations are satisfied (such as obligations for AML training). While firms will often make such matters part of the firm's code of conduct, enabling it to take disciplinary action against staff where relevant, it is important to recognise that failings in these areas could give rise to regulatory concerns as well as HR issues. The code of conduct is the firm's documented expectations of how its staff and management will act in respect of share dealing, engagement with clients and suppliers, and various other matters.

2.1.1 Understand How to Monitor whether a Business is in Compliance with Regulations and Internal Policies and Procedures

Learning Objective

2.2.2 Understand how to monitor whether a business is in compliance with regulations and internal policies and procedures

The common methods used to monitor compliance are:

- interviewing relevant staff, management and directors
- observing the processes in action and seeing evidence of the controls being operated
- testing statistically-based samples of transactions, either in situ or by desk-based review. It is particularly helpful if compliance staff have direct read-only access to relevant systems such that they can take their own samples and do not have to rely on operational staff for providing the material
- reviews of previous reports, audit reports and other key management information such as key performance indicators, breach and complaint trends
- reviewing specific system-produced transaction reports for the compliance function.

2.1.2 Risks of Non-Compliance

Learning Objective

2.2.3 Understand the risks associated with non-compliance for firms and the financial services sector

It is generally accepted that no firm can at all times remain fully compliant with all regulatory requirements. Manual processes are open to error; human beings will make mistakes; fully automated processes can be vulnerable if system problems arise. While any firm may, at times, experience a breach of regulation, it is important that the firm appreciates the significance of such breaches and the potential consequences that could follow. Ultimately, a regulator will have the power to sanction a firm as well as its executive management in the event that the firm fails to uphold the standards expected. It is, therefore, important for the firm to distinguish between isolated failings and situations indicating that a systemic problem exists.

One example of an isolated breach would be where a transaction is misfiled through human error, such that the transaction is delayed and the investor may receive a worse price on their deal. It is important that the firm rectifies such cases. Root cause investigations are a valuable control to confirm that the human error was not caused by a poorly designed process or badly written procedure. Any root cause identified by the firm should be promptly addressed to prevent continued breaches.

The chief risk faced by a firm is that its regulator will take action if it becomes concerned by the level or type of breaches arising, or that the firm is failing to address the fundamental causes of problems. Where the regulator believes the firm's clients are being put at risk, or where it considers the firm is not responding appropriately to the regulator's expectations, the regulator may impose a fine on the firm. Such fines are often made public, which could undermine client confidence in the firm. In some cases, the regulator might also take action against the senior management of the business; those individuals who were personally responsible to the regulator for ensuring the business would be well run.

Aside from the specific cost of any regulatory action taken, the firm is likely to incur substantial additional expense in managing a period of regulatory investigation. Firms under regulatory investigation will often retain external support to help their investigations and build a defensive case – all of which has implications for the firm's profitability.

In extreme cases, the regulator has the power to revoke authorisation, effectively preventing the firm or individual from continuing in business. The regulator must seek to ensure that overall confidence in the financial sector as a whole is maintained, and doing so requires strong action to be taken against those who have failed to operate at the required standards.

2.1.3 Independence of the Compliance Function

Learning Objectives

2.2.4 Understand BIS Principle 5 relating to the independence of the compliance function and senior management accountability

2.2.5 Understand the relationship between compliance and other departments, including 'three lines of defence'

Principle 5 of the BCBS' principles for compliance and the compliance function in banks states that the compliance function should be independent.

The concept of independence does not mean that the compliance function cannot work closely with management and staff in the various business units. Indeed, a cooperative working relationship between compliance function and business units should help to identify and manage compliance risks at an early stage.

The concept of independence involves four related elements:

- Compliance should have a formal status within the firm.
- There should be a group compliance officer or head of compliance.
- Their responsibilities within the firm should not lead to conflicts of interest.
- They should have access to information and personnel.

The independence of the head of compliance and any other staff having compliance responsibilities may be undermined if they are placed in a position where there is a real or potential conflict between their compliance responsibilities and their other responsibilities. It is the preference of the BCBS that compliance function staff perform only compliance responsibilities. The BCBS recognises, however, that this may not be practicable in smaller banks, smaller business units or in local subsidiaries. In these cases, therefore, compliance function staff may perform non-compliance tasks, providing that potential conflicts of interest are avoided. The independence of compliance function staff may also be undermined if their remuneration is related to the financial performance of the business line for which they exercise compliance responsibilities. However, remuneration related to the financial performance of the bank as a whole should generally be acceptable.

Most firms apply the three lines of defence approach or a recognisable variation of it. The first line is operational controls – such as a 'quality check' performed on transactions inputted on the firm's systems to reduce the risk of a processing error. Due to the nature of operational activities, such first-line checks are usually performed only a short period after the initial operational activity so that problem scenarios can be avoided.

Compliance usually provides the second line of defence; the compliance monitoring programme discussed above enables sample-based review of the operational tasks performed to validate the specific performance achieved and to reflect upon whether any improvements might be made to better secure the operational processes against risk.

Finally, the third line of defence is generally delivered by the firm's internal audit function.

The three lines of defence are complementary, each performing its control responsibilities independent of the other lines. The frequency of review may reduce as you progress through the lines of defence, but the depth of critical analysis increases in order to ensure the firm's processes are mitigating risks to the optimal level (given budgets and other organisational limits).

The three lines of defence are a clear and consistent organisational and operational structure, including decision-making powers, reporting and functional links and segregation of duties which are clearly defined, transparent, consistent, complete and free from conflicts of interest.

2.1.4 Compliance Role in Training and Competence

Learning Objective

2.2.6 Understand the role compliance has in training and maintaining competence and awareness: educating staff on compliance issues; acting as a contact point for compliance queries from staff members; providing written guidance to staff

The role of compliance in training is largely in three main areas:

1. Educating staff on compliance issues.
2. Acting as a point of contact for compliance queries from staff members.
3. Providing written guidance to staff.

Educating Staff on Compliance Issues

Education of staff on compliance matters may be completed in a number of different ways, depending on the size and approach of the firm.

If there is a learning and development department responsible for delivering training, then they are likely to be responsible for induction courses and periodic regulatory courses such as those relating to financial crime prevention. The role of compliance is to review the training material and provide advice on updating it to reflect any changes in regulations.

Special workshops or training sessions may be required to be prepared and possibly delivered by compliance staff on specific areas of regulation, such as anti-bribery legislation or new product regulation. They may also provide sessions in groups or individually for directors and senior management who are approved by the regulator; this would be to cover the senior management responsibilities so far as compliance is concerned.

Acting as a Point of Contact

Providing a compliance helpdesk/helpline can be a valuable educational tool. This would deal with day-to-day queries arising from the business where line managers have not been able to answer the query. This can then highlight any areas of the firm and activities where there may be a lack of knowledge and the need for more formal training or guidance to be given. The provision of online facilities with the compliance function producing an FAQ (frequently asked questions) guide can be useful.

Providing Written Guidance to Staff

The compliance department must understand the specific regulations applicable to the business, though most areas of the business simply need to ensure that the work they undertake remains in line with the regulatory requirements. As such, the compliance team will need to provide a range of updates and documentation to support the business areas in maintaining the necessary standards and ensuring that any projects to implement regulatory changes are accurately defined.

There will always be a need for compliance to respond to queries that arise from business-as-usual (BAU) events. In order to remain efficient, and to avoid any systemic concerns from developing, the compliance team should periodically consider whether the BAU questions it has received indicate any underlying concern in a given part of the business. Again, maintaining open and supportive relationships with the business is important for giving compliance visibility of potential concerns.

Depending on the specific activities of the firm, the compliance team may maintain a formal 'house view' of how certain regulations are to be interpreted or applied. Any change to those rules will require the compliance function to update its material and communicate any consequences with the business areas affected. The compliance team might provide periodic internal updates to summarise regulatory themes or specific matters of interest, providing a 'call to action' for the firm to ensure that it is strongly positioned on a matter of regulatory interest.

For firms with a smaller compliance department, these materials might be gained from participation in industry events or trade association discussions. The key point is that the compliance function must ensure it provides guidance to staff in respect of regulatory obligations.

As part of their monitoring programme, the compliance function will review the training and competence policies of the firm and test the record-keeping relating to those staff in approved or supervisory roles. This is to ensure that the training plans and CPD have been completed and, where relevant, that the supervisor or senior manager has assessed the individuals as competent to undertake their role.

2.1.5 Non-Compliance by Individuals

Learning Objectives

2.2.7 Understand how to monitor an individual's compliance with regulations and internal policies and procedures

2.2.8 Understand the range of potential outcomes to remedy non-compliance by an individual within a firm: training and development activities; internal disciplinary measures; external regulatory sanction; legal avenues

The directors and management of a firm have responsibility for the day-to-day managing of staff and providing feedback on any issues arising from an individual's performance. Quality checking and quality assurance processes should be designed to identify non-compliance. If the matter is serious then it may be necessary for management to involve the human resources or personnel department, and if there is a regulatory issue, the compliance function too.

The following list provides examples of methods for the monitoring of an individual's compliance with regulations and internal policies and procedures:

- **Regular appraisal of performance by senior staff** – this may range from daily contact and support/advice provided by those in supervisor, manager or executive roles through to more formal periodic reviews. Periodic reviews may be monthly, quarterly, half-yearly or annual. Appraisals normally are interview-based with written records of areas discussed.
- **Quality checking and assurance processes** – this may take the form of manual checks by a second experienced person. This may range from checking each activity and item of work (ie, checking 100% of the individual's work) through to checking a sample, for example 10%.
- **Exception and error reports** – automated system reports may be used to identify where non-compliance may occur. For example, if an investment manager fails to observe investment and borrowing limits an automated report may be used to warn when a breach occurs.
- **Testing on a periodic basis** – for example, the firm may provide regular (eg, annual) training and refresher training on regulatory subjects and internal policies. These sessions will often involve testing of the individuals to ensure their compliance knowledge is satisfactory.
- **Self-certification by the individual** – a firm may require individuals to sign a declaration periodically (eg, annually) that they have read and understood the firm's policies and procedures, for example, a declaration that the individual has read and understood the policies and procedures relating to client data protection or privacy.
- **Audit trails** – ensuring that the firm maintains adequate records to demonstrate compliance is important. Such records, whether paper- or system-based, may be used to demonstrate an individual's compliance as well as the firm's. In the event that criminal activity is suspected, then a formal audit of the records may be necessary.

The potential outcomes could involve the following:

- **Training and development activities** – this may involve some coaching by an experienced member of staff or it may require the individual being temporarily removed from their role while they are retrained in processes which are compliant.
- **Internal disciplinary measures** – where the individual has acted negligently or repeatedly been non-compliant, then appropriate internal disciplinary measures may be necessary. This may include the giving of a verbal or written warning and a record made on their personal file. Where the behaviour persists, suspension and/or dismissal may be necessary.
- **External regulatory sanction** – in certain cases, it may be necessary for the compliance function to notify the regulator – remember the principle of an open relationship with your regulator! It is possible that the individual may be subject to action, particularly if the breach amounted to serious market abuse; and the firm is at risk too if it failed to have appropriate controls in place or monitor what was going on. A ban and fine for the individual may be levied, quite separate from any action against the firm.
- **Legal avenues** – if the breach is related to money laundering, **insider dealing** or bribery for example, then the regulator may take legal action for any offences committed. Clearly, if convicted of a criminal offence, the individual may face quite severe penalties, not just a fine but a potential custodial sentence.

2.1.6 Business Development

Learning Objective

2.2.9 Understand the role compliance plays in new business development: due diligence; risk assessment; scope of regulation and approval; highlighting material changes in the nature of existing relationships; assessing and reporting potential reputational risks

There are five key aspects to the role compliance plays in the development of new business. These aspects are:

- due diligence
- risk assessment
- scope of regulation
- highlighting material changes in the nature of existing relationships, and
- assessing and reporting potential reputational risks.

Where there is an independent compliance department there tends to be an emphasis on advising the business. In particular, the role of compliance in approving new products has increased significantly and it is recognised as vital to the product development process. This is an area where compliance can add value at an early stage in the product approval process and thereby help to avoid problems later on. It is common at larger firms for there to be written guidelines for new product initiatives, integrating compliance into the process.

Depending on the relationship between the firm's compliance and risk management functions, compliance will either perform or participate in a due diligence review of any new product or service that the firm wishes to introduce. The focus for compliance is to ensure that the regulatory aspects of the new service have been correctly understood and determine any impact of the new service upon the firm's regulatory permissions or capital requirements. At a later point, compliance will need to verify marketing communications and regulatory submissions relating to the new service and may review operational readiness and system test output where the change is substantial.

The wider risk assessment performed in the firm will look at the operational risks of delivering an accurate and timely service in respect of the new product and consider any potential reputational damage that the firm may suffer if problems arise. The firm will also need to ensure that the correct external relationships (eg, partners, clients and suppliers) are in place and ready to support the expanded business – in terms of volumes, capacity and complexity.

3. Managing Regulatory Relationships

3.1 Regulator Relationship

Learning Objectives

2.3.1 Understand the relationship between the firm and regulator

2.3.2 Understand how an effective regulatory relationship can be of strategic importance to a firm: advocating opinion; involvement in consultation; drafting regulatory responses; making representations and applications; obtaining effective guidance

3.1.1 How Regulators Manage the Relationship with Authorised Firms

As a general principle, regulators supervise firms according to the risks they present to the regulator's objectives. They assess risks in terms of their impact (the scale of the effect these risks will have on consumers and the market if they were to happen) and probability (the likelihood of the particular issue occurring).

As noted by the International Organization of Securities Commissions (IOSCO), supervision of market intermediaries' conduct through inspection and surveillance helps to ensure the maintenance of high standards and the protection of investors. These preventative programmes are a necessary complement to investigation and enforcement programmes. The nature and extent of the supervisory relationship with an individual firm depend on how much of a risk the regulator considers the firm could pose. It also may take into account the risks across several firms in the sector (to provide a benchmark) or indeed the market as a whole. It may use different methods or frameworks to assess that risk but generally it will either focus on the firm alone or as part of a sector/industry.

The base level of supervisory intensity depends on impact and probability scores assigned to a firm (or group of firms) which, in turn, help to determine the nature of the relationship that the regulator has with a particular firm.

Medium- and High-Impact Firms

In medium- and high-impact firms, the firm may coordinate work through a relationship manager, who carries out a regular risk assessment and determines a risk mitigation programme proportionate to the risks identified. The precise volume and type of work undertaken will depend on the size and risk rating of the firm concerned.

On a regular basis, the regulator will analyse a firm's financial and other returns and check compliance with notification requirements. Breaches and other indicators of risk may be followed up by the supervisory team with the firm's compliance function.

For high-impact firms, the regulator is likely to apply a closer monitoring regime. This is essentially a planned ongoing schedule of visits to the firm to meet the firm's directors and senior management regularly. In addition, for high-impact firms which are systemic in nature, the regulator may design specific programmes of core work to assess the biggest risks on the prudential and conduct side of the business.

Where possible, the regulator may centralise supervision of all associated firms within a group in a single team and, when appropriate (for example, if it believes the group has an integrated management and/or control structure), produce a combined risk assessment and risk mitigation programme covering all the firms in a group.

Low-Impact Firms

If a firm is assessed as low impact, it may not have a specific risk assessment or risk mitigation programme. These firms are monitored by a combination of base-line monitoring of financial and other returns, action in response to risks identified by this information, thematic exercises to monitor compliance standards in a sector and work as part of sector-wide reviews.

Individually, most small firms pose a low risk to a regulator's objectives. In practice this means, unlike the larger firms, they do not have regular risk assessments and are usually required to send regulatory reports less frequently. Small firms are unlikely to have an individual relationship manager.

However, collectively, small firms pose a risk to a regulator's objectives. The regulator may collect information from a variety of sources such as regulatory returns; analyse the data to identify collective risks; and where necessary investigate the matter further (eg, using questionnaires or targeted firm visits); and then communicate the results of the research to the industry. The aim is to change the behaviour of small firms in a way that improves standards across the industry.

3.1.2 Building the Relationship

Building a good relationship with the regulator is a key role for compliance staff. An effective relationship is one that is built on mutual trust and enables open and constructive discussion to take place. Indeed, a commonly accepted principle is that a firm must deal with its regulator in an open and cooperative way and must appropriately disclose to the regulator anything of which it would reasonably expect notice. One of the valuable aspects of a good relationship is the ability of the firm's compliance function to seek an opinion on issues that arise and discuss resolution or perhaps seek an opinion on a planned business development. Similarly, the regulator may wish to seek firms' opinions on a formal, or informal, basis about a regulatory issue that may be affecting the sector or industry.

Obtaining effective guidance at an early stage can clearly be of strategic importance to the firm and save a great deal of time and effort. A constructive relationship with the regulator enhances the opportunity for such dialogue.

Responding to consultation papers issued by the regulator allows a firm the opportunity to formally express their opinion on forthcoming regulations. It allows the firm further to provide the regulator with information about the practical implications of the proposals being made. It is common for regulators to be accountable for ensuring they understand the business impact and, in some cases, carry out cost-benefit analysis to ensure the proposals are proportionate.

Such responses to consultations may be collated by trade associations and the balance of industry opinion can be analysed and provided to the regulator. This route also allows firms to comment anonymously. However, firms may decide to respond directly as well as through any relevant trade association. When drafting such responses, it is usual to set out details of the firm, its position in the industry and its interest in the consultation being undertaken before going on to respond to the specific points raised in the consultation paper issued by the regulator.

3.1.3 Applications

Obtaining authorisation usually requires a formal application to be made to the regulator. The following are examples of the various types of information required, in this case for a retail financial intermediary firm:

- Staff organisational chart.
- Business plan information.
- Compliance procedures.
- Details of the firm's professional advisers.
- An opening balance sheet.
- A forecast closing balance sheet after 12 months' trading or first year's trading.
- A monthly profit and loss account for the first years of trading.
- A monthly cash flow forecast.
- A copy of the latest annual accounts (if previously traded), and
- A professional indemnity insurance quotation.

3.1.4 Representations

Where a regulator has made a formal decision to refuse an application or proceed with enforcement, it will normally offer an appeals process for firms. The representation may be in writing or it may be an oral representation and will in the normal course be put to persons who may be independent but are appointed by the regulator for the purpose of hearing such representations.

3.1.5 Regulatory Visits

Learning Objective

2.3.3 Understand what to do if your firm is the subject of a regulatory or law enforcement visit: scheduled; unscheduled ('dawn raid')

Scheduled Visit

Medium-sized, as well as selected other firms, can expect to have scheduled visits from their regulator:

- periodically to undertake risk assessments, and/or
- as part of thematic research and investigation, perhaps involving a number of firms across the industry or sector.

Larger firms can expect to receive visits for the same reasons but they may also attend regular meetings to discuss specific areas of their business, and to maintain contact with the senior management to discuss the firm's strategy and corporate plans. In all the above routine-type visits, the firm will normally receive prior notice of the visit and may well receive a request for information to allow the regulator to carry out some desk-based analysis and prepare for the visit. Firms may also, as part of the relationship-building, proactively invite the regulator to their premises to update them on business developments, organisation structure or to present a corporate update and plans for the business over a period.

In all these cases, it is helpful to obtain the cooperation of all relevant areas of the firm who may be involved in the visit. Planning will enable such a visit to run smoothly: prepare the agenda beforehand, book meeting rooms, arrange for relevant directors or managers to be available at the times arranged, arrange refreshments and organise someone to take notes of the meeting(s).

Unscheduled Visit ('Dawn Raid')

Regulators may undertake unscheduled visits where they have an ongoing investigation which may involve a criminal offence such as insider dealing or money laundering. Countries around the world are adding challenges in the form of new laws or the renewed enforcement of existing laws. As national laws are strengthened, and international regulators cooperate on significant investigations, so the likelihood of dawn raids increases.

Unscheduled Visit Procedure

Raids may be carried out at dawn but are usually commenced at the start of the working day. They often take place simultaneously at various offices and homes of key individuals.

A regulator seeking to enter the premises to search for evidence will usually hold a legal search warrant authorising its action. The raid will, therefore, usually be accompanied by police officers. The firm should check that the warrant is in order and ensure that the search team does not exceed the authority granted by the warrant.

The warrant should specify:

- the date on which it was issued
- the legal authority by which it was issued
- the regulatory authority to whom it was granted
- each set of premises to be searched
- the type of articles, materials, or persons sought.

However, the exact nature of warrants will differ between jurisdictions and on the legal basis by which they are issued.

Once inside, the investigators will search through documents, records and computers.

They are likely to have at least one specialist computer forensics expert in the team. The investigators are entitled to take copies of any relevant information. If information is not readily available, then the investigators can ask for it to be compiled. They may also be in possession of a search and seizure order, in which case they can also take possession of hard drives and original documents. Information or documents that fall within the terms of the warrant may be seized; however, the police may be able to seize other material (eg, incriminating material giving direct evidence of a criminal offence) even if not specified in the warrant.

Legally privileged documents and those that may lead to self-incrimination do not need to be provided. Legal advice should be sought to ensure there are reasonable grounds to believe that privilege exists. The investigators must keep a record of all documents they copy and they will ask someone to sign it before they leave and, at that time, a copy should be taken for the records of the firm.

The warrant also entitles the investigators to interview individuals. Failure to cooperate with any aspect of the raid could be a criminal offence punishable by a prison sentence.

Investigators may be willing to wait for legal representatives to arrive before they commence their search, but they are not obliged to do so.

Advance Preparation

It is good practice for firms to advise their employees about the possibility of dawn raids occurring and brief them on the procedure. It is important for staff to understand the scope of the information they should provide. In particular, they should be aware of the legal consequences of a failure to cooperate and of **tipping off** any other persons who may be involved. Firms should have in place procedures for key staff to follow in the event of a raid, including who should be notified.

Consideration should also be given as to how information is stored and whether legal advice and communications should be filed separately. This is advisable in any event and in the event of a raid, it will avoid the inadvertent disclosure of privileged information. In addition, firms are advised to consider lodging copies of sensitive information with their lawyers. If asked for copies, the firm can advise the investigators that they are in safekeeping and that the solicitors will undertake to hold them pursuant to a court order.

Firms should also consider whether the seizing of individual hard drives would inhibit the operation of the company or if all essential information is held on a central server. Consideration should also be given as to how the company would respond to any media interest and in relation to advising investors as to what has occurred. There should be clear internal policies as to how the company would respond if the activities of an employee or director are the focus of any investigation.

General Checklist in the Event of a Raid

If there is a raid on your property, whether business or residential, it is important that you do the following:

- Check that the warrant has been granted against your premises/abode and that it is signed, dated and sealed and that it is still in date – there will be a window of time for the investigators to make the raid. Ensure that all investigators present are named on the warrant. Exclude entry to anyone attempting to enter who is not named.
- Advise the investigators that you are contacting your legal adviser and will ask them to be present.
- Check the terms of the warrant and the scope of the information which must be provided. Brief employees as to the scope of the warrant and remember you do not have to provide privileged legal advice and you have the right to redact documents which have information in them which is not relevant.
- Cooperate by allowing access to relevant documents and information and advise anyone else involved to cooperate.
- Do not tip off people who may not be present that there is a raid, particularly if you believe that they may also be involved and advise other employees of the same risk. Ask investigators before you notify other offices or directors.
- Keep a list of all the documents copied/supplied/asked for and also any questions which are asked and the answers given. The investigators must provide a list of what they are taking. The two lists should be checked against one another before you accept and sign the investigation record of documents copied/taken.
- Compile a report on the raid.

3.1.6 Breaches

Learning Objectives

2.3.4 Understand what to do if a regulatory breach occurs

2.3.5 Know what types of information must be disseminated to whom in the event of a regulatory breach

Minor regulatory breaches need to be recorded in a breaches log and a record needs to be kept of the resolution of the breach or other action taken. The breach should be reviewed by an appropriate manager to ensure that all relevant action has been taken, including where appropriate, that compensation has been paid or that the client has been restored to their correct position.

Analysis of breaches will be helpful to indicate trends and provide managers and senior managers with information to help control the business, identify any action required and consider any preventative action for the future. Any client impacted by the breach should be notified and provided with an explanation of any action taken.

If the breach is a notifiable breach, ie, of a type the regulations state is reportable to the regulator, then a report should be made (normally within 24 hours of identification). The regulator may request some form of incident report and an explanation of how the breach was discovered, whether investors were at risk, and what remedial action has been taken. It will also wish to understand whether the breach is a single event or evidence of a systemic problem. It is important that relevant directors and senior managers are aware of any breach that is reportable to the regulator and ensure that the information provided accurately reflects the issue, the action already taken to rectify the position (and prevent recurrence), and any ongoing areas of activity.

3.1.7 Confidential Information

Learning Objectives

2.3.6 Know what information may be disseminated and what should remain confidential if financial crime is suspected or detected

2.3.7 Know what types of information should remain confidential in the normal course of business

If financial crime is suspected or detected, the person discovering the information should report the matter to the firm's **money laundering reporting officer (MLRO)**, or a police officer. If the MLRO, on review of the matter, believes it is suspicious then they should make a suspicious activity report (SAR) to the appropriate law enforcement agency (LEA). Failing to report suspicions is a criminal offence.

If a client is being investigated, the LEA will not usually divulge the source of the initial report although the client may have the right to see relevant papers/reports should they request them. When an MLRO makes an SAR, individual staff names are not passed on as part of the process. Staff should not inform the client that a report is being made about them. This is regarded as tipping off and the staff member may be liable to imprisonment or a fine or both if they were convicted of tipping off.

Staff may refer concerns about specific transactions or other activity to their line manager to obtain advice or guidance. However, the suspicion should still be logged and referred to the MLRO.

An example of suspicion raised by staff might include the following:

1. **Incident summary** – a high level summary of the case, eg, the client did not pass telephone security questions. Such checks may require the client to quote letters from a password, answer a pre-advised security question (eg, providing their mother's maiden name), or confirm their date of birth.
2. **Details of the incident** – details of the case, including reference to dates and amounts, as appropriate. For example:

   'The client called on 27 October 2016, they answered the full name, address and date of birth questions successfully but they sounded male and the account holder on the system is shown as a female. The caller came through the automated valuation line and was querying the valuation; in addition the caller wanted confirmation of how to sell the investment quickly and send the proceeds to a third party. I informed the client that I could not locate an account with the information provided and that they should put their request in writing'.

3. **Reason for suspicion** – an explanation of what made the staff member suspicious regarding the case, eg, the voice did not sound like a female, the caller was clearly interested in selling the investment quickly and wished the proceeds to be sent to a third party.

The SAR will be made to the regulator and/or an appropriate arm of the police that deals with financial crime.

In the normal course of business, the authorised firm will have a duty of care to keep confidential all the client's information, including the details of their investments or bank account. Any personal data will also be subject to relevant data protection or privacy laws. Reporting suspicious activity, therefore, involves sharing confidential information but does not constitute a breach of client confidentiality or data protection/privacy laws in such circumstances.

Such information may only be disclosed where it is necessary for a criminal investigation or in the event of tax evasion; release of the information may be subject to an appropriate court order being served on the firm.

End of Chapter Questions

Think of an answer for each question and refer to the appropriate section for confirmation.

1. State the two responsibilities of an effective compliance function, irrespective of the organisational structure.
   Answer reference: Section 1.1.1

2. Who is responsible for establishing a written compliance policy containing the basic principles followed by management and staff?
   Answer reference: Section 1.1.3

3. What does the Bank for International Settlements (BIS) Principle 6 require of a firm's compliance function?
   Answer reference: Section 1.2

4. What is the purpose of the compliance manual?
   Answer reference: Section 1.3.1

5. What are the three key stages involved in a risk-based approach to a monitoring programme?
   Answer reference: Section 1.5

6. What are the most common methods used to monitor whether a business is in compliance with regulations, internal policies and procedures?
   Answer reference: Section 2.1.1

7. To which types of people might compliance staff provide individual training?
   Answer reference: Section 2.1.4

8. What role might compliance play in the development of new business?
   Answer reference: Section 2.1.6

9. What two factors do regulators use to assess risks?
   Answer reference: Section 3.1.1

10. What type of information can be withheld when providing information?
    Answer reference: Section 3.1.5

11. What is an SAR?
    Answer reference: Section 3.1.7

Chapter Three

Managing the Risk of Financial Crime

This syllabus area will provide approximately 20 of the 100 examination questions

1. Money Laundering, Terrorist Financing and the Standards Required of Firms

1.1 The Concept of Money Laundering and Terrorist Financing

Learning Objective

3.1.1 Understand the concept of money laundering and terrorist financing

Financial services firms must reduce the risk that their services are used for terrorist financing or money laundering purposes. Although these two areas are related, the issues and risks faced by firms differ and so employees need to be aware of both aspects.

Terrorist financing relates to the financial support of organisations or groups that seek to perform terrorist acts and also to any financial transactions undertaken to move such money around the globe in order to enable terror attacks to be carried out. Money laundering has a wider remit and is related to financial transactions aimed at turning money derived from criminal activities ('dirty money') into money which appears to have been legitimately acquired and which can, therefore, be more easily invested and spent ('clean money').

Money laundering can take many forms including:

- handling the proceeds of crimes such as theft, fraud and tax evasion
- handling stolen goods
- being directly involved with, or facilitating, the laundering of any criminal or terrorist property, or
- criminals investing the proceeds of their crimes in a whole range of financial products.

There are similarities between the movement of terrorist funds and the laundering of criminal property and, because terrorist groups can have links with other criminal activities, there is inevitably some overlap between anti-money laundering (AML) provisions and the rules designed to prevent the financing of terrorist acts. There are two main differences to note between terrorist financing and other money laundering activities:

1. Although the overall funds required may be significant, terrorist financing usually involves small amounts of money, making identification and tracking more difficult.
2. The source of funds may be legitimate, thus, making it difficult to identify when the funds become terrorist funds.

The cross-border nature of money laundering and terrorist financing has led to international coordination to ensure that countries have legislation and regulatory processes in place to enable identification and prosecution of those involved.

Examples include:

- The Financial Action Task Force (FATF), which has issued recommendations aimed at setting minimum standards for action in different countries to ensure AML efforts are consistent internationally; it has also issued special recommendations on terrorist financing.
- European Union (EU) directives targeted at money laundering prevention.
- Standards issued by international bodies to encourage due diligence procedures to be followed for customer identification.
- Sanctions by the United Nations (UN) and the EU to deny individuals and organisations from certain countries access to the financial services sector.
- Guidance issued by the private sector Wolfsberg Group of banks in relation to private banking, correspondent banking and other activities.

1.2 Stages of Money Laundering

Learning Objective

3.1.2 Know the stages of the money laundering process: placement; layering; integration

There are three stages to a successful money laundering operation:

- **Placement** – introduction of the money into the financial system. Typically, this involves placing the criminally derived cash into a bank or building society account, a bureau de change or any other type of enterprise which can accept cash, such as a casino.
- **Layering** – involves moving the money around in order to make it difficult for the authorities to link the placed funds with the ultimate beneficiary of the money. This might involve buying and selling foreign currencies, shares or bonds in rapid succession; investing in collective investment schemes; or insurance-based investment products; or moving the money from one country to another.
- **Integration** – at this final stage, the layering has been successful and the ultimate beneficiary appears to be holding legitimate funds (clean money rather than dirty money). The money is regarded as 'integrated' into the legitimate financial system.

Each of these stages impact financial services firms. During the 'placement' stage, the money launderer introduces cash into the financial system. This requires cash in hand to be replaced by some valuable claim on assets or benefits. In recent years, the use of electronic currency (eg, Bitcoin) has raised much interest regarding the disruptive impacts of technology, but should also be considered in the light of money laundering considerations. Any transaction by which someone converts actual currency for an electronic currency could be an example of placement.

For most financial services firms, 'layering' represents the biggest risk – as any transaction that exchanges one asset for another, or changes the registered owners of an asset, could be a step of layering. Because the purpose of layering is to disguise the original source of the money and the eventual end recipient, layering processes will often be protracted and detailed – yet each individual step will be designed to appear innocent, such as the usual activity of an investor managing their affairs. For this reason, the ability to assess behavioural trends in account activity has become increasingly important.

Where a firm processes many thousands of transactions – each of which seem ordinary – they are investing in systems and procedures that look for patterns or series within the transactional data, such as where an investor might change their bank details or address and shortly afterwards redeem their holding. In many cases, such transactions may still be innocent – but the firm must exercise due care.

'Integration' can be more difficult to demonstrate, because the cleaned money may not actually be removed from the financial system. The money launderer's purposes are satisfied providing the illegal source of the money can no longer be identified by firms or law enforcement. In some cases, the integration phase may see the criminal making withdrawals from a bank account, while in others, the money may remain invested in some long-term project or investment. The aim of firms is to ensure sufficient records make it more difficult for the criminal to achieve this stage of integration.

1.3 Role of International Agencies

Learning Objectives

3.1.3 Know the role of international agencies in combating money laundering and the financing of terrorism: United Nations Office on Drugs and Crime (UNODC); International Monetary Fund (IMF); World Bank

3.1.4 Know the role of the Financial Action Task Force (FATF) in combating money laundering and terrorist financing; jurisdictions with strategic deficiencies; the challenge of jurisdictional differences

1.3.1 United Nations Office on Drugs and Crime (UNODC)

UNODC is mandated to assist member states in combating illicit drugs, crime and terrorism. In the Millennium Declaration, member states also resolved to intensify efforts to fight transnational crime in all its dimensions, to redouble the efforts to implement the commitment to counter the world drug problem and to take concerted action against international terrorism.

The Law Enforcement, Organized Crime and Anti-Money-Laundering Unit of UNODC is responsible for carrying out the Global Programme against Money-Laundering, Proceeds of Crime and the Financing of Terrorism, which was established in 1997 in response to the mandate given to UNODC through the United Nations Convention against Illicit Traffic in Narcotic Drugs and Psychotropic Substances of 1988. The Unit's mandate was strengthened in 1998 by the Political Declaration and the measures for countering money laundering adopted by the General Assembly at its 20th special session, which broadened the scope of the mandate to cover all serious crime, not just drug-related offences.

The broad objective of the Global Programme is to strengthen the ability of member states to implement measures against money laundering and the financing of terrorism and to assist them in detecting, seizing and confiscating illicit proceeds, as required pursuant to UN instruments and other globally accepted standards, by providing relevant and appropriate technical assistance upon request.

1.3.2 International Monetary Fund (IMF)

As a collaborative institution with near-universal membership, the International Monetary Fund (IMF) is a natural forum for sharing information, developing common approaches to issues, and promoting desirable policies and standards – all of which are critical in the fight against money laundering and the financing of terrorism. In addition, the IMF's broad experience in conducting financial sector assessments, providing technical assistance in the financial sector, and exercising surveillance over members' economic systems has been particularly helpful in evaluating countries' compliance with the international anti-money laundering/countering the financing of terrorism (AML/CFT) standard and in developing programmes to help them address identified shortcomings.

In 2006, the IMF executive board confirmed the general principle that every Financial Sector Assessment Program (FSAP) and Offshore Financial Center (OFC) assessment should incorporate a full AML/CFT assessment. The IMF has been a substantial contributor in this area, by cooperating with the FATF and the FATF-style regional bodies (FSRBs), conducting AML/CFT assessments alongside the FATF's and FSRBs' peer evaluations of their members' compliance with the FATF 40 Recommendations (see section 1.3.4), providing technical assistance, and contributing to policy development and research.

The IMF launched a donor-supported trust fund – the first in a series of topical trust funds (TTFs) – to finance technical assistance in AML/CFT in 2009. Canada, France, Japan, Korea, Kuwait, Luxembourg, the Netherlands, Norway, Qatar, Saudi Arabia, Switzerland, and the UK committed to collectively provide US$25.3 million over five years to the financing of the TTF to contribute to the strengthening of global AML/CFT regimes, using the fund's proven expertise and infrastructure. Many projects were successfully completed and, due to the continuing high demand for capacity development in this area, a new five-year phase of the TTF started in May 2014. Donors (France, Japan, Luxembourg, the Netherlands, Norway, Qatar, Saudi Arabia, Switzerland and the UK) have together pledged more than US$20 million over the next five years to support this new phase. The IMF's update in March 2016 notes that US$6.5 million is being used annually to help over 30 countries through technical assistance and training.

In 2018, emerging areas in the AML/CFT space were identified including Fintech, correspondent banking and transaction laundering. The increased demand for integrity advice and capacity development lead to the goal of at least one or two assessments per year going forward. Since 2020, IMF staff participate in AML/CFT assessments carried out by other assessor bodies.

1.3.3 World Bank

The World Bank consists of two main organisations: the International Bank for Reconstruction and Development (IBRD) and the International Development Association (IDA). Both the IBRD and the IDA are involved in supporting developing countries and in the case of the IDA making grants to the poorest countries.

Emerging markets are increasingly becoming the venue for large-scale money laundering operations. If left unchecked, this activity will eventually undermine the credibility of the formal financial sector. In its financial sector operations, the World Bank promotes measures to counter the flow of illicit funds into the financial systems of countries and arranges for external assistance. In doing so, the Bank recognises that measures to prevent and detect money laundering activities cannot focus only on banks. Effective measures must also address the securities, insurance, and money-changing sectors.

The Stolen Asset Recovery Initiative (StAR) is a partnership between the World Bank Group and UNODC that supports international efforts to end safe havens for corrupt funds. StAR works with developing countries and financial centres to prevent the laundering of the proceeds of corruption and to facilitate a more systematic and timely return of stolen assets to their country of origin. Somewhere between US$20 and US$40 billion every year is stolen from developing countries through bribery, misappropriation of funds, and other corrupt practices. This figure is equivalent to 15–30% of official development assistance funds.

1.3.4 Financial Action Task Force (FATF)

The FATF is an intergovernmental body whose purpose is the development and promotion of national and international policies to combat money laundering and terrorist financing. The FATF is, therefore, a policy-making body that works to generate the political will necessary to bring about legislative and regulatory reforms in these areas. Over 180 countries participate in the formulation and implementation of the 40 Recommendations.

The FATF's 40 Recommendations on money laundering plus 9 Special Recommendations on countering terrorist financing were combined in 2012 to make 40 Recommendations that cover both money laundering and countering terrorist financing. The main changes included:

- adding tax crimes as predicate offences for money laundering
- the extension of obligations on financial institutions to conduct enhanced due diligence on a risk basis to domestic **politically exposed persons (PEPs)**
- the introduction of more rigorous requirements in relation to the information which must accompany wire transfers
- the requirement for countries to establish mechanisms to record basic company information and to enable financial institutions, competent authorities and others to determine beneficial ownership and conduct appropriate customer due diligence (CDD)
- the introduction of a new step-by-step process for the identification of beneficial ownership and control of companies as part of CDD measures.

The FATF monitors members' progress in implementing necessary measures, reviews money laundering and terrorist financing techniques and countermeasures, and promotes the adoption and implementation of appropriate measures globally. In performing these activities, the FATF collaborates with other international bodies involved in combating money laundering and the financing of terrorism.

What does the FATF do?

- Sets international standards to combat money laundering and terrorist financing; and provides best practice papers and guidance including implementing a risk-based approach.
- Assesses and monitors compliance with the FATF standards; and provides a list of non-cooperative countries for use by countries to help apply Recommendation 21 (see below).
- Conducts studies of money laundering and terrorist financing methods, trends and techniques.
- Responds to new and emerging threats, such as proliferation financing.

The following is an example of a FATF Recommendation (in this instance, Recommendation 21).

Example

Measures to be taken with respect to countries that do not or insufficiently comply with the FATF:

Financial institutions need to give special attention to business relationships and transactions with persons, including companies and financial institutions, from countries which do not, or insufficiently apply the FATF Recommendations. Whenever these transactions have no apparent economic or visible lawful purpose, their background and purpose should, as far as possible, be examined, the findings established in writing, and be available to help competent authorities. Where such a country continues not to apply or insufficiently applies the FATF Recommendations, countries should be able to apply appropriate countermeasures.

The FATF's Working Group on Terrorist Financing and Money Laundering (WGTM) Project Team on Proliferation Financing (PFPT) was created in October 2008 to develop policy options to consider as measures that could be considered in combating proliferation financing within the framework of existing United Nations Security Council Resolutions.

Proliferation financing refers to the act of providing funds or financial services which are used, in whole or part, for the manufacture, acquisition, possession, development, export, transfer or use of nuclear, chemical or biological weapons and their means of delivery and related materials (including both technologies and dual-use goods used for non-legitimate purposes).

The crime of proliferation financing does not require knowledge, intention or negligence. However, when a jurisdiction specifies the responsibilities of financial institutions or a possible criminal offence of proliferation financing, the legal principles governing these two regimes in that jurisdiction will apply, including the roles of knowledge, intention or negligence.

The FATF Recommendations are continuously reviewed and updated. The most recent amendments were to Recommendations 1 and 2 (concerning risk assessment, the risk-based approach and national cooperation and coordination) in October 2020. The amendments concern, amongst others, additional requirements regarding identification, assessment and mitigation of possible breaches or the evasion of proliferation financing-related sanctions, and information exchange between domestic agencies.

1.3.5 Predicate Offences in Financial Crime

Learning Objective

3.1.5 Understand the role of predicate offences in financial crime: fraud; embezzlement; bribery; corruption

According to Article 23 of the United Nations Convention Against Crime (UNCAC), 'laundering of the proceeds of crime' constitutes a criminal offence, when committed intentionally.

Article 23 prohibits:

1. a. the conversion or transfer of property, knowing that such property is the proceeds of crime, for the purpose of concealing or disguising the illicit origin of the property or of helping any person who is involved in the commission of the predicate offence to evade the legal consequences of his or her action
   b. the concealment or disguise of the true nature, source, location, disposition, movement or ownership of or rights with respect to property, knowing that such property is the proceeds of crime.
2. Subject to the basic concepts of its legal system:
   a. the acquisition, possession or use of property, knowing, at the time of receipt, that such property is the proceeds of crime
   b. participation in, association with or conspiracy to commit, attempts to commit and aiding, abetting, facilitating and counselling the commission of any of the offences established in accordance with this article.

A predicate offence is the underlying criminal offence that gives rise to criminal proceeds, which is then the subject of a money laundering charge. The following crimes are examples of predicate offences in financial crime:

Fraud

Fraud is the practice of obtaining value by deceptive means. That value might be obtained in the form of goods or services. This implies that fraud can cover a wide range of illegal activities.

Credit/debit card fraud sees criminals purchase goods or services using the debit/credit card of their victim, and if the true cardholder is not diligent in reviewing their transaction records, such fraud can go unnoticed for long periods.

Larger transactions can also be fraudulent – such as where one party misrepresents their part in a contract.

Securities fraud is a specific type of fraud, where investors are encouraged to enter into investment transactions based on untrue statements about the assets being traded.

Embezzlement

Embezzlement is the act of dishonestly appropriating or secreting assets by one or more individuals to whom such assets have been entrusted.

Embezzlement is a kind of financial fraud. For instance, a clerk or cashier handling large sums of money could embezzle cash from their employer, a lawyer could embezzle funds from clients' trust accounts, a financial adviser could embezzle funds from investors, or a spouse could embezzle funds from their partner. Embezzlement may range from the very minor in nature, involving only small amounts, to the immense, involving large sums and sophisticated schemes.

More often than not, embezzlement is performed in a manner that is premeditated, systematic and/or methodical, with the explicit intent to conceal the activities from other individuals, usually because it is being done without their knowledge or consent.

Often it involves the trusted person embezzling only a small proportion or fraction of the funds received, in an attempt to minimise the risk of detection. If successful, embezzlements can continue for years (or even decades) without detection. It is often only when the funds are needed, or called upon for use, that the victims realise the funds or savings are missing and that they have been deceived by the embezzler.

Bribery

Bribery, a form of corruption, is the giving of money or something else of value, with the intention of influencing the behaviour of the recipient. Bribery constitutes a crime and is defined by Black's Law Dictionary as the offering, giving, receiving, or soliciting of any item of value to influence the actions of an official or other person in charge of a public or legal duty.

The bribe is the benefit bestowed to influence the recipient's conduct. It may be any money, good, right in action, property, preferment, privilege, emolument, object of value, advantage, or merely a promise or undertaking to induce or influence the action, vote, or influence of a person in an official or public capacity.

Corruption

Corruption involves the abuse of power and may range from bribery of high foreign officials to secure some type of favourable action by a foreign government to so-called facilitating payments that allegedly were made to ensure that government functionaries discharged certain ministerial or clerical duties. Corruption can also take place within financial firms where, for example, senior officials or executives use their position to obtain bribes for awarding contracts.

1.3.6 Financial Firms and Crime

Learning Objective

3.1.6 Understand how financial services firms may be utilised for financial crime: Ponzi schemes; boiler rooms; money laundering; offshore trusts; beneficial ownership; cybercrime

By choosing to invest in financial services products, an investor accepts certain risks. However, where the product or service has not been designed with the investor's best interests at heart, they will be exposed to greater risk of loss than they expect. In some cases, an unscrupulous firm or individual might set up a product designed to further their own self-interest rather than to provide a transparent and honest opportunity for investment returns.

Ponzi Schemes

The term 'Ponzi scheme' is used to describe a financial services product that claims a level of investment return that is not supported by the investment activity undertaken. The shortfall between the returns generated and those claimed is made up by using the money of new investors, who have been attracted to the scheme due to the high headline returns being publicised.

For a short time period, such a product can be sustained – provided sufficient new money is received to cover the returns being paid to older investors. However, as this new money is paid out to earlier investors it is not, therefore, put to any investment purpose; the scheme builds up a substantial unpayable debt to its clients.

At some point there will be insufficient new money to sustain the false profits, and the product will collapse – resulting in losses for those investors that unfortunately joined the scheme too late.

Financial services practitioners – particularly those with successful, market-leading products – must, therefore, guard their motivations. A successful honest product may become a Ponzi if those running the product become dependent on the fame of their success, or the fees it provides, and sacrifice their integrity to sustain high performance rates regardless of current market conditions.

Financial services firms must, therefore, be aware of any products they offer which appear to be providing excessive returns and ensure that the firm has not become host to a Ponzi scheme. Similarly, firms acting on behalf of their clients should ensure they perform solid due diligence reviews of any products recommended/supported to reduce the risk of their clients becoming victims of a Ponzi scheme. Warning signs might include an investment approach that the scheme cannot explain or guaranteed/high rates of return at little investment risk.

Boiler Rooms

'Boiler room' scams involve fraudsters selling customers overvalued, if not worthless, securities by means of an intensive selling campaign through numerous salespeople by telephone or direct mail. They do not consider the suitability or the needs of the customer, and the sales tactics used are designed to induce a hasty decision to buy the securities being offered, without disclosure of the material facts about the issuer (hence the name 'boiler room' due to high-pressure selling tactics). Modern techniques include the use of internet bulletin boards to promote certain securities and entice buyers.

Money Laundering

Financial firms are likely to be used predominantly in the first two stages of money laundering. Banks are among the firms likely to be recipients of cash, ie, the placement stage. Other firms, such as fund managers or stockbrokers, may be used as part of the layering stage where the criminals are attempting to disguise the origins of the dirty money by placing layers of transactions between the original deposit and the ultimate receipt of 'clean' money from the redemption of any investments. This clean money will then be used to invest in legitimate businesses which may or may not include financial firms. See section 1.2 for further details on money laundering.

Fines that relate to money laundering include the following:

- **April 2019** – Standard Chartered Bank was fined £102 million by the Financial Conduct Authority (FCA) for failures in AML controls in their wholesale correspondent banking business and branches in the UAE. In addition, the bank reached a settlement of $1.1 billion with the US Treasury for various violations.
- **January 2018** – Western Union settled a $60 million fine with the New York Fed for failing to implement and maintain an effective AML programme aimed to deter criminals' use of its electronic network to facilitate fraud and money laundering.
- **January 2017** – Deutsche Bank was fined £163 million by the FCA and $425 million by the New York State Department of Financial Services (DFS) for carrying out a series of mirror trades and other suspicious transactions through their offices in London, Moscow, and New York.
- **November 2015** – Barclays was fined £72 million by the FCA for failing to minimise the risk of being used for money laundering when transacting for ultra high-net-worth individuals. The FCA found that Barclays reduced its due diligence measures in such cases, rather than recognising the potential increased risk it faced.

- **January 2014** – Standard Bank was fined £7.6 million by the FCA for failing to take reasonable care to ensure that its AML policies were consistently applied in respect of its corporate customers connected with PEPs.
- **December 2012** – US authorities took action against HSBC for money laundering control failures that resulted in $881 million in drug trafficking proceeds being laundered through HSBC Bank US and $660 million in sanctioned transactions being processed through US financial institutions.
- **August 2012** – the Financial Services Authority (FSA) fined Turkish Bank (UK) ltd £294,000 for breaching the **Money Laundering Regulations** 2007 as it did not correctly identify and implement appropriate procedures to deal with the higher risk of money laundering that is connected to correspondent banking.
- **May 2012** – the FSA fined Habib Bank AG Zurich £525,000 and the money laundering reporting officer (MLRO) £17,500 for anti-money laundering control failings. In particular, they failed to establish and maintain adequate controls for assessing the level of money laundering risk posed by their customers and also failed to conduct adequate enhanced due diligence in relation to higher-risk customers.
- **March 2012** – Coutts was fined £8.75 million for AML control failings. During a themed review, the then regulator, the FSA, identified that Coutts did not apply robust controls when starting relationships with high-risk customers and did not consistently apply appropriate monitoring of those high-risk relationships. In addition, the FSA determined that the AML team at Coutts failed to provide an appropriate level of scrutiny and challenge.

Offshore Trusts

A trust is essentially an agreement whereby assets are donated by one person (the donor or settlor) for the benefit of another (the beneficiary) with a third party acting in the interests of the beneficiary until the assets completely become the property of the beneficiary. An offshore trust is such an arrangement located in a different jurisdiction – usually in order to benefit from the taxation regime there, or some other feature. As such, it should be noted that use of an offshore trust is not, therefore, criminal or suggestive that any impropriety exists.

In most cases, the identities and relationships between the parties are clear, though in some cases the trust might be established such that the identity of the beneficiaries is not stated. Such models are referred to as 'orphan structures', and the use of orphan models might be used to disguise the chain of ownership for certain assets – either because the assets have dubious origins or because the beneficiary is trying to evade tax.

Some offshore trusts are, therefore, used by criminals – as are offshore companies, trusts and financial institutions situated in certain financial centres. Slowly, but surely, this is changing with the greater international focus on fighting financial crime whereby offshore centres are taking away the cloak of anonymity which has hidden so many proceeds of crime in the past.

For example, offshore trusts may be used in the layering process of money laundering by moving monies around different accounts; breaking the proceeds down into different amounts and utilising numbered accounts and/or offshore companies with ownership hidden by offshore trusts, **nominee** directors or bearer shares. This can, at this stage, make it almost impossible to trace ownership and if the funds are then moved to other offshore companies or bank accounts, the funds are separated even further from the original amounts. Offshore companies or trusts can then be used to purchase property, both domestic and foreign.

Although offshore trusts may be used by people for legitimate tax avoidance, ie, minimising an individual's or family's tax liability within the tax regulations relating to their country of residence and the offshore centre, such trusts may also be used for tax evasion. While tax avoidance is legal, tax evasion is a crime and any suspicion is reportable as with any financial crime.

Beneficial Ownership

According to FATF, the beneficial owner is the natural person or persons who ultimately own or control a customer and/or on whose behalf a transaction is being conducted. Beneficial owners include those persons who have ultimate effective control over a legal person or arrangement. In order to ensure the firm is not subject to financial crime, it is important to know who the beneficial owner of a transaction is. Know your customer (KYC) processes play an important role in assessing the ownership structure of the client and the ultimate beneficial owner.

The CDD Rule outlines explicit CDD requirements and imposes a new requirement for these financial institutions to identify and verify the identity of beneficial owners of legal entity customers, subject to certain exclusions and exemptions. In the US, the Financial Crimes Enforcement Network (FinCEN) intends that the legal entity customer identifies its ultimate beneficial owner or owners and not 'nominees' or 'straw men'. The CDD Rule requires covered financial institutions to establish and maintain written procedures that are reasonably designed to identify and verify the beneficial owners of legal entity customers. These procedures must enable the institution to identify the beneficial owners of each customer at the time a new account is opened, unless the customer is otherwise excluded, or the account is exempted.

Cyber Crime

Cyber crime refers to the use of computers for illegal means such as fraud, trafficking, identity theft and violating privacy. The increase in the use of computers has resulted in an increase in cyber crime in which criminals seek to exploit human or security vulnerabilities to steal passwords, data or money. The most common forms of cyber crime are:

- Hacking – including social media and passwords.
- Phishing – fake emails asking for security information and personal details.
- Malicious software – including ransom ware.
- Distributed denial of service attacks (DDoS) – ensuring a website becomes unreachable.

The scale and complexity is wide ranging and can vary from a poorly executed email pretending to be from the bank hoping the recipient will click the link and leave their bank details to complex operations such as cryptomining malware attacking digital currencies.

Cyber crime is global, and is for a large part, undertaken by email. The annual cost for 2019 was estimated to be in excess of $3.5 billion. The number of occurrences as well as the cost are expected to be exponentially higher in 2020, largely as a result of the increased vulnerabilities associated with home working during the coronavirus (COVID-19) pandemic.

Although types of cyber crime have been added to laws in many countries, the criminal justice system in most countries is not yet up to date with the severity of the crimes. In the UK, for example, the conviction rate for hacking is relatively high, but the penalty when convicted is low, and typically does not include a prison sentence. In the US, the number of cyber crimes continues to grow, but litigation rates do not, and penalties when convicted do not represent the severity of the crime.

1.3.7 Misstatement of Financial Circumstances

Learning Objective

3.1.7 Understand how a firm or its representatives may collude in the propagation of financial crime: misstatement of financial circumstances; corporate fraud

A misstatement is defined as a difference between the amount, classification, presentation, or disclosure of a reported financial statement item and the amount, classification, presentation, or disclosure that is required for the item to be in accordance with the applicable financial reporting framework.

Accordingly, a material misstatement of the financial statements may arise in relation to:

1. the appropriateness of the selected accounting policies
2. the application of the selected accounting policies, or
3. the appropriateness or adequacy of disclosures in the financial statements.

Misstatements in financial statements can arise from a fraud or error. The difference is that one is intentional. Where the firm or multiple individuals collude it is more difficult to detect misstatements of financial positions. Errors may be detected by auditors, and fraud perpetrated by an employee can be detected – subject to relevant controls being in place. It is more difficult to detect such fraud where two or more employees collude and even more difficult where management is involved.

Typical objectives for such misstatements are:

- **earnings management** – where there is pressure to meet market expectations, minimise tax or inflate earnings to secure bank finance
- **misappropriation of assets** – eg, embezzling receipts through collections accounts, diverting write-offs to personal bank accounts
- **payments for goods not received** – payments may be made to fictitious vendors, or kickbacks received
- **using entity's assets** – for personal use, eg, as collateral for a loan.

Corporate Fraud

Fraud is the use of deception to obtain goods or services, and is a criminal offence in many jurisdictions. As fraud is an illegal action, it follows that any money received as a result of fraud represents proceeds of financial crime.

Corporate fraud arises when an organisation adopts such deceptive means as part of running its business. We have already seen that a firm running a Ponzi scheme will lie to its clients about the use to which their money has been put. However, there are other types of fraud that a company might commit.

The bookkeeping of the firm is often key to corporate fraud events. The money or assets of an investor might be misused (eg, transferred to the company to support its balance sheet), or the money may be embezzled by an unscrupulous employee. The company's financial accounts might be misstated (including deceiving the financial auditor, so the deception remains undetected) so that the company's share price remains higher based on the inaccurate information released to the market.

This century has already witnessed some substantial corporate frauds, which have illustrated the need for all market participants to beware of any firm that seems to be generating unnatural profit levels in comparison with similar organisations. Some examples of corporate fraud are summarised below:

- **Lehman Brothers Holdings inc.** – the fourth largest investment bank in the US filed for Chapter 11 bankruptcy on 15 September 2008. The company experienced substantial losses due to the sub-prime mortgage crisis, owing to the level of gearing now understood as being built into such mortgage products. In the aftermath, executives faced challenges over the earnings they had made during the period in which the firm was failing. The company's auditors were charged by state prosecutors about the accuracy of the financial accounts they approved. No convictions followed.
- **Enron Energy** – the US energy company failed in 2001, in the light of multiple accounting irregularities which had maintained an artificially high share price. Two of Enron's chief executive officers (Kenneth Lay and Jeffrey Skilling) were each convicted of multiple charges – including conspiracy, securities fraud, false statements, and insider trading. They had each sold substantial shareholdings in the company in the period shortly before the accounting frauds became known.
  Audit firm Arthur Anderson faced much scrutiny for its role in the scandal. A corporate conviction for obstruction of justice (relating to the shredding of Enron-related documentation) effectively prevented the firm from practising and the firm was disbanded (even though the criminal conviction was overturned in 2005).
- **Goldman Sachs** – in 2010, the Securities and Exchange Commission (SEC) charged Goldman Sachs with fraud in respect of some sub-prime mortgage-related securities. Goldman created a portfolio of mortgage-backed investments and sold an interest in that portfolio to a number of investors. However, what Goldman did not disclose to the investors is that the portfolio had been assembled in conjunction with a substantial client of the firm, John Paulson, and that he would then trade in the expectation that the portfolio would reduce in value rather than grow. Effectively Goldman enticed investors who would lose their money to Paulson, without disclosing that it had a corporate interest on both sides of the security.
- Steinhoff International, an international retail holding company in the furniture and household goods business, overstated profits for eight years (2009–17) by a total amount of $7.4bn. The accounting fraud involved a small group of executives and outsiders entering into a transaction that substantially inflated the group's profit and asset values. Although Steinhoff first disclosed irregularities in 2017, the accounting fraud was not revealed until 2019.
- Wirecard AG, a fully licensed German bank providing payment services filed for insolvency in June 2020 after disclosing that approximately €1.9bn was missing. The missing funds are mainly attributed to balance sheet irregularities and inflated profits, a practice rumoured to have started in 2008. In November 2020, the assets of the main business unit were sold to Santander.
- Patisserie Valerie, a UK-based patisserie reported significant and potentially fraudulent accounting irregularities requiring an immediate capital injection of £20m. The firm's finance chief was suspended and arrested on suspicion of fraud having opened secret overdraft facilities totalling almost £10 million. Patisserie Valerie's market capitalisation dropped from £446m to £68m in a period of two weeks.

These cases illustrate not only the potential scale of fraud that can arise, but also the way that discovery of such cases can impact other market participants. It is vital that firms ensure their governance structures are sufficiently robust to protect against becoming victims of fraudulent activity.

1.3.8 Tax Evasion and Tax Avoidance

Learning Objective

3.1.8 Know the concepts of facilitation of tax evasion and tax avoidance

Tax avoidance is the use of legally permissible methods to reduce the amount of tax owed. This is generally achieved by claiming permissible deductions, credits and allowances. Tax avoidance is legal and includes aspects, such as transferring assets between spouses, or making pension contributions in order to reduce the level of income that remains subject to income tax. Tax avoidance is enabled by the complexity built into the taxation system, as such complexity can allow individuals to identify legal loopholes and exemptions by which certain monies do not give rise to tax liabilities.

Tax evasion, however, is an illegal practice where a person, organisation, or corporation intentionally avoids paying part or all of their tax liability. Examples might include not paying income tax or VAT when working for 'cash in hand'. Tax evasion would also arise if the capital gains made on investments were not correctly disclosed for taxation calculation. Although the difference between tax evasion and tax avoidance is clear, there is a grey area referred to as 'tax-aggressive strategies'. Most developed countries have what are known as general anti-avoidance rules (GAAR) prohibiting tax-aggressive avoidance.

1.3.9 Dual Criminality, Extradition and Mutual Legal Assistance

Learning Objective

3.1.9 Know the concepts of dual criminality, extradition and mutual legal assistance

Extradition law is an amalgamation of international and domestic law that sets the structure for an individual living in one country to stand trial in another. Generally, extradition is only supported in conditions of 'double criminality' (also known as dual criminality), ie, where the allegation relates to an action that constitutes a crime in both the country where a suspect is being held and the country asking for the suspect to be handed over or transferred to stand trial. In other words, a crime in one country has to also be a crime in the country extraditing you.

Cases of extradition can involve a combination of legal arguments and diplomacy, and can prove controversial. Consider the cases of 'The NatWest Three' or Gary McKinnon, both of which raised questions of political balance within extradition arrangements between the UK and the US.

Under an Organisation for Economic Co-operation and Development (OECD) convention, each country shall, to the fullest extent possible under its laws and relevant treaties and arrangements, provide prompt and effective legal assistance to another country for the purpose of criminal investigations and proceedings brought by a country concerning offences within the scope of the convention and for non-criminal proceedings within the scope of the convention brought by a country against a legal person. The country receiving the request shall inform the country making the request, of any additional information or documents needed to support the request for assistance without delay and if asked, of the status and outcome of the request for assistance.

Where a country makes mutual legal assistance conditional upon the existence of dual criminality, it shall be deemed to exist if the offence for which the assistance is sought is within the scope of this OECD convention. A country shall not decline mutual legal assistance for criminal matters within the scope of the convention on the grounds of bank secrecy.

2. Practical Implications

Learning Objectives

3.2.1 Understand how external financial crime issues may impact on a firm: reputational; systemically; counterparty risk; unreliable market valuations

3.2.2 Understand how financial crime may directly impact a firm: theft of data; theft of assets

2.1 Impact of Financial Crime on Firms

Financial crime can impact a firm in various ways. If a specific crime becomes public knowledge, any firms directly connected with the crime face reputational damage. A previously respected company name can become synonymous with fraud or poor governance, reducing the potential for the firm to gain further clients and retain the business it already holds. The company's reputation will also be impacted if its regulator imposes a public penalty upon it – such as a regulatory fine or reprimand. For example, if a regulator fines a company for failing to satisfy AML rules, other clients may wish to move their affairs to a more respectable firm.

Firms can also be impacted by events taking place in other parts of the industry – even if they have no direct involvement in those events. Financial crime poses a systemic risk for the industry: the risk of collapse of an entire financial system or entire market, as opposed to risk associated with any one individual entity, group or component of a system. Such risks can lead to instability in the financial system with the outcome for one firm being potentially exacerbated by the action or inaction of other financial intermediaries. Because of interdependencies in a system or market, the failure of a single firm or group can cause a cascading failure, which could potentially bankrupt or bring down the entire system or market.

The Madoff Ponzi scheme is an example of such a crime which led to huge losses across the market. The malfeasance at Lehman Brothers prompted a global financial crisis with unprecedented support from governments being needed to prevent the banking system from collapsing.

The market requires participants to have trust in each other – even if that trust is built on regulatory obligations and a fear of sanction. The potential that a firm may be unable to deliver on its promises to another is termed 'counterparty risk' (or sometimes 'default risk'). While it is rare for a firm to not honour its obligations to, for example, pay out on a bond, credit derivative, credit insurance contract, or other trade or transaction, the risk of such failure is increased significantly where financial crime may be a contributing factor. The inability of the counterparty to meet a claim may be the result of financial crime, including fraud, market abuse and misstatements. Again, the Lehman case is an example where the value of **credit default swaps (CDSs)** based on sub-prime mortgages collapsed and many financial institutions faced major losses and potential ruin.

Firms can also face unreliable market valuations which may lead to securities being over- or under-valued as a result of market abuse and misstatements. To counter market abuse, firms have been required to develop sophisticated reporting systems; failure to provide effective reporting can be serious. Transaction reports are vital in detecting and investigating potential market abuse cases. Since the FCA replaced the FSA, it has fined three major institutions for failings in transaction reporting. RBS was fined £5.6 million in 2013, and Deutsche Bank was fined £4.7 million the following year. In 2015, Merrill Lynch was fined £13.3 million for transaction reporting failures over a seven-year period.

2.2 Direct Impacts of Financial Crime

One of the downsides to the rapid development of electronic communications is the portability of data in large quantities, using the internet or small storage devices. Increasingly sophisticated criminals are targeting financial service companies to steal the data they hold on customers.

The data a firm holds about its customers (eg, their personal details, names, addresses, bank details and passwords) are all types of data that are attractive to those attempting, for example, account takeover and credit card fraud.

There are many ways that criminals can target financial firms with a view to stealing data, including:

- infiltrating firms and placing people as employees who download data onto USB sticks
- theft of computers, laptops and data files on tape or disk
- hacking into systems, breaching firewalls and other security systems, using logger tools to gather data, and
- social engineering, deceiving call centre associates into providing information unwittingly.

Once criminals have a customer's personal details, including bank accounts and investments, they can attempt the theft of the customer's assets. They may take over the accounts of their victims, impersonating the customer to instruct a change of address or bank account details. Having usurped the original customer, the criminal will instruct the sale of assets, and have the proceeds sent to the address/bank account they control – often a fraudulently opened bank account, to ensure the account owner name will match the name on the redemption cheque. The criminal then withdraws the cash and absconds with the proceeds. The financial firm may be left with an angry customer and, depending on the circumstances, may have to compensate its customer and reinstate their accounts.

Firms can be subject to asset thefts too. This may be as a result of account takeover, or other fraudulent activity which may be internal or external to the firm. For example, forged transfer of assets and forged sale instructions. This may involve proceeds being directed to bank accounts set up by the fraudsters specifically for the purpose of laundering the proceeds. In some cases the amounts involved can be very significant.

The impact of such thefts can include the following:

- reduced profits and potentially risks to the financial stability of the firm
- damage to the firm's reputation, which may arise from supervisory or other regulatory action, such as fines
- increased costs arising from investigation of theft, forensic work by expert or specialist firms and remediation where required such as new systems and controls
- increased insurance costs following revised premiums based on recent claim experience, or the need to take out additional insurance cover where perhaps the risk had not previously been identified.

2.3 Firms' Responsibilities for Financial Crime Prevention

Learning Objective

3.2.3 Understand the responsibilities of directors and senior management in relation to anti-money laundering (AML), combating financial crime (CFC) and anti-corruption (AC) initiatives

The directors and senior management of an authorised financial firm are expected to:

- identify, and manage effectively, the risks in their businesses and this will include ensuring appropriate action is taken in relation to combating the financing of terrorism (CFT), AML, combating financial crime (CFC) and anti-corruption (AC)
- appoint a **nominated officer** to process disclosures
- appoint an MLRO with certain responsibilities
- ensure the MLRO has adequate resources devoted to AML/CFT
- understand the potential personal liability if legal obligations are not met.

Accordingly, the directors and senior management will ensure the policies and procedures established include systems and controls that:

1. enable the firm to identify, assess, monitor and manage money laundering risk, and
2. are comprehensive and proportionate to the nature, scale and complexity of its activities.

2.3.1 Anti-Money Laundering (AML)

In many respects, compliance with AML is an integral part of the overall compliance requirements of the regulated sector. The expectation is that senior management are aware of and take responsibility for all compliance activity within their institution. This is embodied through senior management being able to provide evidence of having adequate systems and control procedures in place, which should be tested to prove effectiveness. These general compliance requirements obviously also apply to AML and related initiatives. Indeed, there is plenty of evidence of banks having been fined by regulators for failure to meet these requirements.

It is generally expected that senior management establishes the AML policy, setting out how the organisation will comply with the legal and regulatory AML regime; it will set out the reporting framework with the various responsibilities and accountabilities of the employees and management. The internal information systems will set out the application of the risk-based approach and how it is interpreted together with the client and transaction monitoring, record-keeping and reporting criteria.

2.3.2 Combating Financial Crime (CFC)

International efforts to combat financial crime have focused on a number of objectives to:

- reduce financial crime and deter the use of financial systems
- ensure that firms have in place policies and procedures designed to minimise the risk that the firms' businesses may be used as a vehicle for money laundering and other financial crime
- raise consumer awareness of financial crime issues

- contribute to an effective wider fight against crime through international cooperation
- encourage a balanced, joined-up approach to AML and fraud through standards and guidance
- improve the effective use of regulator resources through risk assessment processes
- improve coordination with partner agencies.

The expectation is that businesses are aware of the risk, have appropriate measures to prevent, detect and monitor financial crime, and provide adequate resources to do so – and that:

- trade associations work together closely and provide leadership over fraud management
- senior managers accept that fraud is a significant threat that needs managing strategically and effectively
- more work is done on the risks and scale of fraud and better ways of tackling it, and
- improved organisational cultures and information sharing are developed.

This means that, using a risk-based approach, regulators will be looking for evidence of:

- a strong anti-fraud culture, with the lead being given from the top
- a clear allocation of responsibility for the day-to-day management of the risk
- satisfactory staff training
- robust **know your customer (KYC)** procedures, and how the firm identifies potential criminal behaviour, and
- what management information on fraud is captured and how it is used.

Regulators will be looking for 'reasonable steps' to be aware of, and tackle fraud risks by being able to identify and report on the following:

- Who is responsible for managing fraud risks?
- How many frauds has the firm suffered recently?
- What are fraud losses?
- What **whistleblowing** arrangements are in place and how successful are they?
- How much is spent on preventing and detecting fraud?
- How does the firm monitor the effectiveness of fraud systems and controls?
- What information on fraud goes to the board or senior management?

Regulators have an important role as gatekeeper of those working in regulated businesses (granting authorisation to firms and those individuals seeking to perform **controlled functions**), and another role ensuring that the expected standards of behaviour and practice are met.

Regulators, therefore, monitor firms and individuals to ensure risks are appropriately managed and fraudulent activity reported, confirming that businesses have in place, the systems and controls to meet various legislative requirements. This will include looking at IT and manual systems, separation of duties within a firm, the role of internal audit, risk assessment, mitigation and monitoring programmes, documented policies and procedures, organisational cultures, collection and use of internal information, and reforms following frauds.

2.3.3 Anti-Corruption Initiatives

Corruption and bribery are harmful for business and form important barriers to investment growth. The development of anti-corruption systems, policies and procedures can help prevent corruption. In order to be effective, organisations must commit to an anti-corruption programme from the board down to senior management and lower levels of the organisations. Policies must be put in place and acted upon, with regular monitoring being an integral part of the plan. The UN launched a call for action in 2014, urging governments to introduce anti-corruption measures and good governance as fundamental pillars of a sustainable and inclusive global economy, and that included anti-corruption initiatives in the UN Sustainable Development Goals. More than 250 companies and investors globally have signed up to the Anti-Corruption Call to Action.

2.4 Identifying Money Laundering

Learning Objective

3.2.5 Understand the implications of using a risk-based approach to identifying money laundering

Many types of transactions can potentially conceal money laundering activity – particularly as the layering stage may feature multiple normal transactions in order to obscure the audit trail. To perform a full set of AML checks on every transaction undertaken would impose a significant cost upon the industry. Given the importance of trust to the financial services sector, it is important that firms also appear to trust their clients – rather than performing intrusive identity checks on transactions of trivial value. To help balance this difficulty, the FATF Recommendations note that a risk-based approach to the identification of money laundering is acceptable.

When adopting a risk-based approach, competent authorities and financial institutions must first determine which activities are most likely to conceal money laundering efforts, and also determine how the suspicious nature of such transactions might be revealed.

For example, firms that accept physical cash from clients will generally be considered as higher-risk, as these businesses offer a means for 'dirty money' to find its way into the financial system. In other cases, a minimum value threshold might be applied, below which the firm need only perform limited scrutiny.

Some types of savings and investment products may be determined as being intrinsically lower-risk in terms of potential money laundering activity (eg, a pension scheme, if an investor's money cannot be withdrawn in the short term without incurring a tax charge). In some cases, the firm might be able to accept a certificate from another regulated firm – confirming that the earlier firm has already completed full client identification checks on a mutual client.

The rules recognise the potential that such mechanisms could mean that some cases of abuse are not identified, but that major abuses should still be captured, and that each firm must still ensure that its staff are sufficiently trained to identify any suspicious activity taking place.

2.5 Prevention of Money Laundering

Learning Objectives

3.2.4 Understand the role of the Money Laundering Reporting Officer (or equivalent) in relation to financial crime

3.2.6 Know the measures firms can adopt to inhibit the likelihood of financial crime

Firms must develop and implement a set of measures that are relevant to the type of business it performs, and sufficient to deliver a risk-based control over potential financial crime activity impacting its business. Some of these measures will be structural (eg, ensuring all relevant staff are sufficiently trained to understand the ways in which financial crime could affect the company), while other measures will apply when processing specific transactions.

A firm must carry out a regular assessment of the adequacy of the systems and controls to ensure that it continues to comply with relevant regulations and relevant legal requirements. In identifying its money laundering risk and establishing the nature of these systems and controls, a firm should consider a range of factors, including:

- its customers, products and activity profiles
- its distribution channels
- the complexity and volume of its transactions
- its processes and systems, and
- its operating environment.

Systems and controls must include:

- appropriate training for its employees in relation to money laundering
- appropriate provision of information to its governing body and senior management, including a report at least annually by that firm's MLRO, or another responsible senior executive, on the operation and effectiveness of those systems and controls
- appropriate documentation of its risk management policies and risk profile in relation to money laundering and other financial crime, including documentation of its application of those policies
- appropriate measures to ensure that money laundering and other financial crime risk is taken into account in its day-to-day operation, including in relation to:
  - the development of new products
  - the taking on of new customers
  - changes in its business profile, and
- appropriate measures to ensure that procedures for identification of new customers do not unreasonably deny access to its services to potential customers who cannot reasonably be expected to produce detailed evidence of identity.

A firm should allocate to a director or senior manager (who may also be the MLRO) overall responsibility within the firm for the establishment and maintenance of effective AML systems and controls.

2.5.1 Money Laundering Reporting Officer (MLRO)

The MLRO is responsible for oversight of the firm's compliance with the regulator's rules on systems and controls against money laundering; and the firm should ensure that its MLRO has a level of authority and independence within the firm, and access to resources and information sufficient to enable them to carry out that responsibility. It is a senior role, sometimes referred to as a 'nominated officer', and the incumbent should report at a senior level and be able to take precedence over business lines operating, for example, in an international context. The following sets out the usual responsibilities. It is the MLRO's role to be aware of any suspicious activity in the business that might be linked to money laundering or terrorist financing, and if necessary, to report it. They are responsible for:

- receiving reports of suspicious activity from any employee in the business
- considering all reports and evaluating whether there is – or seems to be – any evidence of money laundering or terrorist financing
- reporting any suspicious activity or transaction to the appropriate law enforcement agency (LEA) by completing and submitting a suspicious activity report (SAR)
- asking the LEA for consent to continue with any transactions that they have reported and making sure that no transactions are continued illegally.

The firm might decide to make the MLRO responsible for other tasks that need to be done to make sure the business complies with money laundering regulations. For example, they could be made responsible for:

- putting in place and operating AML controls and procedures
- carrying out money laundering risk assessments
- record-keeping, and
- training staff in preventing money laundering.

2.6 How Individuals Can Protect Themselves

Learning Objective

3.2.7 Know the measures individuals can adopt to inhibit the likelihood of financial crime

---

Investors can do a number of things themselves to reduce the likelihood that they would be a victim of financial crime. They should:

- keep personal information secure and if disposing of financial/bank statements, use a shredder to shred the statements before disposal
- keep plastic cards in a secure place
- keep documents safe
- keep passwords and PIN numbers secure
- check the qualification and authorised status of any financial adviser, and
- remember that if an investment sounds too good to be true it probably is.

2.7 Sanctions Checking and Politically Exposed Persons (PEPs)

2.7.1 Sanctions Checking

Learning Objective

3.2.8 Understand the rationale behind sanctions screening

Where an individual, company, organisation, or even country is considered to have acted illegally, it is possible for the rest of the global community to take action against that abuse. One mechanism by which such action might be taken is the use of financial sanctions.

Financial sanctions prevent the use and movement of monies relating to certain individuals or organisations considered by the international community to be unfit (usually due to relationships with crime or terrorism). In this way, those committing illegal actions should not be able to benefit financially from those actions – which should, in theory, reduce the motivation to commit those abuses.

Organisations such as the UN maintain a sanctions list, and financial services firms should seek to minimise the risk that they are servicing customers who are subject to financial sanctions. In some countries (such as the UK), legal sanctions are imposed on firms or individuals found to have breached financial sanctions. Aside from any legal penalties, failure to recognise such cases exposes the firm to reputational risk (as bad publicity that a firm indirectly supported terrorism, for example, may result in other people not doing business with that firm).

The international frameworks for financial sanctions do not prescribe the processes which firms have to adopt to achieve compliance with their legal obligations. The guidance below is intended to provide an indication of the types of controls and processes that firms might adopt in order to enable them to comply with sanctions obligations in an effective and proportionate manner.

Firms should have processes to manage the risk of conducting business with, or on behalf of, individuals and entities on the list provided by their government or directly from the UN and other appropriate sanctions lists. Some countries provide a consolidated list (which includes all the names of sanctioned persons and entities under the UN and, for example, EU sanctions regimes which have effect in the country concerned). Firms should consider screening their customers and transactions on a periodic and/or ongoing basis.

The scope and complexity of the screening process will be influenced by the firm's business activities, and according to the profile of the firm. An effective screening process should include the following elements:

- it should flag up potential name matches against the consolidated list and names against which measures have been issued, for example, in the UK under the Counter-Terrorism Act
- potential matches should be reviewed by appropriately trained staff
- where matches are confirmed as true, appropriate action should be taken to freeze the account
- true matches should be reported as soon as is practicable to the relevant LEA or government department, and
- the firm should maintain an audit trail of actions around potential and true matches.

Many firms use automated customer screening software provided by a commercial provider; other firms rely on manual screening. Firms may consider whether and what type of screening software to use in line with the nature, size and risk profile of their business. A key element of a screening system is that it will flag potential matches clearly and prominently. Firms should document the reasons for choosing whichever screening method they decide to use.

Where commercially available automated screening software is implemented, firms should understand its capabilities and limits, and make sure it is tailored to their business requirements, data requirements and risk profile. Firms should also monitor the ongoing effectiveness of automated systems. Where automated screening software is used, firms should be satisfied that they have adequate contingency arrangements should the software fail and should periodically check the software is working as they expect it to.

It is important to consider 'fuzzy matching' (a term used to describe partial or potential matches). Some software solutions identify possible matches where data – whether in official lists or in firms' internal records – is misspelled, incomplete, or missing. They are often tolerant of multinational and linguistic differences in spelling, formats for dates of birth, and similar data. A sophisticated system will have a variety of settings, enabling greater or less fuzziness in the matching process, as appropriate to the risk profile of the business.

The generation and resolution of an undue number of false positives may have a negative impact on the efficacy of the resolution process. Firms should, therefore, consider the level of appropriate human intervention to assess which results may be false positives.

All customers should be screened during the establishment of a business relationship or as soon as possible after the business relationship has commenced. Firms should be aware of the risks associated with screening customers after a business relationship has been established and/or services have been provided, ie, that they may transact with a sanctioned party in breach of sanctions prohibitions. Firms must be aware of the absolute restrictions embedded in the financial sanctions regime. Where there is any delay in screening, firms risk breaching the legislation.

A firm must apply enhanced due diligence measures on a risk-sensitive basis in any situation which by its nature can present a higher risk of money laundering or terrorist financing. As part of this, a firm may conclude, under its risk-based approach, that the standard evidence of identity is insufficient in relation to the money laundering or terrorist financing risk, and that it must obtain additional information about a particular customer.

As part of a risk-based approach, therefore, firms may need to hold sufficient information about the circumstances and business of their customers for two principal reasons:

- to inform their risk assessment process, and thus manage their money laundering/terrorist financing risks effectively, and
- to provide a basis for monitoring customer activity and transactions, thus increasing the likelihood that they will detect the use of their products and services for money laundering and terrorist financing.

2.7.2 OFAC Sanctions

The Office of Foreign Asset Control (OFAC) is part of the US Department of the Treasury and acts under presidential national emergency powers, as well as the authority granted to it by specific legislation. OFAC has the right to impose controls on transactions and to freeze assets under US law. In addition, they administer and enforce economic and trade sanctions, many of which are based on the United Nations Security Council (UNSC) resolutions and other international mandates. OFAC is responsible for the administration of the specially designated nationals (SDN) list which contains individuals and organisations with whom US citizens and permanent residents are prohibited from transacting and doing business with.

Under Chapter VII of the UN charter, the sanctions process of the UN typically starts with a matter of concern taken up by the Security Council. At an early stage, knowing the Security Council may impose sanctions can be sufficient to prevent escalation or outbreak of conflict. Sanctions are a last resort imposed in a variety of instances, including in the combating of terrorist financing and proliferation finance.

The sanctions process can be depicted as follows[1]:

Sanctions are imposed by means of a UNSC resolution establishing a sanctions regime and a sanctions list. Names of countries, individuals and groups on a sanctions list may change over time with names added to and removed from the list. Sanctions committees are subsidiary organs of the Council and are composed of all 15 of the Council's members. The role of the sanctions committees is to implement, monitor and provide recommendations to the Council on particular sanction regimes.

Committees meet regularly to consider reports from expert panels and to meet with Member states, UN actors and international organisations. Sanctions need to be implemented with due regard for human rights.

The range of sanctions can vary from comprehensive financial and trade sanctions to more targeted measures, such as arms embargoes, travel bans, financial or diplomatic restrictions.

1 https://news.un.org/en/story/2016/05/528382-un-sanctions-what-they-are-how-they-work-and-who-uses-them

01732 368678

Sanctions Measures

2.7.3 Politically Exposed Persons (PEPs)

Learning Objective

3.2.9 Understand the purpose behind screening individuals: risk-based approach; politically exposed persons (PEPs)

PEPs are individuals who have (or have had) a high political profile, or who hold (or have held) public office. Such persons can pose a higher money laundering risk to firms as their position may make them vulnerable to corruption. This risk also extends to members of their immediate families and to known close associates. PEP status itself does not incriminate individuals or entities. It does, however, put the customer, or the beneficial owner, into a higher risk category. A PEP is defined as:

> *'an individual who is or has, at any time in the preceding year, been entrusted with prominent public functions and an immediate family member, or a known close associate, of such a person'.*

EU Directive 2006/70/EC sets out the implementing measures for defining PEPs, and so provides a definition of positions that constitute prominent public functions. That definition includes:

- heads of state, heads of government, ministers and deputy or assistant ministers
- members of parliaments
- members of supreme courts, of constitutional courts or of other high-level judicial bodies whose decisions are not generally subject to further appeal, except in exceptional circumstances
- members of courts of auditors or of the boards of central banks
- ambassadors, charges d'affaires and high-ranking officers in the armed forces
- members of the administrative, management or supervisory boards of state-owned enterprises.

This definition is reinforced in 4MLD and maintained in subsequent editions of MLD, and extended to include members of the governing bodies of political parties; as well as directors, deputy directors and members of the board or equivalent function of an international organisation. In addition, the definition of a PEP extends to direct family (spouse or equivalent, children and their spouses (or equivalent), and parents) as well as close associates. In this context, close associates are:

- natural persons who are known to have joint beneficial ownership of legal entities or legal arrangements, or any other close business relations, with a PEP
- natural persons who have sole beneficial ownership of a legal entity or legal arrangement which is known to have been set up for the de facto benefit of a PEP.

In all six categories, the definition excludes middle- and junior-ranking officials. The governmental legislative/judicial positions noted in the first five categories may relate to posts at national or community (ie, EU) level.

Firms are required to take a risk-based approach to PEPs and need to:

- have appropriate risk-based procedures to determine whether a customer is a PEP
- obtain appropriate senior management approval for establishing a business relationship with such a customer
- take adequate measures to establish the source of wealth and source of funds which are involved in the business relationship or occasional transaction, and
- conduct enhanced ongoing monitoring of the business relationship.

3. Policies, Procedures and Controls Required of Firms

Learning Objectives

3.3.1 Understand the risks to a firm posed by its clients, products and delivery systems

3.1 The Risks Posed to a Firm

Similar to individuals, firms are also exposed to financial crime risks when they perform financial services for clients.

Some of these risks arise because of the firm's clients: are they honest, or seeking to deceive the firm to achieve criminal outcomes? Other risks arise in respect of the different products that the firm may offer: products such as individual savings accounts (ISAs) or pensions allow certain tax benefits, and the firm should be alert to the risks associated with tax evasion. The delivery systems chosen by the firm to provide its services can also affect the financial crime risks that the firm is managing; for example, it is important that the firm is confident that any instructions it receives are made by the actual customer (rather than a criminal seeking to impersonate the customer in order to take over the account and acquire the assets). The mechanisms that the firm can use to validate a person's identity will vary for different communication channels: telephone calls enable ID questions to be asked; written material must contain all necessary information; and electronic communications are usually protected by some form of username and password.

The firm must be able to recognise such areas of risk and understand how these different elements apply to its own business model. In this respect, senior management should ask themselves a number of questions.

For example:

- What risk is posed by the firm's customers?
  - Does the client satisfy the definition of a PEP, and is the firm able to give such an account the extra care required?
  - Is a customer based in, or conducting business through, a high-risk jurisdiction – and is the firm equipped to perform the additional due diligence that may be required?
  - Is the customer's own business within a sector that places them at a higher risk of exposure to financial crime or corruption? A firm would not want to be associated with a customer who could be exposed as committing or facilitating financial crime – both from a public relations perspective, and due to the practical implications of 'dirty money' being found to have passed through the firm's financial products as market transactions.
- What risk is posed by a customer's behaviour?
  - Has the firm established relevant controls over dealing patterns and trends, to identify whether a customer is performing unusual deals that could be suspicious?
  - How would the firm react if a customer asks questions about the levels of secrecy regarding a transaction – or requests additional secrecy measures?
  - Is a customer seeking to transfer assets or money to the firm in such a way that the origin of wealth or the source of funds cannot easily be verified?
  - If the customer is not a private individual, is the operator of the account willing to provide relevant information about the underlying owners and controllers?
- What risk is posed by the way the customer became a customer?
  - Was the firm able to complete the necessary due diligence review of the customer?
  - Where the customer came to the firm via a financial intermediary, is the firm confident in the due diligence material provided by that intermediary?
  - Was the customer accepted after distance communication only, or was a face-to-face meeting held?
- What risk is posed by the products/services the customer is using?
  - Does the product allow payments to third parties?
  - Could the product be used to enable inappropriate assets to pass through the firm?
  - Does the product include other features that could enable money laundering or terrorist financing?

The firm must, of course, consider all these factors against its normal expectations for the type of business it performs and the clients it intends to service.

3.2 Understanding the Controls

Learning Objective

3.3.2 Understand the controls a firm should have in place to minimise its risk to fraud, money laundering and terrorist financing, including a training programme

Firms are exposed to the risk that its business will become a victim of fraud or will be used by someone performing money laundering or seeking to support terrorist organisations. The firm must, therefore, assess where such risks primarily reside: what processes, products, and client types pose the greatest risk of being abused in this way. Having assessed the risk, senior management must then ensure that appropriate controls are designed and implemented to mitigate this risk.

In respect of fraud, firms must recognise the potential for both internal and external fraud. Internal fraud relates to the actions taken within the company: an employee misusing their position to enrich themselves at the expense of the company or its employees. Quality control checks (to ensure accuracy of processing) and segregation of duties (to ensure that work must pass through separate departments before payment is released) are examples of controls that can reduce the risk of internal fraud occurring.

As regards money laundering and terrorist financing, managing and mitigating the risks will involve:

- measures to verify the customer's identity
- collecting additional information about the customer, and
- monitoring transactions and activity, to determine whether there are reasonable grounds for knowing or suspecting that money laundering or terrorist financing may be taking place.

Part of the control framework will involve decisions as to whether verification should take place electronically, and the extent to which the firm can use customer verification procedures carried out by other firms. Firms must determine the extent of their CDD measures on a risk-sensitive basis depending on the type of customer, business relationship, product or transaction.

To decide on the most appropriate and relevant controls for the firm, senior management should ask themselves what measures the firm can adopt, and to what extent, to manage and mitigate these threats/risks most cost effectively, and in line with the firm's risk appetite.

Examples of control procedures include:

- introducing a customer identification programme that varies the procedures in respect of customers appropriate to their assessed money laundering/terrorist financing risk
- requiring the quality of evidence – documentary/electronic/third-party assurance – to be of a certain standard
- obtaining additional customer information, where this is appropriate to their assessed money laundering/terrorist financing risk, and
- monitoring customer transactions/activities.

Risk management is generally a continuous process, carried out on a dynamic basis. A money laundering/terrorist financing risk assessment is not a one-time exercise. Firms must, therefore, ensure that their risk management processes for managing money laundering and terrorist financing risks are kept under regular review. A firm should, therefore, keep its risk assessment(s) up to date. An annual, formal reassessment might be too often in most cases, but still appropriate for a dynamic, growing business. It is recommended that a firm revisits its assessment at least annually, even if it decides that there is no case for revision. Firms should include details of the assessment, and any resulting changes, in the MLRO's annual report.

3.3 Effective Training

Learning Objective

3.3.2 Understand the controls a firm should have in place to minimise its risk to fraud, money laundering and terrorist financing including a training programme

It is essential that the firms train their employees in respect of fraud, money laundering controls, and the prevention of terrorist financing in order that staff will be able to recognise suspicious events, and will know how to escalate any such suspicions.

Key criteria for a training programme include:

- understanding the internal controls established, and the risks they are intended to mitigate (eg, controls intended to prevent internal fraud)
- staff responsibilities under the firm's arrangements for the prevention of money laundering and terrorist financing, including those for:
  - obtaining sufficient evidence of identity
  - recognising and reporting knowledge or suspicion of money laundering or terrorist financing
- the identity and responsibilities of the nominated officer and the MLRO
- the potential effect on the firm, on its employees personally and on its clients, of any breach of that law
- the content and frequency of training reflecting the risk assessment of the products and services of the firm and the specific role of the individual
- appropriate assessment at the end of a training session to ensure it has been effective.

In addition, selected or relevant employees should be given regular appropriate training in order to be aware of:

- potential fraudulent activity
- the criminal law relating to money laundering and terrorist financing, and
- the regulations or guidance issued by the regulator.

Staff will find it helpful to have illustrations of the type of situation that may be unusual, and which in certain circumstances might give rise to reasonable grounds for suspicion.

Training programmes may also include:

- examples of fraudulent activity – whether previously identified within the firm itself, or relevant cases from similar firms
- the nature of terrorism funding and terrorist activity, in order that staff are alert to customer transactions or activities that might be terrorist-related, and
- trends and the changing behaviour and practices among those involved in money laundering and financing terrorism.

3.4 Effective Suspicious Activity or Transaction Reporting

Learning Objective

3.3.3 Know the criteria for an effective suspicious transaction reporting system

An appropriate system of reporting must be in place whereupon:

- All staff must raise an internal report where they have knowledge or suspicion, or where there are reasonable grounds for having knowledge or suspicion, that another person is engaged in money laundering, or that terrorist property exists.
- The firm's nominated officer must consider all internal reports.
- The firm's nominated officer must make an external report to the relevant LEA as soon as is practicable if they consider that there is knowledge, suspicion, or reasonable grounds for knowledge or suspicion, that another person is engaged in money laundering, or that terrorist property exists.
- The firm must seek consent from the LEA before proceeding with a suspicious transaction or entering into arrangements.
- The firm must freeze funds if a customer is identified as being on the sanctions list on the government website of suspected terrorists or sanctioned individuals and entities and make an external report to the relevant authority in its home state.

Firms need to ensure that detailed records are maintained, relating to any suspicious transaction activity – whether as part of the reporting system or as separate records. Such record-keeping should include:

- Details of any disclosures made regarding enquiries on a case.
- The reasons why a SAR/suspicious transaction report (STR) was, or was not, submitted.
- Any communications made with or received from the authorities, including the LEA, in relation to the SAR/STR.
- Where relevant, details of the need for prior consent to be received from the LEA before releasing the proceeds of a transaction – together with details of any such consent received.

The firm's nominated officer must report suspicious approaches, even if no transaction takes place. Any actions required should be kept under regular review.

It is normally a criminal offence for anyone, following a disclosure to a nominated officer or to the LEA, to do or say anything that might either tip off another person that a disclosure has been made or prejudice an investigation.

End of Chapter Questions

Think of an answer for each question and refer to the appropriate section for confirmation.

1. What are the three stages of money laundering?
Answer reference: Section 1.2

2. What is the purpose of the Financial Action Task Force (FATF)?
Answer reference: Section 1.3.4

3. Give two examples of predicate offences in financial crime.
Answer reference: Section 1.3.5

4. How does a Ponzi scheme work?
Answer reference: Section 1.3.6

5. What are typical cyber crime activities?
Answer reference: Section 1.3.6

6. Describe how a material misstatement of financial statements may arise.
Answer reference: Section 1.3.7

7. What is the difference between tax avoidance and tax evasion?
Answer reference: Section 1.3.8

8. Explain the concept of dual criminality.
Answer reference: Section 1.3.9

9. Since replacing the Financial Services Authority (FSA), the Financial Conduct Authority (FCA) has fined three major institutions for failings in transaction reporting. Of what magnitude were these fines?
Answer reference: Section 2.1

10. What are the direct impacts of financial crime?
Answer reference: Section 2.2

11. Name three responsibilities of senior management in relation to financial crime.
Answer reference: Section 2.3

12. What factors should a firm consider when assessing the adequacy of its financial crime prevention systems and controls?
Answer reference: Section 2.5

13. How can individuals protect themselves from financial crime?
Answer reference: Section 2.6

14. When should a firm apply enhanced due diligence?
Answer reference: Section 2.7.1

15. List the range of the United Nations (UN) sanctions.
Answer reference: Section 2.7.2

16. Where do the Office of Foreign Assets Control (OFAC) powers originate from?
Answer reference: Section 2.7.2

17. What is included on the specially designated nationals (SDN) list?
Answer reference: Section 2.7.2

18. In applying a risk-based approach to financial crime prevention, what factors should a firm consider?
Answer reference: Section 3.1

19. What controls should be put in place to mitigate the risk a firm faces in respect of money laundering?
Answer reference: Section 3.2

20. Give three examples of the content of a training programme relating to the detection and prevention of fraud, money laundering and terrorist financing.
Answer reference: Section 3.3

21. What action should be taken if a customer is identified as being on the sanctions list?
Answer reference: Section 3.4

Chapter Four

Ethics, Integrity and Fairness

This syllabus area will provide approximately 19 of the 100 examination questions

1. Ethics

Learning Objective

4.1.1 Understand how ethical principles relate to the financial services industry: regulatory standards; professional codes of conduct; internal codes of conduct

1.1 Relating Ethical Standards to the Financial Sector

Regulators believe that they have an obligation to consider and make judgements about the ethics and values of the firms they regulate. Making judgements about behaviours is more than just setting regulations and expecting firms to comply; having a compliance culture is simply not enough. What is needed is an ethical culture in the firm which embodies the values underlying the whole regulatory structure – values which lead to proper protection for consumers of financial services, to proper information for customers, and behaviour in the markets which maintains public confidence in them, and which enables financial crime to be fought effectively.

History reveals that many British firms across various industries were originally established as a reflection of the beliefs of their founders; Cadbury and Quaker Oats being two commonly cited examples from the industrial era. Equally, there are examples in the financial sector. Lloyds and Barclays grew from the Quaker movement; Halifax Building Society was created to help the working classes achieve the benefits of home ownership. Over time, others entered these markets – many simply keen to provide a good service and earn a reasonable capital return, rather than directly following ideological purposes – and the original founders of a company will be replaced. As a market evolves and competition matures, the initial motivations of participants may, therefore, become less visible – particularly if the market begins to display examples of abuse.

While the Western financial sector has arguably moved some way from the ideological roots of some founding firms, the Islamic finance industry is still a relatively young market and still displays its strong ethical underpinning. The **Quran** gives moral guidance governing property and wealth, the obligation to make charitable distributions, and the role of wealth creation. The structuring and underlying criteria of Islamic finance are overseen by Shariah supervisory boards (SSBs). The Islamic financial system should, therefore, contribute to the major socio-economic goals of Islamic society.

Meanwhile, as awareness of market activity and investment processes increased, certain investors sought services that reflected their own ethical values – notably an attitude towards smoking, armaments, and environmental issues. Ethical finance is, therefore, concerned with investment decisions being underpinned and with environmental, social and/or ethical factors.

An example of ethical finance is money invested with an ethical provider that will be reinvested into institutions that benefit the environment locally, regionally, or globally, such as organic farming enterprises and human rights issues.

1.2 Regulatory Standards

Most regulators set out standards and principles which they expect businesses and key individuals to observe. These may include:

- **Integrity** – a firm must conduct its business with integrity.
- **Customers' interests** – a firm must pay due regard to the interests of its customers and treat them fairly; and provide them with information which is clear, fair and not misleading; and advice which is suitable.
- **Market conduct** – a firm must observe proper standards of market conduct.
- **Client assets** – a firm must arrange adequate protection for clients' assets when it is responsible for them.

By setting such standards and principles for firms and key individuals, the regulator aims to ensure that the culture and operation of a firm meets the spirit, as well as the letter, of the regulations.

1.3 Professional Codes of Conduct

For any industry in which trust is a central feature, demonstrable standards of practice and the means to enforce them are a key requirement. Hence, the proliferation of professional bodies in the fields of health and wealth – areas in which consumers are more sensitive to performance and have higher expectations than in many other fields.

The terms 'code of ethics' and 'code of conduct' are often used interchangeably. However, using the term 'ethics' implies conformity with standards of behaviour and personal morality and does not imply compliance with rules and guidance relating to professional dealings. The latter is more appropriately described as a code of conduct. Where it is considered that more specific guidance on standards of professional practice would be beneficial, such standards might be set out in an appropriately entitled document, or in regulatory standards. Examples of professional codes follow.

1.3.1 The Chartered Financial Analyst (CFA) Institute – Code of Ethics and Standards of Professional Conduct

One of the professional institutes with a global reach is the CFA Institute whose members follow a code of ethics and standards of professional conduct which were created in the 1960s and are continuously reviewed and updated as required. The code and standards have promoted the integrity of CFA Institute members and have served as a model for measuring the ethics of investment professionals globally, regardless of job function, cultural differences or local laws and regulations.

The CFA Institute Code of Ethics includes the requirements that members and candidates must:

- act with integrity, competence, diligence, respect and in an ethical manner with all stakeholders, such as clients and others in the profession
- place the profession above their own interests
- exercise independent professional judgement
- encourage others to act in a professional and ethical manner
- uphold the rules governing capital markets
- exercise continuing professional development.

Full details of the code and standards can be obtained from the Institute's website at www.cfainstitute.org

1.3.2 The Chartered Institute for Securities & Investment (CISI) Code of Conduct

Professionals within the securities and investment industry owe important duties to their clients, the market, the industry and society at large. Where these duties are set out in law, or in regulation, the professional must always comply with the requirements in an open and transparent manner. Members of the CISI are required to meet the standards set out within the CISI's Principles.

These Principles are also known as the Lord George Principles in recognition of the contribution made to standards of integrity by the late Lord George FSI(Hon). They impose an obligation on members to act in a way beyond mere compliance, and to support the underlying values of the CISI.

The Principles are shown in the following table, with a column indicating the main stakeholders in connection with application of the relevant Principle. However, members should be aware that the list is not exclusive and, in some instances, the Principles are applicable to more than one stakeholder.

The Principles	Stakeholder
Personal Accountability – to strive to uphold the highest levels of personal and professional standards at all times, acting with integrity, honesty, due skill, care and diligence to avoid any acts, either in person, in a remote working environment or digitally which may damage the reputation of your organisation, your professional body or the financial services profession.	Self, clients, regulators, colleagues, market participants, firm, profession, society
Client Focus – to put the interests of clients and customers first by treating them fairly, being a good steward of their interests, never seeking personal advantage from confidential information received and utilising client data only for a defined purpose.	Clients
Conflict of Interest – being alert to and actively manage fairly and effectively any personal or other conflicts of interest, obeying legislation and complying with regulations to the best of your ability, ensuring you are open and cooperative with all your regulators, challenging and reporting unlawful or unethical behaviour.	Clients, market participants, regulators
Respect for Market Participants – to treat all counterparties and business partners with respect, to observe proper standards of market integrity, good practice, conduct and confidentiality required to maintain the highest level of mutual trust.	Clients, market participants
Professional Development – to strive continually for professional excellence, committing to Continuous Professional Development (CPD) and promoting and supporting the development of others.	Profession, clients, colleagues
Aware of Capabilities – to decline to act on any matter about which you are not competent or qualified unless you have access to such advice or assistance to carry out the work in a professional manner, taking into account the nature of the individual mandates given by your customers and counterparties.	Clients, profession, market participants
Respect Others and the Environment – to treat everyone fairly and with respect, supporting opportunity for all, embracing diversity and inclusion and ensuring that the environmental impact of your work is considered.	Society, colleagues, clients, regulators, market participants, profession, professional body
Speak Up & Listen Up – to be active in speaking up and encouraging others to do so by listening up, promoting a safe environment for all and recognising the responsibilities you have to the communities in which you operate.	Society, colleagues

Material breach of the Code of Conduct would be incompatible with continuing membership of the CISI and may result in disciplinary action. Members who find themselves in a position which might require them to act in a manner contrary to the Principles are encouraged to:

1. Discuss their concerns with their line manager.
2. Seek advice from their internal compliance department.

3. Approach their firm's non-executive directors or audit committee.
4. If unable to resolve their concerns and, having exhausted all internal avenues, contact the CISI for advice (email: principles@cisi.org).

1.4 Internal Codes of Conduct

Many firms in financial services have adopted their own internal codes of conduct and ethics which they communicate to staff and customers. Such codes may reflect the aim of good ethical behaviour as well as regulatory compliance. See the following example:

Example

Code of Conduct

As an industry leader, we want to set an example in the marketplace when it comes to ethical values and professional standards. The Code of Conduct provides a clear approach for how we expect all members of the Board of Directors and employees to conduct themselves. Only by operating within this framework can we maintain and strengthen our reputation for integrity, fair dealing and measured risk-taking. Our vision is to become the world's most admired bank. Our client-focused, capital-efficient strategy is designed to help realise this ambition and is reinforced by our principles of being a proactive, principled partner to our clients.

Our Ethical Values

- **Integrity** – A reputation for integrity is essential for our long-term success.
- **Responsibility** – We take responsibility for our actions and honour our commitments to our stakeholders.
- **Respect** – We treat our employees with respect and fairness.
- **Compliance** – We strive to maintain an exemplary control and compliance culture.
- **Confidentiality** – We treat confidential information as such and do not disclose any non-public information unless required to do so by law.
- **Trust** – We are committed to behaving in an ethical and professional manner.

Our Professional Standards

- **Service and Excellence** – We are committed to being a proactive, principled partner to our clients.
- **Risk Culture** – Our business is based on disciplined and intelligent risk-taking.
- **Transparency** – We seek constructive, transparent and open dialogue with our stakeholders.
- **Adherence to Laws and Regulations** – Members of the Board of Directors and employees are expected to comply with all applicable laws, regulations and policies.
- **Sustainability** – We conduct our business with a long-term view to support environmental and social sustainability.
- **Commitment** – We value the efforts of our employees and strive to create a work environment that is designed to attract, develop and retain talent.

1.5 Applying an Ethical Approach

Learning Objectives

4.1.2 Understand the impact of the following when applying an ethical approach within an organisational or team environment: self-interest; fiduciary responsibilities; the role of the agent; the role of stakeholders; the role of the group or team

4.1.3 Understand the advantage of ethical behaviours and decision-making over rule-based compliance

1.5.1 Self-Interest

Self-interest generally refers to a focus on the needs or desires (interests) of oneself. By extension, it can mean:

- individualism, a philosophy stressing the worth of individual selves
- psychological egoism, the view that humans are always motivated by self-interest
- ethical egoism, the ethical position that moral agents ought to do what is in their own self-interest
- hedonism, the school of ethics which argues that pleasure is the only intrinsic good
- Epicureanism, a philosophical system related to hedonism
- enlightened self-interest, a philosophy which states that acting to further the interests of others also serves one's own self-interest
- indirect self-interest, any situation in which the interests of others match one's own, so that serving one will lead to serving the other.

When an ethical approach is to do the right thing and to ensure customers are treated fairly, the needs of the customer may be placed before the self-interest of the individual or the interest of the team or firm. A firm's corporate culture and attitude to ethics are set by the behaviour of the board and the executive. Therefore, if a senior member of management is seen to bend the regulations to favour the firm or themselves, junior staff are likely to follow their example.

1.5.2 Fiduciary Responsibilities

The term 'fiduciary duty' originates from the Latin *fiduciarius*, meaning '(holding) in trust'; from *fides*, meaning 'faith' and fiducia, meaning 'trust'. It is a legal or ethical relationship of confidence or trust regarding the management of money or property between two or more parties, most commonly a fiduciary and a principal. The fiduciary (for example, a corporate trust company or the trust department of a bank) holds a fiduciary relation or acts in a fiduciary capacity to the principal (for example, a person whose funds are entrusted to it for investment).

In a fiduciary relation, the principal places confidence, good faith, reliance and trust in the fiduciary whose aid, advice or protection is sought in some matter. The fiduciary should always act in the sole benefit and interests of the principal. The recruitment and training of the firm's staff who undertake these services will feature an ethical competency requirement.

1.5.3 The Role of the Agent

Investors will often seek the advice of agents such as independent financial advisers, when purchasing financial products and services. The agent may be completely independent of any bank, fund manager or insurance company in order to give the client unbiased advice or tied agents who sell only the products from one provider. Independent agents typically charge a fee or commission for such advice, agreed to by the client. The agent will often arrange the purchase on the client's behalf either through an exchange or direct from the product provider. The client is relying on the trustworthiness of the agent to provide them with good advice and to ensure the suitability of any investment recommended.

Even after the UK regulator's Retail Distribution Review (RDR) banned many types of commission payments, some product providers offer agents a commission when they sell their products to the agent's clients. From an ethical perspective, there is a risk that the agent may be tempted to prioritise the products from a provider who pays the highest commission rather than the product most suitable for their client. Regulators have sought to prevent such outcomes, requiring transparency and disclosure of the commission received. The Markets in Financial Instruments Directive (MiFID) II introduces similar bans on the payment of commission within the European Union (EU). Another potential adverse impact of commission payments is that unless the rates are fixed, product providers may compete by offering increasing levels of commission.

Tied agents can be salaried and/or in receipt of commission or bonuses for sales. In these cases, the agent is clearly the agent of the product provider rather than the investor. To ensure they are fair, clear and not misleading, they should inform the investor of their tied status and that their advice is limited to the range of products and services offered by the product provider they act for, and not the full range of products available from the market.

1.5.4 The Role of Stakeholders, Groups and Teams

A firm is a combination of groups and teams working to achieve outcomes, supported by, and accountable to, a range of stakeholders. Some of those stakeholders represent the executive leadership of the firm; others are non-executive (such as shareholders). The role of stakeholders will vary, as does the application of codes of conduct. The CISI Code of Conduct, for example, is intended to provide direction to members regarding their behavioural obligations when dealing with all stakeholders involved in the activity of financial services.

At the corporate and institutional level, this means operating in accordance with the rules of market conduct, dealing fairly and honestly with other market participants and not seeking to take unfair advantage of either. Competition should be fostered, but the rules and standards of behaviour enable markets to function smoothly, alongside the actual regulations which provide direction for the technical elements of market operation. Firms have an ethical responsibility to their clients over and above complying with the regulatory framework and legal responsibilities.

External stakeholders (eg, shareholders of the firm, creditors, local and national governments) have a role in holding the executive leadership to account for their implementation of the firm's ethical stance. Groups and teams within the organisation will, in most cases, own that implementation and must recognise their responsibility to the firm for ensuring their daily work reflects the ethical position of the firm.

1.5.5 The Advantage of Ethical Behaviours and Decision-Making

The main criticisms of rules-based compliance are that the rules become outdated as the market evolves, they become too complex and detailed, and those gaps in the rules become loopholes which unscrupulous firms will exploit.

In addition to the shift towards principles-based regulation (setting the required outcomes, rather than the means of achieving them), there has been renewed focus on professional integrity. If those in the industry act in an ethical manner, the motivation for abuse will be reduced, resulting in various advantages.

Clients will have increased trust in firms and practitioners if they are confident that ethical standards are being applied. Firms may be able to change the way in which they oversee certain tasks, reducing the costs associated with monitoring activity and increasing the value of their findings. If firms can show that they can act in line with such ethical standards, over time, it should enable the regulators to reduce the prescriptive aspects of the rulebook, confident that firms will not seek to exploit such additional freedoms.

1.5.6 Senior Management and Ethical Standards

Learning Objective

4.1.4 Understand the importance of senior management leadership in developing and maintaining ethical standards

Culture can be described, but not easily defined. It cannot be imposed on an organisation by just putting in a programme; it must be recognised by those inside who are employed, and those outside who come into contact with the business.

At its most basic, corporate culture expresses itself in the behaviour of individuals and in the way a business is run. Staff members are sensitive to management style. When faced with a business problem, a manager has to balance the legitimate requirements of attaining business objectives and the ethical requirements of honesty and integrity in the way this is achieved.

If staff see from their managers' decisions that the prevailing culture is one of trust, integrity and openness, they generally will feel comfortable at work and be proud of the organisation. This is likely to be reflected in their own dealings with others.

For an ethical culture to be successful, it must have regard for all of those people and organisations who are affected by it.

An ethical approach helps minimise the negative effects of employee behaviour while ensuring a firm and its industry sustain healthy competition as well as socially responsible behaviour in the long run. Put simply, ethics control costs that cannot be controlled directly or may not be known. Setting up an ethics policy and instilling a sense of ethics into all employees is, however, a substantial task. Determining what can actually be considered ethical is challenging and it is tempting to shape an ethics policy to be self-serving.

Maintaining ethical standards is a necessity and requires management to build a culture of ethics. An organisation can only maintain ethical standards if senior management considers setting ethics as a top priority. Accordingly, management needs to embrace strong ethics while enforcing tough standards for all employees from the board and senior managers down to the lowest levels of employment. An ethical organisation can strengthen its resolve to behave responsibly only by developing its ranks into ethical professionals, so that current and future leaders will follow solid ethics and help their firm succeed in the long term.

As ethics attempt to address unknowns, it is difficult for management to isolate unethical behaviour by an individual until the fallout of those decisions occurs. This is further hindered by the fact that unethical behaviour typically occurs without the company's knowledge; thus, ethics rely on trust. To build trust, employees can be tested by management setting them up for ethical successes. Creating an ethical professional relies on management shaping the behaviour of employees where leaders can easily identify and guide individuals who may find it difficult to understand the real benefits of pursuing an ethical approach.

Maintaining ethical standards is a continuous effort that requires professional and workplace development. Ethical violations can be minimised by instilling a strong sense of ethics in employees when business leaders have influence over their subordinates' behaviour. Management can maintain strong ethical standards in their organisations by making it a requirement that all employees take ethical considerations into account when making decisions, but a strong ethics culture must be built over time.

The role of senior management in developing and maintaining strong ethical standards is recognised by regulators across the world. In some countries, it has become the standard for firms to appoint chief ethics officers to assist in the delivery and maintenance of ethical programmes designed to raise the ethical standards employed by financial firms.

1.5.7 Ethical Decision-Making and Training

Learning Objectives

4.1.5 Know how training programmes can be used to promote ethical decision-making

IOSCO Recommendations for Developing an Effective Ethics Training Programme

An effective training programme needs to do more than communicate a code of conduct; it needs to give employees an increased level of confidence and comfort when making business decisions that address ethical challenges. Guiding principles, practical decision-making models and training must be accompanied by company leadership dedicated to ethical decision-making. With these building blocks in place, financial services professionals will be able to develop a culture centred on ethical conduct that should become one of their greatest assets.

Effective training contains the following components:

1. **Basic Approach to Successful Ethics Training**
    a. Help employees understand ethical judgement.
    b. Give employees ethical expectations and rules.
    c. Identify specific industry/profession areas of concern.
    d. Help employees understand their own ethical tendencies.
    e. Offer a realistic and practical view of the challenges in ethical decisions.
    f. Practise and return with questions.

2. **Strategy Designed to Follow the Creation of a Code of Ethics**
    a. Help employees understand the code and its usefulness.
    b. Review the code's provisions with a focus on how these provisions apply to job responsibilities.
    c. Learn what behaviours and decision-making processes the organisation wants employees to apply when confronting ethics challenges.
    d. Raise questions about ambiguities or uncertainties resulting from the code's language and examples.
    e. Practice applying the standards communicated by the code to 'typical' ethics challenges faced by employees.
    f. Learn what the organisation wants employees to do when:
        i. facing ethical uncertainties
        ii. observing ethical misconduct, or
        iii. perceiving pressures being applied (to oneself or others) to commit ethical misconduct.

3. **Practical Advice for Developing a Comprehensive Ethics Training Programme**
    a. Start with company values and an ethics code of conduct.
    b. Involve executive management and secure adequate funding.
    c. Develop a range of materials.
    d. Consider innovative delivery strategies.
    e. Know when not to use technology.
    f. Tailor to firm operations.
    g. Integrate key ethics concepts into training courses.
    h. Make training programmes both global and local.
    i. Evaluate the programme.
    j. Consider using case studies from both inside and outside the industry.
    k. Consider a train-the-trainer/cascading process.
    l. Consider outside trainers.

Finally, there must be a mechanism for periodic review of the code of ethics programmes.

Creating an Ethical Culture

Experts emphasise that the goal of ethics training should not be to simply convey knowledge of the standards or the law, but rather to create an ethical culture in which employees are guided by a shared ethical compass that incorporates the principles behind the standards and the law.

In order to achieve this, an organisation has several options, the most effective being a 'values-based cultural approach'. This approach seeks to motivate employees to aspire to ethical conduct, encourage them to question authority where ethics are at stake, and to hold them accountable for ethics violations. Furthermore, this values-based approach requires the sincere commitment of leadership at all levels, including paying ongoing attention to key issues such as fair treatment of employees, rewards for ethical conduct, concern for external stakeholders, and consistency between words and actions.

An organisation would need to do the following:

- Instil the basics. An ethics or compliance function and articulated professional ethics standards are the foundations on which the other parts are built.
- Develop a well-known policy of 'programme follow through' which not only tries to detect violators but also follows up on the ethical concerns raised by employees. This is key, as it helps to demonstrate that the company and, specifically, the company leadership, are committed to an ethical culture.
- Recognise that ethical and effective leadership creates 'an ethical tone' in companies, which employees detect and to which they respond. This ethical leadership should not be overlooked or understated as employees look to their leaders and managers for their own ethical tone. Thus, employees will have a more serious view of ethics if they perceive that their leaders and managers pay attention to, and promote, ethical behaviour.
- Make ethics discussions a part of normal day-to-day activities. Ethics discussions should be woven into the corporate culture by making the discussions and ethics concerns part of the norm.
- Implement a simple rewards system for ethical conduct that demonstrates the company's endorsement of an ethical culture and gives additional public examples of the company's focus on ethical actions.
- Reinforce ethical standards on a regular, repeating basis.
- Monitor and keep in touch with employee concerns about ethics. This provides valuable insight both into where, and how, real ethics violations are going to occur, and how employees perceive the ethical culture within the company.

2. Market Integrity

2.1 Fair and Orderly Markets

Learning Objective

4.2.1 Understand the benefits of a fair and orderly market

4.2.2 Understand the implications of false and misleading statements, behaviours and practices

The benefits of fair and orderly markets broadly mirror the objectives and benefits of regulation (see chapter 1, section 1.1). The benefits include:

- Investors will have the confidence to invest in securities issued by businesses which need to raise capital.
- They help to establish the environment to encourage economic development and wealth creation.
- They allow the transfer of capital between enterprises at fair prices for minimal cost.
- They successfully provide liquidity through the speed and ease with which capital transfers can be affected, and buyers and sellers are able to locate counterparties willing to trade a wide range of securities at acceptable prices quickly and efficiently.
- Investors can be reassured that settlement and delivery of stock will take place.

- Information will be readily available to ensure transparency.
- The way in which securities trades are handled and cleared will be controlled and rules adopted aimed at limiting the volatility of security prices.
- Significant resources will be applied to the identification and prevention of market abuse.

Orderly markets depend upon the availability of accurate information. The integrity of the market can be affected when a party provides false or **misleading statements** regarding financial or other matters.

Publication of misleading financial statements might result in asset values being over- or under-stated, which may in turn affect share prices and potential takeover and merger activity.

It is, therefore, important that a firm's behaviours and practices uphold market integrity. Where a firm provides false information, or acts improperly in some similar manner, market operations are impacted. Where such behaviour is then identified and made public, confidence in the market and its participants can be severely shaken. Regulators will, therefore, impose significant penalties on firms that release false or misleading information to the markets.

2.2 Price-Sensitive Information

Learning Objectives

4.2.3 Understand what type of information may be deemed to be price-sensitive non-public information

4.2.5 Know what activities can constitute 'insider dealing'

Directors and other senior staff members of a company have access to various types of corporate information relating to company performance (eg, budgeting and forecasting material, corporate accounts, or details of new contracts being entered into). In the event the company is listed on a stock market, this information may have an impact on the share price and is referred to as 'price-sensitive information'. It would not be ethical for those inside the company to benefit from their knowledge of such information.

As such, listed companies must establish controls and protocols to limit the ability of those with access to price-sensitive information (including their immediate family members) to trade shares in the company during key periods of the business cycle (eg, in the months before publication of the company accounts). The company will also require that its senior management maintain the confidentiality of price-sensitive information, so that the individual does not share the information with anyone who can deal in the company's shares in the light of the information obtained from the company insider.

An example of insider trading would be when a company insider trades in the knowledge of confidential information or passes information to another person in order to benefit from stock market activity. These would constitute a criminal offence in most jurisdictions and are punishable by a prison sentence and/or a fine.

Inside information is information that:

- relates to particular securities or to one or more particular issuers (ie, it is not so wide as to apply to securities or issuers of securities generally); it could, however, include information about the particular market or sector the issuer is active in
- is specific or precise
- has not been made public, and
- is price sensitive (ie, if it were made public, it would be likely to have a significant effect on the price of any securities).

Some of these criteria may seem quite subjective; for example, what is specific or precise? Legislation generally gives some assistance in interpretation; for example, it may include a (non-exhaustive) list of what 'made public' means. For example, information becomes public when it is:

- published in accordance with the rules of a regulated market to inform investors (eg, a UK-listed company making an announcement through a regulated information service (RIS)), or
- contained within records open to the public (eg, a new shareholding that is reflected in the company's register of shareholders).

An individual commits the offence of insider dealing if they:

- deal in price-affected securities when in possession of inside information
- encourage someone else to deal in price-affected securities when in possession of inside information, or
- disclose inside information, otherwise than in the proper performance of their employment, office or profession.

For a deal (ie, an acquisition or a disposal of price-affected securities) to fall under the insider dealing legislation, it must take place on a regulated market, or through a professional intermediary – otherwise, the legislation does not apply.

Insider trading can only be committed by an individual holding inside information as an insider; it cannot be committed by a company. However, by arranging for a company to deal, an individual could commit the offence of encouraging it to do so. The offence of encouraging someone to deal need not result in an actual deal for the offence to have been committed (though it may be unlikely that the offence will come to light, if no deal results).

2.3 Ways in which Individuals Legally Possess Price-Sensitive Non-Public Information

Learning Objective

4.2.4 Understand how individuals may legally possess price-sensitive, non-public information

2.3.1 Market Makers

As long as a market maker can show that they acted in good faith in the course of their business as a market maker, they will not be deemed guilty of insider dealing. So, a market maker (or their employees) could hold unpublished price-sensitive information as an insider and continue to make a market in that security.

2.3.2 Market Information

An insider is not guilty of dealing or encouraging others to deal if they can prove that the information they held was 'market information', and that it was reasonable for them to act as they did despite having the information at the time. Market information includes information such as the fact that the sale of a block of securities is under consideration, or the price at which such a transaction is likely to be done.

2.3.3 Price Stabilisation

Rules generally permit the market price of a security to be 'stabilised' in connection with a new issue in order to manage volatility. These are known as the 'price stabilisation rules'; and as long as these rules are being followed, then the participants are not deemed to be insider dealing.

2.4 Market Integrity Controls (including Chinese Walls)

Learning Objective

4.2.6 Understand how systems and controls can minimise exposure to strategies and behaviours that might impair market integrity: information barriers/'Chinese walls'; insider lists (including watch and restricted lists); personal account dealing; gifts and entertainment; conflicts of interest policies; whistleblowing

2.4.1 Chinese Walls

A **Chinese wall** is the term given to arrangements made by a firm to manage conflicts of interest where information held by an employee in one part of the business must be withheld from (or, if this is not possible, at least not used by) the people working in another part of the business.

There is no requirement for a firm to have Chinese walls in place; they are just one example of how to manage conflicts of interest. However, the regulator normally requires that if a firm establishes and maintains a Chinese wall, it must:

- withhold or not use the information held, and
- for that purpose, permit its employees in one part of the business to withhold the information from those employed in another part of the business.

A firm only needs to do so if at least one of those parts of its business is carrying on regulated activities, or another activity carried on in connection with a regulated activity.

Where a firm adopts Chinese walls, they must be correctly maintained – including taking reasonable steps to ensure that these arrangements remain effective and are adequately monitored.

Example of a Chinese Wall in Operation

When a common-platform firm establishes and maintains a Chinese wall, it allows the persons on one side of the wall, eg, corporate finance, to withhold information from persons on the other side of the wall, eg, the equity research/market-making arm, but only to the extent that one of the parts involves carrying on regulated activities, ancillary activities or MiFID ancillary services.

The effect of the Chinese wall rule is that the corporate finance department may have plans for a company that will change the valuation of that company's shares. The equity research/market-making arm on the other side of the wall should have no knowledge of these plans; consequently, the inability to pass this knowledge on to clients is not seen as a failure of duty to their clients.

A firm will not be guilty of the offences of market manipulation, market abuse or be liable to a lawsuit when the failure arises from the operation of a Chinese wall.

In order to manage conflicts of interest and ensure the fair treatment of clients, firms need to have policies and procedures in place such as information barriers (reporting lines); remuneration structures; segregation of duties; policy of independence. The procedures and measures provided for must:

- be designed to ensure that relevant persons engaged in different business activities involving a conflict of interest of the kind specified above carry on those activities at a level of independence appropriate to the size and activities of the common-platform firm and of the group to which it belongs, and to the materiality of the risk of damage to the interests of clients
- include some of the following as necessary and appropriate for the common-platform firm to ensure the requisite degree of independence:
    - effective procedures to prevent or control the exchange of information between relevant persons engaged in activities involving a risk of a conflict of interest if the exchange of that information may harm the interests of one or more clients
    - the separate supervision of relevant persons whose principal functions involve carrying out activities on behalf of, or providing services to, clients whose interests may conflict, or who otherwise represent different interests that may conflict, including those of the firm
    - the removal of any direct link between the remuneration of relevant persons principally engaged in one activity and the remuneration of, or revenues generated by, different relevant

- persons principally engaged in another activity, when a conflict of interest may arise in relation to those activities
  - measures to prevent or limit any person from exercising inappropriate influence over the way in which a relevant person carries out services or activities
  - measures to prevent or control the simultaneous or sequential involvement of a relevant person in separate services or activities when such involvement may impair the proper management of conflicts of interest.

If the adoption or the practice of one or more of those measures and procedures does not ensure the requisite level of independence, a firm must adopt such alternative or additional measures and procedures as are necessary and appropriate.

2.4.2 Insider Lists (including Watch and Restricted Lists)

Regulated/unregulated firms and issuers who handle inside information must have strong systems and controls to ensure confidentiality and prevent the risk that the inside information they hold is improperly disclosed contrary to any regulator market abuse regime. It is equally important that senior management at regulated/unregulated firms and issuers establish (and are seen to establish) a robust anti-leaking culture within their organisations. Some principles, policies and procedures for handling inside information are shown in Appendix 6.

An issuer, usually an investment bank or stockbroker, must ensure that it and persons acting on its behalf or on its account, draw up a list of those persons working for them, under a contract of employment or otherwise, who have access to inside information relating directly or indirectly to the issuer, whether on a regular or occasional basis.

As part of developing the Market Abuse Directive (MAD), the European Commission published two templates for maintaining an insider list (one template to record permanent insiders, the other to record those who are insiders only in respect of a particular event or period of time).

Both templates require the following information to be recorded for each insider identified by the issuer:

- first name
- surname
- birth surname (if different)
- date of birth
- national identification number (if applicable)
- personal telephone numbers
- personal full home address
- professional telephone number
- company name and address (ie, any company associated with the insider)
- the person's function and reason for being an insider
- the date and time the individual was added to the list.

In addition, for a temporary insider, the date and time from which the individual ceased to be classed as an insider should also be recorded. Standard layouts of insider lists in other jurisdictions may vary. An insider list needs to be updated promptly and should clearly state the date and time it was created and last updated. In case the issuer is not able to ensure the confidentiality of the relevant inside information, they must have measures in place which enable public disclosure to be made via an RIS as soon as possible.

Before the details are made public, information in relation to a merger, acquisition or a corporate action such as a rights issue are clearly sensitive. During the sensitive period, the risk of insider dealing and market manipulation greatly increases. The perception that participants in an offering exploit material information and/or trade with a view to influencing the offer price and/or change their proprietary positions is potentially damaging to the fair and efficient operation and integrity of regulated markets.

During the sensitive period, participants in an offering should implement trade review and surveillance procedures usually known as watch lists (sometimes referred to as grey lists), which permit trading in the securities on the list, subject under close scrutiny by the firm's compliance department, and restricted lists, which restrict or prohibit trading in the securities on the list.

A restricted list is a mechanism established within a financial services firm to identify any securities that the firm's staff are (at that time) not permitted to trade. The firm will add a security to its restricted list during any period when the firm is in possession of sensitive information about that security or its issuer. An example is when the firm is involved in a material transaction of the issuer, the details of which are confidential and may also be price sensitive. As inclusion on a restricted list will often mean that the firm and the issuer are engaged in some business/transaction, it is important that the restricted list (or details of the securities included) should not be communicated to anyone outside the trading areas of the firm or to anyone external to the firm.

The compliance department plays an important role during the sensitive period. When an employee becomes aware of material information regarding a security, they should immediately inform the compliance officer. The compliance officer must then decide on the trading restrictions, if any, that are appropriate in the circumstances. In particular, the compliance officer must decide whether to place the security on the firm's watch list or restricted list. The compliance officer must also consider the appropriateness of any trading restrictions in the context of the firm being a member of a financial group.

Participants in an offering should establish adequate internal controls over the trades carried out by their managers, employees and other related persons. Examples of issues the compliance function should be alert to in relation to inside information and which may give regulators cause for concern may include the following:

- The distribution of restricted lists to all staff working in the firm, regardless of function. Distribution should be restricted to those with a need to know.
- A failure by senior management/compliance to understand what information had been made available at 'private side' conferences that were subject to non-disclosure agreements (NDAs). While it is positive that such NDAs are signed off by compliance or senior management, knowledge of the firms and information discussed at such conferences is vital for proactive monitoring of subsequent trading.
- A general failure by firms to adopt clear desk policies. This leaves firms vulnerable to a leakage of inside information both to staff who are not insiders and to outside contractors who may have access to the firms' offices, particularly outside normal office hours. It is expected that firms adopt appropriate controls in order to protect the security of inside information.
- While IT controls may be in place involving system passwords and file protections, it is necessary to consider extending the full range of market abuse controls to contractors and employees alike. Some external contractors may have access to sensitive information, but not be subject to personal account trading restrictions or market abuse training.

2.4.3 Personal Account (PA) Dealing

Besides from the mechanisms described above, which tend to affect certain employees or managers in certain situations or in respect of certain investments, financial services firms will have arrangements in place to minimise the risk of a conflict of interest when their employees deal in investments on their own account. Under MiFID, these rules regarding 'personal account dealing' are applicable to individuals defined as 'relevant persons'. In simple terms, a 'relevant person' means anyone working for the firm (from directors of the firm or any of its **appointed representatives**, to any natural person involved in providing services to the firm – such as an outsourced services provider).

Conflicts of interest can be subjective, depending on the specific role an individual fulfils, and the specific information they possess. Therefore, each firm will design its personal account (PA) dealing policy according to its own business context and activity. In some cases, all members of staff will be expected to apply the policy in a common manner; in some companies the personal account dealing policy will apply differently as the individual progresses up the corporate hierarchy. The intention is to protect staff against the suggestion that they acted improperly under a conflict of interest, so the policy may restrict the following types of activity:

1. entering into a personal transaction that is contrary to the MAD; involves misuse or improper disclosure of confidential information, or conflicts with the firm's duties to a customer
2. improperly advising or procuring that anyone else enters into a transaction that (if it had been done by the employee themselves) would have fallen foul of the above or of a 'relevant provision', or
3. improperly disclosing information or opinion, if they know or should know that the person to whom they have disclosed it is likely to enter into a transaction that (if it had been done by the employee themselves) would have fallen foul of the above or of a relevant provision or encouraging someone else to do so.

Clear PA dealing policies should be in place and all PA dealing requests should be signed off by an appropriately empowered individual. It is not appropriate for senior managers to be able to sign off their own PA dealing. Firms must keep records of all personal transactions notified to them, and of any authorisation or prohibition made in connection with them.

Relevant persons may include close relatives or co-habitees.

The arrangements must ensure that the affected employees are aware of the restrictions on personal transactions and of the firm's procedures in this regard. The arrangements must be such that the firm is informed promptly of any such personal transaction, either by notification of the transaction, or by some other procedure enabling the firm to identify it.

When outsourcing takes place, the arrangements must be such that the outsource service provider maintains a record of personal transactions undertaken by any relevant person and provides it to the firm promptly on request.

The rules on personal account dealing do not apply to:

- deals under a discretionary management service, if there is no prior communication between the portfolio manager and the relevant person (or any other person for whose account the transaction is being executed) about the deal

- deals in units/shares in certain classes of a fund, if the relevant person (and any other person for whom the deals are affected) is not involved in the management of the fund.

The compliance function should ensure that:

- Staff are reminded periodically of the firm's PA dealing rules which should be readily available to them via a compliance manual or staff handbook, eg, a reminder via a regular email.
- Induction and refresher training, as part of the regulatory suite of training sessions or online elearning modules, should be provided on an annual basis. Attendance or completion of such training should be recorded.

2.4.4 Gifts, Benefits in Kind and Entertainment

The firm needs to be sure that none of their board members, managers or staff are induced to act improperly.

Gifts and benefits in kind must never be accepted if they might give rise to the suspicion that the recipient's judgement is likely to be influenced. Staff must report to the compliance function, all gifts and benefits offered to them in the course of business, for example, by means of a Gifts and Benefits Form.

Failure to report a gift or benefit in kind is often deemed a disciplinary offence and may constitute grounds for dismissal. Employees should be asked to familiarise themselves with the firm's policy. Firms should keep a record of gifts and benefits received; it is quite normal to set a minimum level for this and to require prior approval of compliance where the amount is over a set level.

While entertainment, such as lunch or attending a sporting event (eg, golf days), has been quite normal practice, and broadly acceptable, a number of UK firms have in recent years been less willing for their staff to accept such invitations. Lavish gifts, such as holidays, should never be accepted. The compliance officer will also need to take into account the employee's position and level. A junior member of staff may be influenced by a gift of a much lower value than that for, say, the chief executive.

2.4.5 Conflicts of Interest Policies

In general, firms must seek to:

- take all reasonable steps to prevent conflicts of interest from giving rise to a material risk of damage to the interests of clients
- implement and operate an effective written policy for identifying and managing conflicts of interest
- specify in the conflicts policy, certain procedures and measures to ensure appropriate independence and further steps if these prove inadequate
- disclose the conflict to the client, if the arrangements under the firm's policy are not adequate to prevent material risks of damage to a client, and
- in considering their own policy in respect of their duties to their clients, take account of any circumstances, of which the firm is, or should be aware, which may give rise to a conflict of interest arising as a result of the structure and business activities of other members of the group.

As far as market integrity is concerned, one of the key areas where conflicts of interest may arise, is in relation to the production and dissemination of investment research on listed companies and their securities.

Firms must also ensure that they have arrangements designed to satisfy the following conditions in place:

- Financial analysts and other relevant persons who know the likely timing/content of investment research which is not yet publicly available or available to clients and which cannot be inferred from information that is available, cannot undertake personal transactions, or trade for others, until the recipient of the investment research has had a reasonable opportunity to act on it. Certain exceptions may apply, such as the receipt of an instruction from an execution-only client and a market maker acting in good faith.
- In cases not covered by the above, firms cannot undertake personal account transactions without prior approval from the firm's compliance or legal department and then only in exceptional circumstances.
- The firm and any person involved in the production of research must not accept inducements from those with a material interest in the subject matter of the research.
- Firms may not promise issuers favourable research coverage.
- Issuers, relevant persons other than financial analysts, or anyone else must not be allowed to review draft investment research which includes a recommendation or target price, other than to verify compliance with the firm's legal obligations.

A key control for dealing with conflicts of interest is ensuring that appropriate disclosures are made including the following:

- Disclosure by the firm of any relationships and circumstances that may reasonably be expected to impair the objectivity of the research recommendation.
- When the disclosure would be disproportionate in relation to the length of the research recommendation, the firm must make clear and prominent reference to such a place where disclosures can be directly and easily accessed by the public.
- Disclosure of any significant shareholder relationship between the firm (or any affiliated company) and the relevant issuer (the company which is the subject of the investment research recommendations), including at least:
    - shareholdings exceeding 5% of the total issued share capital held by the firm or affiliated company
    - shareholdings exceeding 5% of the total issued share capital of the firm or any affiliated company held by the relevant issuer.
- Any other financial interests held by the firm or any affiliated company in relation to the relevant issuer which are significant in relation to the research recommendation.
- If applicable, a statement that the firm or any affiliated company is party to any other agreement with the relevant issues relating to the provision of investment banking services.
- In general terms, the effective organisational and administrative arrangements set up within the firm for the prevention of avoidance of conflicts of interest with respect to research recommendations, including information barriers.

2.4.6 Whistleblowing

Increasingly, regulators rely on whistleblowers in their battle against market abuse. A whistleblower is a person (typically an employee) who exposes any kind of information, behaviour, or activity deemed illegal, unethical, or incorrect within a private or public organisation. Regulators and companies encourage staff to speak up, and through legislation, regulation, and internal procedures, protection for these individuals is improving.

In the US, whistleblowers involved with the securities markets are provided incentives and protection by the Dodd–Frank Wall Street Reform and Consumer Protection Act (2010).

In the UK, the Public Interest Disclosure Act 1998 provides a framework of legal protection for individuals who disclose information, so as to expose malpractice and matters of similar concern. It protects whistleblowers from victimisation and dismissal.

Firms need to put in place appropriate arrangements that allow staff to raise concerns about any malpractice with their manager, a senior executive or an independent function like compliance. If they feel uncomfortable raising the matter internally, the firm should also provide details of an external body such as private or charitable services. In some cases, regulators themselves provide a telephone hotline or an email address for staff to contact.

Firms need to have a written policy and procedures in place which are communicated to staff on induction and periodically.

3. Fair Conduct

Learning Objective

4.3.1 Understand expected compliant standards of behaviour for firms and individuals: honesty & fair trade; acting in best interest

3.1 Honesty and Fair Treatment

The key attributes of a successful industry are a good reputation and the trust of the public. A vital part of maintaining a strong reputation and trust is dealing with investors and customers honestly and fairly.

A firm must pay due regard to the interests of its customers and treat them fairly. Firms should conduct business with due skill, care and diligence; take reasonable care to organise and control affairs responsibly and effectively with adequate risk management systems; provide clear, fair and not misleading information to meet client needs; and ensure the suitability of their advice and discretionary decisions for customers.

The following are the expected outcomes set out by the UK's Financial Conduct Authority (FCA) for customers in the retail area from a fair approach:

- **Outcome 1** – Consumers can be confident that they are dealing with firms where the fair treatment of customers is central to the corporate culture.
- **Outcome 2** – Products and services marketed and sold in the retail market are designed to meet the needs of identified consumer groups and are targeted accordingly.
- **Outcome 3** – Consumers are provided with clear information and are kept appropriately informed before, during and after the point of sale.
- **Outcome 4** – Where consumers receive advice, the advice is suitable and takes account of their circumstances.
- **Outcome 5** – Consumers are provided with products that perform as firms have led them to expect, and the associated service is of an acceptable standard and as they have been led to expect.
- **Outcome 6** – Consumers do not face unreasonable post-sale barriers imposed by firms to change product, switch provider, submit a claim or make a complaint.

Firms are expected to be able to demonstrate that they are consistently treating their customers fairly and delivering fair outcomes relevant to their business. A firm needs to be able to:

- demonstrate that senior management have instilled a culture whereby they understand:
  - what the fair treatment of customers means
  - where they expect their staff to achieve this at all times, and
  - where (a relatively small number of) errors are promptly found, put right and learnt from
- appropriately and accurately measure performance against all customer fairness issues materially relevant to its business, and be acting on the results
- deliver those fair outcomes, and
- have no serious failings – whether seen through management information (MI) or known to the regulator directly.

Regulators will take into account a firm's record in these areas when carrying out risk assessments of the firm and its supervisory approach. It is in the firm's interest to be able to demonstrate that treating customers fairly and honestly goes beyond just words and is followed through in practice.

3.2 Acting in Best Interest

Similarly, regulators expect firms and individuals to act in the best interest of their clients. Where any conflict of interest arises, the expectation is that it will be resolved in the best interests of the client.

Firms are also expected to act in the customer's best interest with regard to advice, ensuring the suitability of the advice and any investments recommended. They should, for example, avoid any bias in their recommendations which might arise as a result of commission or other remuneration.

3.3 How does Fairness Impact on Firms?

Learning Objective

4.3.2 Understand how the concept of fairness impacts on financial services firms

Fairness is difficult to define as it involves a subjective assessment by one participant in the relationship in relation to the treatment they have received from the other. Different people may have different expectations of fairness, which complicates the position of a firm trying to assess if its actions have been fair to a particular customer or market segment.

In the UK, the regulator introduced a focus on treating customers fairly (TCF). The TCF regulations clarify that fair is 'the same', ie, in the regulator's eyes, it would be viable under certain circumstances for the firm to treat two clients in different ways, yet maintain that both clients had received fair treatment.

Firms should, therefore, ensure that any policy material is carefully worded where any aspect of fairness is being considered, to ensure that the policy can be consistently applied and demonstrated as being part of the company's approach to doing business. Other aspects that the firm might consider from the perspective of fairness include:

- incorporating the concept in the firm's strategy so that it is reflected in any new products and services
- observing compliance standards
- embedding fairness through the training of staff and measurement through monitoring compliance with the standards and other management information
- the need for transparency and detailed disclosure to clients and counterparties and the provision of information which is clear, fair and not misleading
- the provision of unbiased advice and recommendations which are in the interests of investors.

3.4 Financial Advice – Relevant Legal Concepts and Considerations

Learning Objective

4.3.3 Understand legal concepts and considerations relevant to financial advice

The relationship between an adviser and their client is subject to the following legal concepts and considerations:

- **Law of contract and capacity** – the client will normally enter into an agreement with the adviser for the provision of advice. Capacity relates to the ability of the client to enter into a contract, minors (children) and the incapacitated may require someone to contract on their behalf. In the case of children, an appropriate adult (eg, a parent or guardian) and for the incapacitated, an appointed legal personal representative or someone appointed by an appropriate court.

- **Law of agency** – the adviser may act on behalf of the client for such activities as buying and selling investments in the client's name or collecting income. In giving instructions, the adviser becomes an agent of the client and their actions may be binding on the client.
- **Legal identity** – the legal person is a physical body that has rights and duties on the one hand and certain behaviours and capability, eg, to contract, on the other. Companies and other entities are also legal bodies in law, with defined rights and duties. Incorporated bodies are entities in their own right with defined rights and duties, while unincorporated bodies are collectives in which rights and duties are held against its members.
- **Property ownership** – where advice is given, ownership of assets will normally vest in the name of the client, although some advisory firms may also offer custodial or trust services. In the latter case, assets may be registered in the name of a nominee or trustee.
- **Powers of attorney** – the client appoints one or more individuals to act on their behalf. The client may use a power of attorney, for example, where they wish another to take decisions on their behalf, in anticipation of some incapacity or perhaps in cases where they may be going overseas for a period.
- **Law of succession** – this may be an important consideration where the client wishes to pass on assets to their heirs, or otherwise make provision for them.
- **Insolvency and bankruptcy** – this is an important consideration in that advice may be necessary to ensure the client does not contravene laws relating to insolvency or bankruptcy.
- **Use of trusts** – this is a legal arrangement whereby assets are managed by a person, persons or organisation for the benefit of another. It is quite common in inheritance or estate planning to use trusts to reduce the impact of tax, or to ensure an appropriate provision is made for dependants on the death of an individual.

3.5 Senior Management Responsibilities, Management Information and Corporate Culture

Learning Objective

4.3.4 Understand the role senior management play in maintaining fair conduct: senior management responsibilities; management information; corporate culture

The firm's executive management should expect to be questioned on how they maintain fair conduct and treatment of customers. This will form an integral part of the assessment regulators will make of the firm. They will also need to demonstrate that the firm's MI is picking up the issues regulators may discover during periodic reviews of the business. The following expectations of regulators help senior management identify barriers to delivery of treating customers fairly outcomes in the culture of the firm:

- Leadership is central – where there is strong leadership with a clear vision of what treating customers fairly means for the firm, there is more likely to be a corporate culture which is geared towards delivering fair consumer outcomes.
- The integration of fair conduct and treatment into the firm's strategy is very important – in any developments in significant new products or target markets, or outsourcing arrangements, we would expect fair treatment implications for customers to be an automatic feature of those strategies. As current market conditions cause firms to alter their strategic direction, senior management should consider the implications for customers an integral part of their planning.

- Decision-making within the firm will also impact controls, including MI, which are also important so that senior management in the firm can satisfy themselves that the customer is being treated fairly.
- People issues – recruitment, training and competence – firms can influence the delivery of fairer outcomes by recruiting staff with appropriate values and skills, training staff effectively and assessing their competence. Topically at present, reward or remuneration strategy is key.

4. Fair Dealing

Learning Objective

4.4.1 Understand how associated but non-transactional activities impact on the firm: product design and marketing; financial promotions/advertising; client documentation; fair contracts

4.1 Product Design and Marketing

Regulators typically authorise and regulate firms and ensure that the people who manage them are competent to do so. They may also regulate the design and marketing of financial products, particularly retail products. The extent to which regulators get involved in the detailed regulation of products varies across the world, but once again the financial crisis has prompted regulators to re-assess their approach and make changes where they think it appropriate. Regulators assess whether firms ensure that the fair treatment of customers is built into their governance and oversight arrangements.

What they look for may include:

- **Governance and oversight:**
  - a board engaged in ensuring products deliver the right outcomes for consumers
  - clearly allocated responsibilities for oversight of product governance
  - the effective inclusion of control functions such as compliance in oversight arrangements
  - policies and procedures that support the design of products appropriate to a specified target market
  - a design process that leads to an appropriate matching of products to the needs of the target market
  - clear consideration of what customer usage or needs the product would not fulfil.

- **Target market:**
  - a target market that is plausible in terms of size or shape, and
  - products designed to meet customer needs – not simply copying a competitor's product.

- **Distribution:**
  - controls in place that ensure the distribution channels and strategy are compatible with the target market
  - details of the target market, product features and risks being accurately conveyed to distributors
  - interactions and communications with distributors that are likely to lead to fair customer outcomes, and
  - the firm taking action to address any mismatches between the actual distribution/sales and the intended target market.

4.2 Financial Promotions/Advertising

Firms must ensure that communications relating to investment business, including financial promotions are fair, clear and not misleading. The way in which this is achieved should be appropriate and proportionate and take account of the means of communication and what the communication is intended to convey. So, for example, communications aimed at professional clients may not need to include all the same information as those aimed at retail clients.

It is normal for the compliance function to review such promotions and approve them; the review is to ensure that it complies with the rules governing financial promotions which may also include advertising standards.

Firms should ensure that:

- any risk to a client's capital is made clear
- any quoting of yields gives a balanced impression of both the short-term and long-term prospects for the investment
- any complex charges for products or services are communicated fairly, clearly and in a manner which is not misleading
- the firm's regulator is named.

In some cases, the firm's promotional literature might be used by other firms (eg, distributors or intermediaries) when selling those packaged products. Any firm relying on promotional materials produced by another party should:

- take reasonable care to establish that an authorised firm has confirmed that the promotion complies with the rules
- take reasonable care that it communicates it only to the type of recipient it was intended for
- as far as it is (or should be) aware, the promotion is still fair, clear and not misleading, and has not been withdrawn by the other party
- ensure that the materials give a fair and not misleading impression of the producer of the product.

4.3 Client Documentation

A regulated firm will need to provide various pieces of documentation to its clients. The specific documents are determined by the role the firm is fulfilling, the types of activities it is undertaking, and the types of assets concerned – the following list illustrates a number of key documents:

- **key product information**, including a prospectus, terms and conditions and details of complaint and compensation procedures
- **suitability report**, based on an assessment of the client's needs and their risk appetite
- **contract note or deal confirmation**, showing the details of any transaction performed (eg, the asset, the price, the number of shares)
- where provided, details of **cancellation or cooling-off rights**, ie, where the investor has the right to change their mind
- **regular statements**, showing, for example, any additional investments and income reinvested
- **tax certificates** relating to income earned/distributed
- **annual and interim reports**, issued by the product provider and where appropriate or required regular valuations.

4.4 Fair Contracts

Firms should, in good time before a retail client is bound by any agreement relating to investment business or ancillary services or before the provision of those services, whichever is earlier, provide that client with:

- the terms of any such agreement, and
- the information about the firm and its services relating to that agreement including authorised communications, conflicts of interest and the firm's authorised status.

Firms should provide the agreement and information in durable medium or via a website, where the website conditions (as defined in the Glossary of the FCA/**Prudential Regulation Authority (PRA) Handbook** and Article 3 of the MiFID implementing directive) are satisfied. A firm may provide the agreement and the information immediately after the client is bound by any such agreement if:

- the firm was unable to provide the agreement in good time prior to the carrying out of investment business for the client due to the agreement being concluded using a means of distance communication which prevented the firm from doing so
- the deal was done by telephone, the firm makes a record of the call and the investor confirms they wish to proceed.

A firm should establish a record that includes the agreement between itself and a client which sets out the rights and obligations of the parties, and the other terms on which it will provide services to the client. The records should be maintained for an appropriate period, normally whichever is the longer between:

- five years
- the duration of the relationship with the client, or
- in the case of a record relating to certain pension transfers, indefinitely.

The Unfair Contract Terms Act 1977 is an Act of Parliament of the UK which regulates contracts by restricting the operation and legality of some contract terms. It extends to nearly all forms of contract and one of its most important functions is limiting the applicability of disclaimers of liability. The terms extend to both actual contract terms and notices that are seen to constitute a contractual obligation.

The Act renders terms excluding or limiting liability ineffective or subject to reasonableness, depending on the nature of the obligation purported to be excluded and whether the party purporting to exclude or limit business liability is acting against a consumer.

4.5 Client and Counterparty Objectives and Risk Profile

Learning Objectives

4.4.2 Understand the factors to consider prior to entering into a transaction: client/counterparty objectives; client/counterparty risk profile; affordability; suitability of the investment

4.4.3 Understand factors that should be considered at the point of sale: clear information; suitability of advice

The goal of both parties to a contract is that the delivery and settlement of the transaction will take place. Where a deal takes place on a regulated market, the client will have reasonable assurance that the counterparty, for example a market maker, has met minimum requirements for admission to membership of the exchange or market. The counterparty will look to the broker's track record for reassurance that the client will pay the consideration for the purchase of an investment or deliver the stock if the client is selling. The use of delivery versus payment (DvP) systems provided by recognised exchanges serve to provide reassurance and confidence to both parties. In the case of exchange-traded derivatives, there will be a **central counterparty (CCP)** which will stand behind the settlement and clearing of transactions.

In the case of off-exchange transactions, there will be greater risk that the counterparty may not deliver. The difficulties with credit default swaps (CDSs) and the inability to deliver the underlying sub-prime mortgage-based assets proved to be a major illustration of the failure of markets to recognise the risks involved and led to the collapse of Lehman Brothers, a significant counterparty to many traders.

The role of the compliance function is to ensure that appropriate due diligence is undertaken both on clients through thorough know your customer (KYC) assessments and on market counterparties. The KYC process will also involve the firm in ensuring they have a full understanding of the client's risk appetite.

4.6 Affordability/Suitability of the Investment

It is the responsibility of the firm to ensure that contracts being transacted are within the means of the client and are appropriate given their risk profile.

Regulators' suitability rules exist to ensure that firms providing services of advice or investment management take reasonable steps to ensure that personal recommendations (or decisions to trade) are suitable for their clients' needs. When a firm makes a personal recommendation, or is managing a client's investments, it should obtain the necessary information regarding the client's:

- knowledge and experience in the investment field relevant to the specific type of designated investment business
- financial situation, and
- investment objectives, enabling the firm to make the recommendations, or take the decisions which are suitable for the client.

A firm should provide a retail client with a suitability report if it makes a personal recommendation that the client:

- invests in a packaged product such as a mutual fund or regular savings scheme linked to such a fund or investment company
- buys, sells, surrenders, converts or cancels rights under, or suspends contributions to, a personal pension scheme
- elects to make income withdrawals or purchases a short-term annuity
- enters into a pension transfer or pension opt-out, or
- takes out or modifies a life assurance policy.

4.7 Point-of-Sale Factors

Certain obligations will arise at the point of sale. Trade confirmation information needs to be provided to the investor in respect of MiFID transactions, which must provide clear information on the trade executed with/for the client. Where the firm has provided financial advice to the client, specific documentation will be provided in which the firm explains why the advice provided was correct and appropriate to the position of the client. This material can often be lengthy – not only because of the complexity of aspects of the advice process, but because firms are keen to demonstrate to both regulators and ombudsmen, the basis on which advice was provided.

Given the potential financial and reputational implications of a sustained ombudsman investigation, firms providing advice will be keen to demonstrate why certain approaches were rejected or certain types of investment assets dismissed from their planning – as otherwise, in the future, it might be claimed that the adviser did not consider all the asset types that should have been discussed.

4.8 Post-Sale Factors

Learning Objective

4.4.4 Understand post-sale factors that may impact on the firm: handling complaints in line with international standards; avenues of redress; expected and actual product performance; safeguarding customer money and assets; reporting requirements

---

4.8.1 Handling Complaints in Line with International Standards

The International Standards Organisation (ISO) provides a Standard (ISO 10002) to guide companies in the handling of complaints and in which they may gain accreditation. This is a general standard which may be adopted subject to local regulatory requirements.

The Standard sets out guiding principles (including in respect of responsiveness and objectivity in complaint handling) before considering the different operational stages of a complaint. The Standard provides a framework by which a firm can consider whether its complaint-handling approach is sufficient.

This is in respect of stages such as:

- receiving a complaint
- acknowledging a complaint
- investigating a complaint
- responding to a complaint, and
- closing a complaint.

4.8.2 Avenues of Redress

Contacting the Firm Directly

The normal process when a client has a complaint is for them to first approach the firm to seek resolution. Regulators will normally encourage the client to contact the firm directly as soon as possible. Typically, regulated firms are required to investigate complaints promptly and reply to them within an appropriate period, eg, eight weeks.

Contacting the Financial Ombudsman

If an investor is not satisfied with the firm's response, an ombudsman service may be able to help. The Financial Ombudsman Service (FOS) offers (a usually) free independent service for settling disputes between financial services firms and their customers.

The Ombudsman will ask the firm to explain what happened and then decide whether to uphold the complaint. Clients should usually contact the Ombudsman within a fixed period of receiving the original response from the firm (eg, six months). In the UK, the Ombudsman can now make awards of up to £150,000.

Taking Civil Action through the Courts

If the client remains unsatisfied, as a last resort they can take the case to court. However, the client cannot usually take their complaint to court if they have already been through a complaints scheme or accepted an Ombudsman's decision.

4.8.3 Expected and Actual Product Performance

The expected investment performance and the actual performance may vary, of course, due to market movements, the economic conditions and the performance of individual companies. Where the firm provides ongoing advice as part of its service, the firm will be expected to review the performance of the client's investments, provide periodic valuations and update the client on progress against the client's original investment objectives.

4.8.4 Safeguarding Customer Assets and Client Money

Firms should, when holding client assets in safe custody, make adequate arrangements to safeguard clients' ownership rights, especially in the event of the firm's insolvency and to prevent the use of safe custody assets belonging to a client on the firm's own account, except with the client's express consent.

Firms should also introduce adequate organisational arrangements to minimise the risk of loss or diminution of the client's safe custody assets. Firms must take the necessary steps to ensure that client money is held in an account or accounts identified separately from any accounts used to hold money belonging to the firm.

National rules will confirm how such segregation is achieved – in particular, the actions required when a firm receives client money. For example, a UK firm that operates the 'normal approach' to segregation must promptly place client money received into one or more accounts opened with any of the following:

- a central bank
- a Banking Consolidation Directive (BCD) credit institution (a credit institution that has its registered office in a European Economic Area (EEA) state)
- a bank authorised in a third country
- a qualifying money market fund.

There have been a number of high-profile and high-value penalties issued by the UK regulator, and it is notable that in many of these cases there was no actual loss by any investor. Rather the FCA is responding to the failure of the firm to establish and maintain processes and procedures that deliver compliance, and the risk exposure that arises where such controls are deficient.

5. Environmental, Social and Governance (ESG)

Learning Objective

4.5.1 Know what is meant by environmental, social and governance (ESG)

4.5.2 Know the main international ESG initiatives: Task Force on Climate-Related Financial Disclosures (TCFD); United Nations supported Principals for Responsible Investment (PRI)

4.5.3 Understand the importance of initiatives on environmental and corporate responsibility

Also known as ethical investment, sustainable investment, and socially responsible investment, environmental, social, and governance (ESG) refers to any area of the financial sector where the ESG and ethical principles of the investor (whether an individual or institution) influence which organisation or venture they choose to place their money with. It also encompasses how an investor might use their power as a shareholder to encourage better environmental and social behaviour from the companies they invest in. ESG are non-financial performance indicators to assess the impact of the firm or the investment on society.

climate related risk

5.1 International ESG Initiatives

Taskforce on Climate-Related Financial Disclosures (TCFD)

The TCFD is established by the Financial Stability Board (FSB) with the goal to develop recommendations for more effective climate-related disclosures. The aim of the disclosures is to promote more informed investment, credit, and insurance underwriting decisions and, in turn, enable a better understanding of concentrations of carbon-related assets in the financial sector and the exposure of the financial system to climate-related risks. A better understanding of the financial implications associated with climate change will empower market participants to channel investments to sustainable and resilient solutions, opportunities, and business models.

The TCFD has issued their recommended disclosures in 2017 structured around four identifiable themes:

1. **Governance**
   - Describe the board's oversight of climate-related risks and opportunities.
   - Describe management's role in assessing and managing climate-related risks and opportunities.

2. **Strategy**

   - Describe the climate-related risks and opportunities the organisation has identified over the short, medium, and long term.
   - Describe the impact of climate-related risks and opportunities on the organisation's businesses, strategy and financial planning.
   - Describe the resilience of the organisation's strategy, taking into consideration different climate-related scenarios, including a two degrees Celsius or lower scenario.

3. **Risk Management**

   - Describe the organisation's processes for identifying and assessing climate-related risks.
   - Describe the organisation's processes for managing climate-related risks.
   - Describe how the processes for identifying, assessing, and managing climate-related risks are integrated into the organisation's overall risk management.

4. **Metrics and Targets**

   - Disclose the metrics used by the organisation to assess climate-related risks and opportunities in line with its strategy and risk management process.
   - Disclose Scope 1, Scope 2, and, if appropriate, Scope 3 greenhouse gas (GHG) emissions, and their related risks. The three Scopes are different classifications relating to a company's emissions, for instance, emissions resulting from the company's operations or from employee commuting.
   - Describe the targets used by the organisation to manage climate-related risks and opportunities and performance against targets.

The TCFD has developed specific additional guidance for the financial sector as well as non-financial groups for recommendations related to strategy, risk management and metrics, and targets as identified in the below table.

Availability of Additional Guidance

		Strategy			Risk Manangement			Metrics and Targets		
	Industries and Groups	**a)**	**b)**	**c)**	**a)**	**b)**	**c)**	**a)**	**b)**	**c)**
Financial	Banks	Yes			Yes			Yes		
	Insurance companies		Yes	Yes	Yes	Yes		Yes		
	Asset owners		Yes	Yes	Yes	Yes		Yes	Yes	
	Asset managers		Yes		Yes	Yes		Yes	Yes	
Non-Financial	Energy		Yes	Yes				Yes		
	Transportation		Yes	Yes				Yes		
	Materials and buildings		Yes	Yes				Yes		
	Agriculture, food and forest products		Yes	Yes				Yes		

United Nations-Supported Principles for Responsible Investment (PRI)

The UNPRI defines its mission as follows:

> *'We believe that an economically efficient, sustainable global financial system is a necessity for long-term value creation. Such a system will reward long-term, responsible investment and benefit the environment and society as a whole.*
>
> *The PRI will work to achieve this sustainable global financial system by encouraging adoption of the Principles and collaboration on their implementation; by fostering good governance, integrity and accountability; and by addressing obstacles to a sustainable financial system that lie within market practices, structures and regulations'.*

In order to achieve this mission, the UNPRI issued the following six principles in 2006:

- **Principle 1**: We will incorporate ESG issues into investment analysis and decision-making processes.
- **Principle 2**: We will be active owners and incorporate ESG issues into our ownership policies and practices.
- **Principle 3**: We will seek appropriate disclosure on ESG issues by the entities in which we invest.
- **Principle 4**: We will promote acceptance and implementation of the Principles within the investment industry.
- **Principle 5**: We will work together to enhance our effectiveness in implementing the Principles.
- **Principle 6**: We will each report on our activities and progress towards implementing the Principles.

The principles are voluntary and an aspirational set of investment principles offering a range of options for the incorporation of ESG into investment practice.

5.2 Impact of Initiatives on Environmental and Corporate Responsibility

Corporate social responsibility (CSR) is a form of corporate self-regulation integrated into the business model of a company. CSR policy functions as a built-in, self-regulating mechanism whereby a business monitors and ensures its active compliance with the spirit of the law, ethical standards, and international norms. ESG criteria are a set of standards used by socially responsible investors to screen potential investments.

The goal of CSR is to embrace responsibility for the company's actions and encourage a positive impact on the environment, consumers, employees, communities, stakeholders and all other members of the public sphere.

Furthermore, CSR-focused businesses proactively promote the public interest by encouraging community growth and development, and voluntarily eliminating practices that harm the public sphere, regardless of legality. CSR is the deliberate inclusion of public interest into corporate decision-making, that is the core business of the company or firm, and the honouring of a triple bottom line: people, planet, and profit.

In crowded marketplaces, companies strive for a unique selling proposition that can separate them from the competition in the minds of consumers. CSR can play a role in building customer loyalty based on distinctive ethical values. Several major brands like to highlight their ethical values. Business service organisations can benefit too from building a reputation for integrity and best practice. However, once CSR is placed at the heart of the firm's market positioning, any failure to live up to those ideals will undermine customer trust and have a substantial negative impact on the organisation.

In addition to the ones mentioned in section 5.1 above, there are a number of other initiatives in global ethical CSR which either include financial services, or are specific to improving the reputation of the financial sector.

The Organisation for Economic Co-operation and Development (OECD) has issued a number of reports, guidelines and principles including:

- a 'Strategic Response to the Financial and Economic Crisis'.
- Guidelines for Multinational Enterprises.
- Principles of Corporate Governance.
- Convention on Combating Bribery.

The OECD Guidelines for Multinational Enterprises are recommendations to multinational enterprises operating in, or from, adhering countries. They provide voluntary principles and standards for responsible business conduct in areas such as employment and industrial relations, human rights, environment, information disclosure, combating bribery, consumer interests, science and technology, competition, and taxation. (See: www.oecd.org/daf/inv)

In addition, the International Organization of Securities Commissions (IOSCO) has published a Model Code of Ethics which recommends that firms adopt the following ethical principles:

- integrity and truthfulness
- promise keeping
- loyalty (fully disclosing conflicts of interest)
- fairness to the customer
- doing no harm to the customer or the profession, and
- maintaining confidentiality.

It is important to ensure that any code of ethics is more than mere statements. There must also be a robust ethics education programme in place.

End of Chapter Questions

Think of an answer for each question and refer to the appropriate section for confirmation.

1. Name three of the standards and principles set out by regulators which they expect business and key individuals to observe.
   Answer reference: Section 1.2

2. Name the three Chartered Institute for Securities & Investment (CISI) Code of Conduct Principles appropriate to a firm.
   Answer reference: Section 1.3.2

3. What would be included in an internal code of conduct?
   Answer reference: Section 1.4

4. What is a fiduciary duty?
   Answer reference: Section 1.5.2

5. How can technology be used to support the promotion of ethical decision-making?
   Answer reference: Section 1.5.7

6. Name four of the benefits of fair and orderly markets.
   Answer reference: Section 2.1

7. What are Chinese walls?
   Answer reference: Section 2.4.1

8. What arrangements must a firm have in place under personal account (PA) dealing? policy
   Answer reference: Section 2.4.3

9. What could be classed as a lavish gift? Holiday
   Answer reference: Section 2.4.4

10. What are the six fair approach outcomes for customers in the retail area?
    Answer reference: Section 3.1

11. Name four of the legal concepts and considerations that adviser and client relationships are subject to.
    Answer reference: Section 3.4

12. Who should expect to be questioned on how they maintain fair conduct and treatment of customers?
    Answer reference: Section 3.5

13. What do regulators look for when ensuring that fair treatment of customers is built into governance and oversight arrangements?
    Answer reference: Section 4.1

14. What is covered under the Unfair Contract Terms Act 1977?
Answer reference: Section 4.4

15. What is the limit that the UK's Financial Ombudsman can award an eligible complainant?
Answer reference: Section 4.8.2

16. Who can a firm open an account with in order to hold client money?
Answer reference: Section 4.8.4

17. What is the general expectation for ESG?
Answer reference: Section 5.1

Chapter Five

Governance, Risk Management and Compliance

This syllabus area will provide approximately 17 of the 100 examination questions

1. Corporate Governance

1.1 Objectives of Corporate Governance

Learning Objective

5.1.1 Understand the objectives of corporate governance

Effective corporate governance practices are essential to achieving and maintaining public trust and confidence in the banking system, which are critical to the proper functioning of the financial sector and economy as a whole. Poor corporate governance can contribute to bank failures, which can pose significant public costs. Such failures also have the potential to impact on any applicable deposit insurance system, and there is the possibility of broader macroeconomic implications (such as contagion risk and impact on payment systems). This was illustrated in the financial crisis that began in mid-2007.

In addition, poor corporate governance can lead markets to lose confidence in the ability of a bank to properly manage its assets and liabilities, including deposits, which could in turn trigger a bank run or liquidity crisis. Indeed, in addition to their responsibilities to shareholders, banks also have a responsibility to their depositors and to other recognised stakeholders. The legal system in each country determines the responsibilities a domestic bank may have to its shareholders, depositors and other relevant stakeholders – and so these responsibilities may vary across jurisdictions.

The Organisation for Economic Co-operation and Development (OECD) Principles of Corporate Governance define corporate governance as involving:

'a set of relationships between a company's management, its board, its shareholders, and other stakeholders'.

Corporate governance also provides the structure through which the objectives of the company are set, and the means of attaining those objectives and monitoring performance are determined. Good corporate governance should provide proper incentives for the board and management to pursue objectives that are in the interests of the company and its shareholders and should facilitate effective monitoring. The presence of an effective corporate governance system, within an individual company or group and across an economy as a whole, helps to provide a degree of confidence that is necessary for the proper functioning of a market economy.

From a financial services sector perspective, corporate governance involves the manner in which the business and affairs of a firm are governed by its board and senior management, including how they:

- set the firm's strategy and objectives
- determine the firm's risk tolerance/appetite
- operate the firm's day-to-day business
- protect the interests of depositors, meet shareholder obligations, and take into account the interests of other recognised stakeholders, and
- align corporate activities and behaviour with the expectation that the firm will operate in a safe and sound manner, with integrity and in compliance with applicable laws and regulations.

1.2 Senior Management Leadership

Learning Objective

5.1.2 Understand the importance of senior management leadership, accountability and personal responsibility

It is the responsibility of the board of directors to set out the governance structure for the organisation, to make sure it is implemented as intended, and to provide effective supervision over senior management. Members of the board need to act with honesty and integrity and need to be independent. Members of the board of directors and senior managers of financial institutions performing key roles need to be approved by the regulator to execute their function.

Approval needs to be obtained from the regulator prior to the senior manager performing their role. Criteria may vary by regulator, but typically include prior experience, character, and education. The requirement for senior management approval applies to all institutions that operate within the jurisdiction, although they may differ based on the size of the operation. Senior managers and members of the board can be held directly and personally accountable if they did not take reasonable steps to prevent or stop a breach in regulatory requirements.

The **Senior Manager and Certification Regime (SM&CR)** in the UK banking industry was introduced in 2015 with the aim of reducing damage to consumers and to strengthen market integrity. It replaces the approved persons regime for senior management and encourages senior management to take responsibility for their actions. In addition, there is a strong focus on improved conduct and governance structures. As part of the SM&CR, each senior manager must have a statement of responsibilities (SoR) setting out their roles and responsibilities. Senior management functions include the following:

- Chief Executive.
- Executive Director.
- Partner.
- Chair of Audit Committee.
- Compliance oversight.
- Money Laundering Reporting Officer (MLRO).

Under the SM&CR, senior managers have to take personal responsibility for their actions and are held accountable. Clear personal responsibility and accountability aims to reduce harm to customers and strengthen market integrity. Although senior management is ultimately personally responsible, this does not mean they should not delegate. The delegation of tasks is perfectly permissible, but reasonable steps must be taken to ensure the delegated tasks are discharged appropriately.

1.3 Monitoring Corporate Governance

Learning Objective

5.1.3 Understand the role of the compliance function in implementing and monitoring corporate governance standards

A firm's corporate governance standards need to reflect the regulations and practices of the various jurisdictions in which the firm operates. The compliance function should, therefore, provide a key contribution to the formulation of these standards, in particular to ensure that all relevant regulatory aspects are included.

Regulators will have local expectations of corporate governance – whether due to international standards, obligations of European Union (EU) or other local or regional legislation/regulation, or their own domestic concerns – and so the compliance function should ensure that the firm's approach will be satisfactory.

A corporate governance manual is designed to help executives and others understand the governance framework and approach pertaining to their business. Strong governance is a vital ingredient in a successful, growing and dynamic business. The more successful a business becomes, and the faster it grows, the more important a corporate governance manual is in decision-making, risk-taking and helping executives remain in control of their business. A corporate governance manual also explains the corporate and management structure of a business.

As part of its work as the firm's second line of defence, the compliance function should also include a review of these governance standards as part of its monitoring activity. This monitoring should include the regulatory standards relating to corporate governance, and also the activity of those board members and senior management in positions of significant influence. Any deviations should be reported to an appropriate level of management and, in case of material deviations, to the board.

1.4 Unitary and Dual (Two-Tier) Boards

Learning Objective

5.1.4 Know the main corporate governance structures in UK/US, Europe: unitary board; two-tier structure

There are two types of board structures. The unitary board – typically found in the UK and US and the dual board which is common in Europe.

The unitary board of directors is characterised by one single board comprising both executive and non-executive directors. The dual board consists of a supervisory board and an executive board of management where there is a clear separation between the functions of supervision and management.

In a two-tier structure, a management board manages the company's business operation but is accountable to, and supervised by, a supervisory board elected by shareholders.

Despite this structural difference between unitary and dual-board systems, the similarities in actual board practices are significant. Both types of systems comprise a supervisory function and a managerial function.

The board of directors in a unitary board and the supervisory board in the two-tier system are usually elected by shareholders (though in some European countries, employees will also elect one or more supervisory board members). Typically, both the unitary board and the supervisory board in the two-tier structure appoint the members of the managerial body. In addition, both the unitary board and the supervisory board usually have responsibility for ensuring that financial reporting and control systems are effectively functioning and to ensure the company complies with laws and regulations.

1.5 Effective Management

Learning Objective

5.1.5 Understand the impact of business and/or management structures on the effective management of the compliance function: matrix structures; silo structures; maintaining independence

1.5.1 Matrix Structures

Traditional business hierarchy models saw individuals receiving authority from the person above them. Responsibilities would cascade down from a single point, eg, the board-level compliance director would establish a compliance structure which apportioned responsibility to their senior managers, who in turn would retain teams to ensure the work is performed.

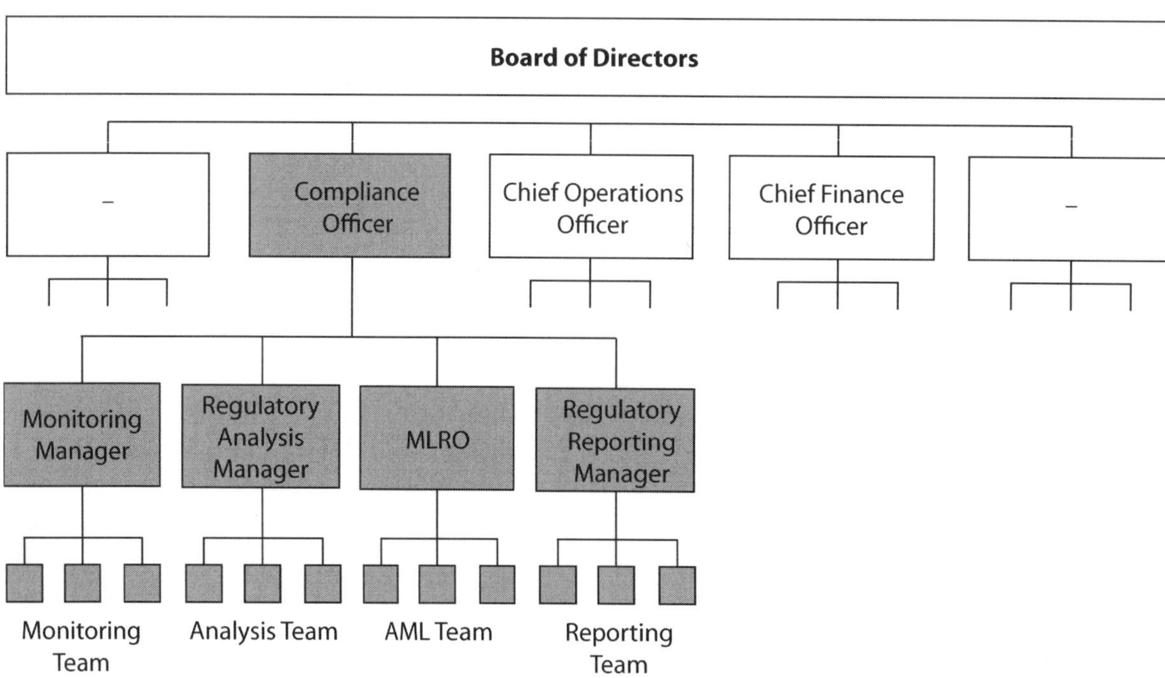

While successful in terms of accountability, the increasing size and complexity of financial institutions highlighted limitations of such a model. Such organisations need a balance between detailed knowledge of the products and services being provided by each business unit alongside the need for other disciplines to be centrally delivered by core teams of skilled personnel.

This need to balance efficient common services across an organisation (mirroring the traditional hierarchy) with dedicated activity within each business unit has led to a growth of 'matrix structures' within firms. The principle is that an individual may serve two or three managers rather than just one, having accountability to their functional manager for the delivery of services to a particular business unit, and having responsibility to, for example, the chief executive of that business unit for their contribution. Models can become more complex, with the individual having a functional responsibility across the wider business while also having specific responsibility to a particular business unit.

In a compliance setting, a member of the team may, therefore, have a responsibility to the compliance director in respect of their contribution to the compliance team's objectives (for example, performing regulatory analysis of consultation papers to determine what changes the firm might need to implement) while also having a matrix reporting line to the chief executive officer (CEO) of a particular business unit where that person has applicable detailed compliance experience. The following diagram illustrates such a matrix structure, with dotted lines representing the matrix reporting lines to respective CEOs:

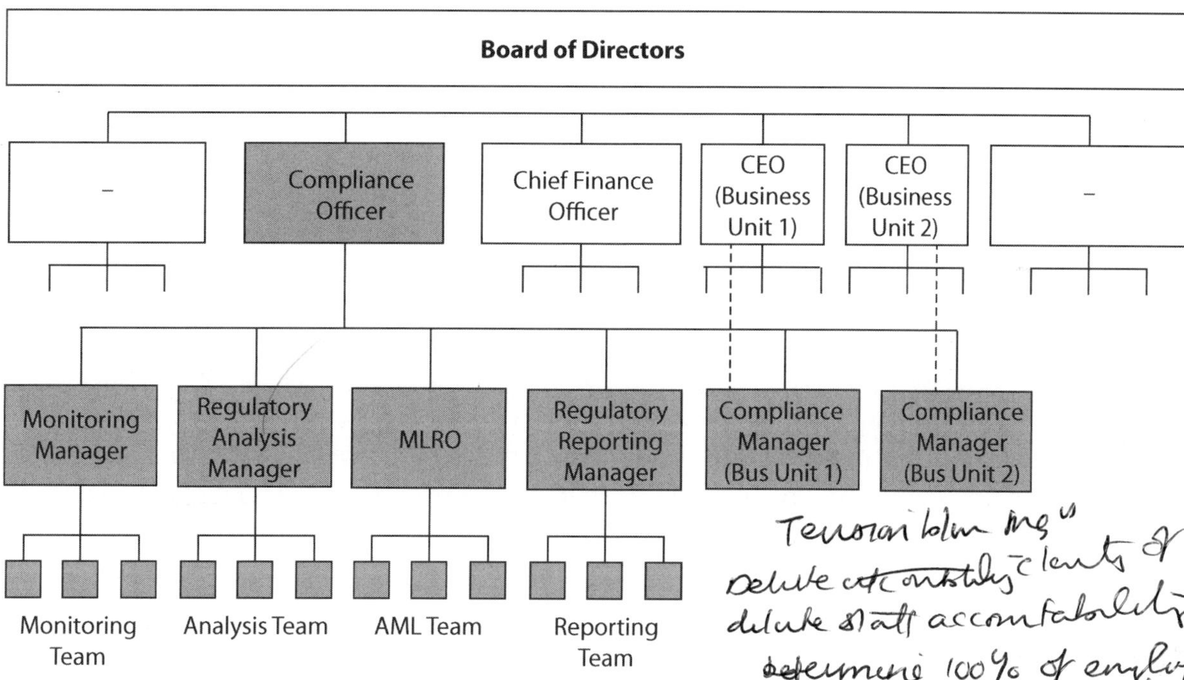

Such an approach should lead to a more flexible servicing model, as members of the team build and apply experience in multiple contexts to benefit the business overall. However, firms also must be careful to ensure that the implementation of matrix structures does not dilute staff accountability and clarity in the roles that each person fulfils. There can also be tensions if the managers in the matrix structure continue to expect that they can determine 100% of the employee's activity – forgetting that the employee has a matrix responsibility to another manager covering a portion of their time.

isolated grp of workers report to line mgr or functional manager function replicated in each silo

1.5.2 Silo Structures

Larger organisations may operate in a silo structure, where isolated groups of workers report to a line or functional manager. Imagine columns on a page with a line manager above each column and a group of workers inside each column under the manager of the division. As these groups operate independently, it is not unique to discover functions replicated in each silo.

In an information technology organisation, for instance, you might discover software programmers in the sales office, some more in the accounting department, and still more in corporate headquarters, because each of these functioning units has a programming demand.

Such a structure is illustrated here, with the shaded boxes reflecting activity within the responsibility of a single director. Multiple functions are repeated in each office, as determined by the local requirements, with some functions being undertaken in multiple locations.

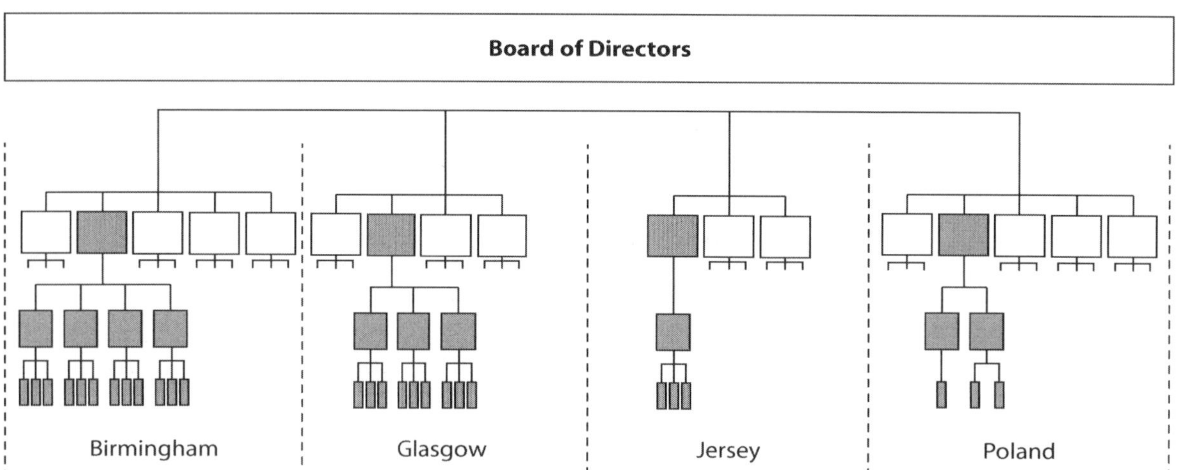

This has implications for all parts of the business, as such a structure is likely to become inefficient due to effort being duplicated in multiple areas. For compliance, there is an additional concern that replication of functions (eg, monitoring, advisory, regulatory analysis) in different locations can lead to inconsistency of the control infrastructure, and could ultimately undermine the clarity and consistency of liaison with regulators. The accountability of each person might be increased as they are responsible for delivering their specific function, though the overall structure must be robust to deliver group cohesion and cost control.

1.5.3 Maintaining Independence

Regardless of the structure chosen, the compliance function should clearly be independent within the firm. This involves four related elements:

1. The compliance function should have a formal status within the firm.
2. There should be a group compliance officer or head of compliance with overall responsibility for coordinating the management of the firm's compliance risk.

3. Compliance function staff, and in particular the head of compliance, should not be placed in a position where there is a possible conflict of interest between their compliance responsibilities and any other responsibilities they may have.
4. Compliance function staff should have access to the information and personnel necessary to carry out their responsibilities.

1.6 Audit Contribution to Governance

Learning Objective

5.1.6 Understand how auditing contributes to prudential corporate governance, accounting and reporting requirements: audit committees; internal audit; external auditors

The board should recognise and acknowledge that independent, competent and qualified internal and external auditors, as well as other internal control functions (including the compliance functions), are vital to the corporate governance process in order to achieve a number of important objectives. Senior management should also recognise the importance of the effectiveness of these functions to the long-term soundness of the firm.

The board and senior management can enhance the ability of the internal audit function to identify problems with a firm's risk management and internal control systems by:

- encouraging internal auditors to adhere to national and international professional standards, such as those established by the Institute of Internal Auditors
- promoting the independence of the internal auditor, for example by ensuring that the internal audit function reports to, or has direct access to, the board or the board's audit committee
- recognising the importance of the audit and internal control processes and communicating their importance throughout the firm
- utilising, in a timely and effective manner, the findings of internal audits and requiring timely correction, by senior management, of identified problems, and
- engaging internal auditors to judge the effectiveness of the risk management and compliance function, including the quality of risk reporting to the board and senior management, as well as the effectiveness of other key control functions.

The board and senior management:

- are responsible for the preparation and fair presentation of financial statements in accordance with applicable accounting standards in each jurisdiction, as well as the establishment of effective internal controls related to financial reporting
- can also contribute to the effectiveness of external auditors in order to ensure that the firm's financial statements fairly represent the financial position and performance of the company in all material respects by, for example, including in engagement letters the expectation that the external auditor will be in compliance with applicable domestic and international codes and standards of professional practice.

Non-executive board members should have the right to meet regularly – in the absence of senior management – with the external auditor and the heads of the internal audit and compliance functions. This can strengthen the ability of the board to oversee senior management's implementation of the board's policies and to ensure that the firm's business strategies and risk exposures are consistent with risk parameters established by the board.

Senior management should promote strong internal controls and should avoid activities and practices that undermine their effectiveness. For example, senior management should ensure there is effective segregation of duties where conflicts could arise. They should also exercise effective control over employees in key business positions. This latter point has proven especially problematic where managers have failed to question employees who generate revenues or returns out of line with reasonable expectations (eg, where supposedly low-risk, low-margin trading activity generated unexpectedly high returns) for fear of losing either revenue or the employee.

1.7 What does Due Diligence Mean?

Learning Objective

5.1.7 Know the purpose and key elements of due diligence: identification; selection; fitness & propriety

Offers to purchase an asset are usually dependent on the results of due diligence analysis. This includes reviewing all financial records plus anything else deemed material to the sale. Sellers could also perform a due diligence analysis on the buyer. Factors that may be considered are the buyer's ability to purchase, as well as other items that would affect the purchased entity or the seller after the sale has been completed. Due diligence serves to confirm all material facts with regard to a sale and is a key activity in good governance, serving to identify and limit risks. This is a way of preventing unnecessary harm to either party involved in a transaction. Generally, due diligence refers to the care a reasonable person should take before entering into an agreement or a transaction with another party.

For example, a due diligence investigation with regard to hedge funds refers to an in-depth review of a hedge fund's activity, conducted in order to ensure that the fund is in compliance with its prospectus. It is a roadmap for existing and potential investors in understanding whether a specific fund will meet their investment horizon, risk tolerance and investment strategy.

Such due diligence of a US hedge fund would, therefore, include an examination of factors such as:

- a fund snapshot
- disclosed investment strategy
- historical returns
- assets under management (a copy of the fund's portfolio from the custodian is usually requested)
- audited financial statements if the fund is regulated by the US Securities and Exchange Commission (SEC)
- fund's terms and details
- regulatory registration, if any
- risk factors
- valuation.

The results of due diligence will help to determine the selection of an investment or indeed confirm whether a takeover might proceed. Part of the due diligence process will be to review the senior management involved to ensure their fitness and propriety; this is to verify they are financially sound and have appropriate skills, knowledge and experience. Due diligence will also be required in respect of other contractual relationships entered into by a firm, including the providers of material outsourced functions and the appointment of custodians.

1.8 Corporate Governance Training

Learning Objective

5.1.8 Understand how an effective training programme can contribute to good corporate governance

The commercial argument supporting corporate governance is simple – well-run companies produce better results. Much emphasis has been placed on the best practice of managing formal external relationships; establishing transparency; and emphasising legal, timely and trustworthy information. Research suggests that companies with better corporate governance are more valued than others with less sophisticated systems. Studies also show that those enterprises with good corporate governance are far less likely to be involved in survival and recovery planning.

From a regulatory perspective, it is important that the board and senior management fully understand their governance responsibilities and have the opportunity to test their knowledge periodically. The use of scenarios to discuss key governance and regulatory challenges can be an effective method of training.

A training programme for corporate governance would cover the following:

- Key governance issues:
  - managing conflicts, the unitary board and the balance of power
  - stakeholder management
  - managing financial and non-financial risk
  - communication and narrative reporting
  - transparency and disclosure.
- The board:
  - role and composition of the board: balance and independence
  - roles of executive and non-executive directors (including senior independent directors (SIDs))
  - roles of the chairperson and CEO
  - directors' duties
  - corporate social responsibility (CSR)
  - board induction, training and effectiveness
  - professional development
  - board performance evaluation
  - reporting internal control and risk management
  - corporate reporting, including governance reporting, and risk management
  - stakeholder management
  - communication, shareholder activism and engagement
  - investor relations.

- The annual general meeting (AGM) and annual report.
- The company secretary's role:
  - responsible for governance through the chairperson
  - advising and guiding the board.

1.9 Enhancing Corporate Governance – Background to the Bank for International Settlements (BIS) Principles

Learning Objectives

5.1.9 Understand the factors behind the formulation of the BIS Principles for enhancing corporate governance

5.1.10 Know the BIS Principles for enhancing corporate governance

Given the important financial intermediary role of banks in an economy, the public and the market have a high degree of sensitivity to any difficulties potentially arising from any corporate governance shortcomings in banks. Corporate governance is, thus, of great relevance both to individual banking organisations and to the international financial system as a whole, and merits targeted supervisory guidance.

The Basel Committee on Banking Supervision (BCBS) has had a longstanding commitment to promoting sound corporate governance practices for banking organisations. The BCBS's guidance assists banking supervisors and provides a reference point for promoting the adoption of sound corporate governance practices by banking organisations in their countries. The principles also serve as a reference point for the banks' own corporate governance efforts.

The BCBS's 2006 guidance drew from the Principles of Corporate Governance that were published in 2004 by the OECD. The OECD's widely accepted and long-established Principles aim to assist governments in their efforts to evaluate and improve their frameworks for corporate governance and to provide guidance for participants and regulators of financial markets.

The BCBS's 2006 Principles targeted key issues of corporate governance. Primary points in the 2006 guidance included:

- the board should be appropriately involved in approving the bank's strategy
- clear lines of responsibility should be set and enforced throughout the organisation
- compensation policies should be consistent with the bank's long-term objectives, and
- the risks generated by operations that lack transparency should be adequately managed.

Subsequent to the publication of the BCBS's 2006 guidance, there have been a number of corporate governance failures and lapses, many of which came to light during the financial crisis that began in mid-2007. These included, for example, insufficient board oversight of senior management, inadequate risk management and unduly complex or opaque bank organisational structures and activities.

Against this background, the BCBS decided to revisit its 2006 principles. Having reviewed and revised these principles, it reaffirmed their continued relevance and the critical importance of their adoption by banks and supervisors to ensure effective implementation of the principles.

The key areas where the Committee believes the greatest focus is necessary are highlighted below:

1. **Board practices**

   The board should actively carry out its overall responsibility for the bank, including its business and risk strategy, organisation, financial soundness and governance. The board should also provide effective oversight of senior management.

   To fulfil this responsibility, the board should:

   - exercise sound objective judgement and have and maintain appropriate qualifications and competence, individually and collectively
   - follow good governance practices for its own work as a board, and
   - be supported by competent, robust and independent risk and control functions, for which the board provides effective oversight.

2. **Senior management**
   - Under the direction of the board, senior management should ensure that the bank's activities are consistent with the business strategy, risk tolerance/appetite and policies approved by the board.

3. **Risk management and internal controls**
   - A bank should have an independent risk management function (including a chief risk officer or equivalent) with sufficient authority, stature, independence, resources and access to the board.
   - Risks should be identified and monitored on an ongoing firm-wide and individual entity basis, and the sophistication of the bank's risk management and internal control infrastructures should keep pace with any changes to the bank's risk profile (including its growth) and to the external risk landscape.
   - Effective risk management requires frank and timely internal communication within the bank about risk, both across the organisation and through reporting to the board and senior management.

4. **Compensation**
   - The banks should fully implement the Financial Stability Board's (FSB – formerly the Financial Stability Forum) Principles for Sound Compensation Practices (FSB Principles) and accompanying Implementation Standards (FSB Standards) or the applicable national provisions that are consistent with the FSB Principles and Standards.

5. **Complex or opaque corporate structures**
   - The board and senior management should know, understand and guide the bank's overall corporate structure and its evolution, ensuring that the structure (and the entities that form the structure) is justified and does not involve undue or inappropriate complexity.
   - Senior management, and the board as appropriate, should understand the purpose of any structures that impede transparency, be aware of the special risks that such structures may pose and seek to mitigate the risks identified.

6. **Disclosure and transparency**
   - Transparency is one tool to help emphasise and implement the main principles for good corporate governance.

The BCBS's guidance is intended to assist banking organisations in enhancing their corporate governance frameworks and to assist supervisors in assessing the quality of those frameworks. It is not, however, intended to establish a new regulatory framework on top of existing national legislation, regulation or codes. The implementation of the principles should be proportionate to the size, complexity, structure, economic significance and risk profile of the bank and the group (if any) to which it belongs.

The application of corporate governance standards in any jurisdiction is naturally expected to be pursued in a manner consistent with applicable national laws, regulations and codes. The BCBS recognises that some countries have found it appropriate to adopt legal frameworks and standards (eg, for publicly traded firms) as well as accounting and auditing standards. Such frameworks and standards tend to be particularly relevant for larger or publicly traded banks or financial institutions. Whatever the case may be, supervisors are encouraged to periodically check their frameworks and standards for consistency with relevant BCBS guidance.

BCBS guidance refers to a governance structure composed of a board and senior management. The BCBS recognises that there are significant differences in the legislative and regulatory frameworks across countries regarding these functions (such as adopting a unitary or two-tier board structure). Owing to these differences, the terms board and senior management are used not to identify legal constructs, but rather as a way to refer to the oversight function and the management function, depending on which tasks are assigned to the different functions by the applicable law within each jurisdiction. Recognising that different structural approaches to corporate governance exist across countries, the guidance encourages practices that can strengthen checks and balances and sound corporate governance under diverse structures. The 14 principles are outlined in the following table:

The BIS Principles for Enhancing Corporate Governance

Principle 1	The board has overall responsibility for the bank, including approving and overseeing the implementation of the bank's strategic objectives, risk strategy, corporate governance and corporate values. The board is also responsible for providing oversight of senior management.
Principle 2	Board members should be and remain qualified, including through training, for their positions. They should have a clear understanding of their role in corporate governance and be able to exercise sound and objective judgement about the affairs of the bank.
Principle 3	The board should define appropriate governance practices for its own work and have in place the means to ensure such practices are followed and periodically reviewed for improvement.
Principle 4	In a group structure, the board of the parent company has the overall responsibility for adequate corporate governance across the group and ensuring that there are governance policies and mechanisms appropriate to the structure, business and risks of the group and its entities.
Principle 5	Under the direction of the board, senior management should ensure that the bank's activities are consistent with the business strategy, risk tolerance/appetite and policies approved by the board.
Principle 6	Banks should have an independent risk management function (including a chief risk officer or equivalent) with sufficient authority, stature, independence, resources and access to the board.
Principle 7	Risks should be identified and monitored on an ongoing firm-wide and individual entity basis, and the sophistication of the bank's risk management and internal control infrastructures should keep pace with any changes to the bank's risk profile (including its growth), and to the external risk landscape.
Principle 8	Effective risk management requires robust internal communication within the bank about risk, both across the organisation and through reporting to the board and senior management.
Principle 9	The board and senior management should effectively utilise the work conducted by internal audit functions, external auditors and internal control functions.
Principle 10	The board should actively oversee the compensation system's design and operation and should monitor and review the compensation system to ensure that it operates as intended.
Principle 11	An employee's compensation should be effectively aligned with prudent risk-taking: compensation should be adjusted for all types of risk; compensation outcomes should be symmetric with risk outcomes; compensation payout schedules should be sensitive to the time horizon of risks; and the mix of cash, equity and other forms of compensation should be consistent with risk alignment.
Principle 12	The board and senior management should know and understand the bank's operational structure and the risks that it poses (ie, 'know-your-structure').
Principle 13	Where a bank operates through special-purpose or related structures, or in jurisdictions that impede transparency or do not meet international banking standards, its board and senior management should understand the purpose, structure and unique risks of these operations. They should also seek to mitigate the risks identified (ie, 'understand-your-structure').
Principle 14	The governance of the bank should be adequately transparent to its shareholders, depositors, other relevant stakeholders and market participants.

2. Key Risk Types, their Application and Impact on the Compliance Function

2.1 Risk and Uncertainty

Learning Objective

5.2.1 Understand the difference between risk and uncertainty

Many things in life are not certain, and we manage these issues in our everyday lives. Consider the question of whether you will arrive at work on time tomorrow morning, and the number of events that could prevent success: whether the car will start, whether the roads will be clear, whether the trains will be operating – and that is before we consider less likely factors (for example, hurricanes, unseasonal snowfall, or earthquake damage).

As you probably felt when reading those last few items, one of the ways we handle uncertainty in our personal lives is through assessing whether certain events or outcomes are likely. The same is true when we consider professional matters.

Uncertainty is a general concept that simply recognises the potential of different outcomes arising. Uncertain matters tend to be vague rather than measurable; science or statistics are unable to help us make decisions. However, where we are able to use data or probability theory to assess and analyse potential outcomes, we are able to talk in terms of 'risk'.

One of the challenges facing a risk professional is, therefore, to identify areas of general uncertainty within a company, and then to deploy tools and analysis in order to quantify those issues as recognised risks – which can then be managed. A key aspect is, therefore, determining the likelihood of outcomes arising, ie, assigning probabilities to matters of uncertainty in order to assess risk, and thus provide better information to senior management for decision-making.

However, to accurately quantify an event's probability of occurring, we need large amounts of observable, repeating data that can be grouped and analysed. This sort of data is available for credit and **market risk** analysis, but business risk has much less 'repeatable' data. Many business risk events (including operational risk) are rare events – and, in some cases, have not yet occurred.

Nevertheless, this technical difference between risk and uncertainty should not stop firms from protecting themselves against the negative consequences of less quantifiable events.

2.2 External Sources of Risk

Learning Objective

5.2.2 Know the key external sources of business risk and their potential impact

External risks arise from changes in:

- the global economy
- the political arena
- the competitive environment
- social and market forces, and
- technological innovation.

Further business risks are also posed by unexpected shocks and natural events, and the actions of external stakeholders and third parties.

2.2.1 Economic Risk

The economy, in its simplest terms, consists of the interaction between individuals and firms, and the allocation of their limited resources to maximise their financial positions. In other words, the economy is shaped by human behaviour, whether as individual consumers or as collectively arranged organisations.

Therefore, a firm has to understand the current and potential future patterns of human behaviour that will affect the products or services it sells. For example, during an economic boom, a failure to anticipate an imminent downturn will result in firms continuing to increase their stocks using current input prices of raw materials. They will then find they need to reduce the prices of their finished goods to sell them in a recession. Equally, financial services firms with securitised mortgages on their books will find it difficult to sell them if there is a fall in house prices.

2.2.2 Political Risk

Wealth creation and its distribution tend to be viewed in different ways by different political parties. Therefore, a change in government will generally affect the financial sector and may be the cause of a rise, or fall, in the markets. This will depend upon the economic strategies that commentators expect the new leadership to implement.

Other political events, such as changes in economic policy, or tax law, will also affect the financial sector. Political changes, being so closely linked to the economy, can affect financial services firms in three main ways:

- A rise or fall in the markets in which firms invest.
- An increase or decrease in demand for the products which the industry sells.
- Changes to the legislative and regulatory environment in which financial services firms operate.

2.2.3 Risks from the Competitive Environment, Social and Market Forces

Firms are affected by the performance of other companies, especially those operating in related industries and markets. For example, if a competitor gains a critical mass of market share, it may become too expensive for some of the other firms to continue servicing the remaining customers. This will force one or more of them to exit that part of the market. On the other hand, if a close competitor fails, there may be scope to buy parts of their business at below their market price.

Firms in the finance sector are also particularly susceptible to certain changes in social and market forces, such as:

- the propensity to save
- attitudes to living on credit
- house prices and their relationship to demographic changes.

2.2.4 Technological Risk

The development of new technology is behind many of the increases in productivity that create economic growth.

For example, computerisation changed the way in which businesses organise their operations. 'Interconnectedness' is also affecting how information and data are transmitted, how businesses and people communicate, and how, when and where people work. The availability of fast and efficient telecommunications has enabled new ways of reaching customers and organising internal resources. In the past, workers may have had to relocate to where employers delivered their services. Now, a bank can 'outsource' individual functions to lower-cost overseas locations.

In addition, internet services mean that expensive branch networks are no longer a prerequisite for success in the financial sector. Information management has also improved – both in terms of firms making use of consumer data, and consumers gaining access to more information about products and services. Firms that do not anticipate or keep up with technological change, or which specialise in older technology investments, risk falling behind.

2.2.5 Shocks and Natural Events

We live in an age of instant media coverage and shocks or natural events in one part of a country have the potential to adversely affect the national, or even the global economy. For example, after the 2004 Indian Ocean earthquake and tsunami, the Thai prime minister assessed the cost of damage at $510 million. It was estimated that the disaster would reduce Thailand's 2005 GDP by 0.5%.

There was very little that firms in the affected areas could have done in advance to prepare for the tragedy, but firms which had planned in advance for generic disasters were able to recover operations more quickly than those who had not.

The same is also true to some extent of the events of the 9/11 attacks in the US – with the exception that operational recovery did not necessarily enable continued business because:

- the debris from the collapsing towers and the general chaos in the area meant the closure of the New York Stock Exchange (NYSE), as well as brokerage houses and banks in the Wall Street area
- the grounding of all aeroplanes prevented the clearing of cheques and the distribution of paper currency, creating uncertainty for financial institutions.

Despite this event having occurred in the US, the interrelationship between the financial markets and economies of the UK and the US caused the UK FTSE 100 to fall by 12%.

Coronavirus (COVID-19) Pandemic

The COVID-19 pandemic which, at the time of publication of this workbook is still ongoing, has resulted in the global shutdown of economies and businesses. Some, like supermarkets, have fared well and increased their business. Others, such as the hospitality industry and non-essential businesses have lost out as a result of having to close their business for extended periods. The impact on the global economy is estimated to be three times more harmful than the 2008 crisis.

Although financial institutions have reduced credit restrictions to assist companies throughout the pandemic, businesses continue to be assessed on their credit worthiness. Default risk – the risk a borrower is unable to meet their debt obligations – has been negatively impacted during the pandemic, and this is expected to continue for some time after the pandemic ends.

From a compliance perspective, the pandemic has resulted in additional risks such as an increased vulnerability to cyber crime, and the challenges associated with the sudden move to remote working. Although technologically most firms seem to have coped well with these changes, working from home has created a larger potential of data protection breaches, and the associated loss of interconnectivity between staff may result in patterns of behaviour related to market abuse and fraud being overlooked. Policy, processes, and procedures will need to be amended to cater for the new working environment.

2.2.6 Risks from Stakeholders and Third Parties

External stakeholders that cause business risk typically include a firm's parent company, any major institutional investors and any particularly large or important customers.

1. **The parent company**
    - Where the parent owns more than one business it will take a 'global view' and this, at times, may cause it to question or alter the plans of its subsidiary firms.
    - Unless parent firm expectations are carefully managed during the formulation of the plans, this can cause great inconvenience to the subsidiary firm. Quite often, by the time the plans are ready to be shared with the parent, staff may have been hired and external research may have been commissioned. Key customers may even have been consulted as part of the planning process.
    - In some cases, particularly where the firm is a 'start-up' or embarking on a diversification of service, the 'parent' role may be held by a venture capital firm. This can bring a different set of expectations, such as a goal of achieving a certain level of financial return over a defined time period, or achieving a market listing.

2. **Major institutional investors**
   Where institutional shareholders own large shareholdings in the firm, this gives them influence through voting rights. If these stakeholders have different views on, for example, the competence of certain board members, then in some cases there may be little that the firm can do to prevent them pushing for change.

3. **Large customers**
   If a firm has an over-reliance on a particular customer, that relationship needs to be carefully managed. This is particularly important as there are often other firms in the industry that could provide the same services to this customer. Over the longer term, the firm should aim to dilute this risk by increasing its customer base.

   The key to managing stakeholder risk is to:
   - build relationships at senior levels
   - understand their agenda and how it may differ from the firm's own agenda
   - manage expectations with any new developments.

   Other third parties that can also be a source of business risk might include:
   - brokers
   - solicitors
   - IT and data suppliers
   - outsourced back-office administrators
   - advisers/industry consultants.

It will be important for the firm to ensure that, where possible, it can source equivalent goods and services from alternative suppliers. That way, if a third party defaults or delays delivery, there should be no service interruption to the firm's customers.

2.3 Internal Sources of Risk

Learning Objective

5.2.3 Know the key internal sources of business risk and their potential impact

2.3.1 Strategic Risk

The Committee of European Banking Supervisors (CEBS) defines **strategic risk** as:

> *'the current or prospective risk to earnings and capital arising from changes in the business environment and from adverse business decisions, improper implementation of decisions or lack of responsiveness to changes in the business environment'.*

In simple terms, strategic risk takes two forms:

1. Is the strategy right?
   - Producing the wrong strategy can be one of the most serious mistakes a board can make.

2. Is the strategy being properly implemented?
   - Failing to implement even the best of strategies may also lead a firm to extinction.
   - Does the board know whether, and how well, its strategy is being implemented?
   - If the strategy is not implemented, is this because the firm is being run by inexperienced or lax management? Or is the strategy so complex that it is impossible to implement?

2.3.2 Operational Risk

The BIS defines operational risk as *'the risk of loss arising from processes, people, systems or external events'*. The BIS states that operational risk is inherent in all banking products, activities, processes and systems, and that the effective management of operational risk has always been a fundamental element of a bank's risk management programme. Therefore, having a sound operational risk management programme in place is a reflection of the effectiveness of the board and senior management in administering its portfolio of products, activities, processes and systems.

2.3.3 Financial Risk

At the simplest level, for a company to stay in business its revenues must match or exceed its costs. Any agreement by the firm to offer credit terms to its customers creates a financial risk that the customer may not pay. Similarly, financial risk arises any time a firm deploys its corporate resources ahead of receiving payment for services – such as any investment to build up stock.

Sadly, financial risk is not limited to the internal informed decisions of a firm; it can also arise where a participant in the market is acting improperly. If the finances of a firm are 'glossed' to cover up losses, itself a breach of the Corporate Governance Code, the pretence can be kept up only for a limited time before the firm runs into liquidity problems. Unless the underlying finances of a firm are sound, the firm will be 'found out' when markets or other environmental factors change. However, when the firm becomes insolvent there will be insufficient resources left to pay all its creditors. Another source of financial risk stems from the use of gearing. Also known as leverage, gearing is the ratio of a firm's debts to the value of its equity. A company which, on paper, looks sound, but which has become over-geared can suffer disproportionately if interest rate rises cause its debt to become more expensive, or if its revenues fall to a level too low to repay its debt. For these reasons, it is important that any firm offering credit terms to its customers should seek to obtain evidence of financial soundness in order to manage the associated financial risks.

2.3.4 Legal, Regulatory and Reputational Risk for Financial Services Firms

Financial services firms' failure to comply with legislation and regulations may result in serious consequences including financial penalties and loss of reputation (see section 3 of this chapter).

2.4 Effective Risk Management

Learning Objective

5.2.4 Know the components and practical application of an effective risk management process

Risk management should identify what could go wrong, evaluate which risks should be dealt with, and implement strategies to address those risks. Firms that take pre-emptive action to identify their risks and formulate a response plan will be better prepared and have a more cost-effective way of dealing with them if those risk events do occur.

The key elements of a simple risk framework are:

- risk policies and governance at board level
- risk oversight – often performed by a dedicated risk management function, often organised by risk type and performing the following tasks:
  - identifying risks
  - assessing risks
  - ensuring that risks are appropriately controlled
  - monitoring and reporting on the risks and their associated controls
  - day-to-day risk management – this activity is inseparable from good business management and must be owned by the business units, not the risk function.

2.5 Assessment of Risks

Learning Objective

5.2.5 Understand how the impact of risks on a firm's business activities are assessed and managed including operational resilience

2.5.1 Assessing External Risks

A number of different techniques are used to arrive at an understanding of a firm's business risk profile. Here are some examples.

- **PESTLE analysis** – this is an analysis of the external macro environment in which a business operates. This environment will inevitably contain factors which are beyond the firm's control or influence, but which are, nevertheless, important to be aware of when developing new products, businesses or strategies. Risks are considered under the following headings:
  - political
  - economic
  - social
  - technical
  - legal
  - environmental.

- **Business continuity/disaster recovery planning** – a company must take reasonable steps to ensure that its services are robust given the various risks that affect its operations. IT systems and infrastructure should be designed to include resilience against isolated failures of individual components, yet problems can arise that prevent the firm's primary processes from being completed. Disaster recovery planning covers the most significant threats facing the ongoing activities of the business – such as the inability to use a building or data centre as a result of fire, flood, or loss of utilities. Disaster recovery events generally require firms to relocate their staff to alternative premises for a period, until the primary facilities can again be used. It is a rare event for a firm to implement a full disaster recovery. The parallel discipline of business continuity planning requires the firm to establish protocols that would be invoked where physical premises remain serviceable yet some other event makes it impossible for certain services to be delivered in the usual manner. For example, the loss of telecommunications links may prevent some tasks from being performed in the normal manner, though as other processes remain operational it may not be a sound decision to implement full disaster recovery and relocate staff to alternative premises. The tension between restoring the lost service and completing other tasks needs to be understood. Thorough planning, and testing through desktop exercises, will enable the firm to understand the time frames within which a business continuity event must be resolved before the firm will instead declare an emergency and invoke full disaster recovery, for example, moving all functions onto a back-up IT infrastructure.
- **Business process analysis** – this involves:
  - examining each high-level business process
  - describing both the internal processes and external factors which can influence those processes.

Having identified the external business risks on which to focus, each one should then be assessed so that the risks can be considered and prioritised in order of 'potential damage'. This is preferable to simply tackling the ones that look most straightforward or interesting.

One of the simplest methods of assessing risks is the creation of a ranking hierarchy, which is a method of ranking risks in order of their significance to the firm. As noted earlier, it is necessary to turn general uncertainty into manageable risk – which requires analysis. Such assessments may be subjective (based on the experience of the professionals involved) or objective (being supported by historical data) or both. In either event, the ranking decision depends on two criteria: the likelihood of the risk being realised, and the magnitude of the impact.

The likelihood of the risk can be represented as a range of probabilities that correspond to a rating. For example, depending on the business area being measured, the following ratings might be used:

Likelihood Probability Ratings

Very low	less than 1%	rating score = 1
Low	1% or more, but less than 5%	rating score = 2
Medium	5% or more, but less than 10%	rating score = 3
High	10% or more, but less than 20%	rating score = 4
Very high	20% or more	rating score = 5

Impact Loss Ratings

The impact of the risk is the potential loss if the risk occurs. This can be represented as a monetary range, and also assigned a rating in line with the size and financial reserves of the firm. For example:

Very low	less than £5 million	rating score = 1
Low	£5 million or more, but less than £20 million	rating score = 2
Medium	£20 million or more, but less than £50 million	rating score = 3
High	£50 million or more, but less than £100 million	rating score = 4
Very high	£100 million or more	rating score = 5

A simple overall risk assessment is arrived at by multiplying the likelihood rating scores with the impact rating scores:

Risk score = likelihood score × impact score

However, in devising any mathematical model, it is necessary to consider the behaviour of numbers. The simple formula above would give a value of '5' where a 'very low' likelihood is combined with a 'very high' impact – yet a score of '6' when a 'low' likelihood is combined with a 'medium' impact. Compliance and risk professionals designing a risk assessment should, therefore, give careful consideration to the correct weighting of results, which may lead them to use non-linear scales or other weighting factors to yield tailored outcomes suitable for the context of their business.

2.5.2 Assessing Internal Risks

Internal drivers of business risk are typically identified through a combination of techniques, such as the following:

- Structured brainstorming – an example of this is SWOT analysis that focuses participants' attention systematically on the firm's:
  - strengths
  - weaknesses
  - opportunities
  - threats.
- Industry best practice benchmarking performed by external consultants.
- Scenario analysis, including **stress testing** and reverse stress testing.
- Risk assessment workshops – going through the firm's corporate goals to bring out the factors that could prevent each goal from being met.
- Discussion with external auditors – external auditors who are often well placed to give advice on potential areas of business risk (even if such risks fall outside the scope of the usual audit activity).

Having identified the key internal drivers of business risk, each one then needs to be assessed. As in the external business risk discussion above, the risks are usually scored by impact and likelihood, so they can be ranked and prioritised for mitigation effort.

2.5.3 Risk Appetite

Risk appetite, or risk tolerance, is the level(s) of loss that the firm is willing to accept in its different businesses over a specified time horizon at a given level of confidence, ie, the level of expected loss that the firm will not (or cannot) mitigate.

In the risk versus uncertainty discussion above, we considered the differences in the amount of data available for assessing the likelihood of credit and market risk losses compared to that which is available for assessing the likelihood of business and operational risk losses. Risk appetite will need to be expressed in different ways for different risk types, to reflect the relative ease of assigning probabilities to the losses caused by each type.

For example, for more easily quantifiable risks the risk policy might include:

- a tolerance for direct financial loss, or
- specific risk measures, such as credit or market **value at risk (VaR)** metrics.

For less easily quantifiable risks, the policy might specify non-financial statements, such as:

- 'Our disaster recovery plans ensure that, following the loss of our main premises, the firm will reopen for business within eight hours.'
- 'The firm has no appetite for reputational risk. All external communications must be approved by the head of marketing.'

At the group level, the firm will need to tie its overall risk profile, which in effect is its current default risk tolerance, to its level of available risk capital.

Setting a risk appetite tends to be an iterative process, and often needs both a top-down and a bottom-up approach.

The top-down approach involves the board and senior management:

- identifying threats to the firm's objectives
- relating them to the 'coverage' available from the firm's capital/earnings/assets, and
- recognising that holding capital is not always the best mitigant for every risk and using scenario analysis to enable appropriate responses to be devised for each threat.

The bottom-up approach requires line management to adopt:

- a set of departmental 'acceptable occurrence' levels for errors and losses
- an appropriate set of **key risk indicators (KRIs)** which can be tracked against predefined tolerances.

The escalation mechanism for tolerance breaches also needs to be defined so that the bottom-up approach can be linked to the top-down approach.

2.5.4 Risk Register

Having identified and then assessed the various internal and external business risks facing the firm, and ranked the risks to decide the priority order for mitigation, the next stage is to construct a risk register (also known as a 'risk log').

This is simply a list of the identified risks, linked to the business objectives whose success would be threatened if the risk materialised. The overall risk score is used to sort the risks so that the list runs from the most significant to the least significant. Each risk is assigned to an owner or lead person and then the mitigating actions would be listed, along with their deadlines for completion.

Finally, the sources of assurance and oversight would be given in order to allow periodic re-assessment of the risk and the status of the mitigating controls which the actions will have implemented. Both 'assurance' and 'oversight' refer to the mechanisms used by the firm to provide an objective view on the quality of each risk's management.

Mitigating controls are ways in which the likelihood and impact of a risk are reduced. They could include, for example, managerial sign-off of work before it leaves the department, or perhaps an IT system that requires a second member of staff to verify inputs for accuracy.

In summary, the usual column headings for a risk register are:

- business objective
- description of associated risk
- risk ranking
- lead person or department
- action plan
- target and completion dates
- sources of assurance and oversight (which may or may not be the lead person or department)
- mitigating controls.

2.5.5 Operational Resilience

Following the financial crisis in 2008, regulators have strongly focused on the financial **operational resilience** of banks to ensure the stability of the financial system. Increasing complexity and interconnectivity have made financial institutions vulnerable to operational disruptions such as the temporary loss of IT systems. The COVID-19 pandemic appeared unexpectedly and clearly shows the need for firms to be able to suddenly amend their working processes which, in turn, has resulted in a larger vulnerability to cyber crime. Although COVID-19 is an extreme event, firms need to be able to respond to the challenges caused by uncertain events.

2.5.6 Risk Management

Learning Objective

5.2.6 Understand the key aims of the risk management function, the risk committee and their relationship with the compliance department

The resources to coordinate and monitor risks of all types are generally provided by a centralised risk management function which is independent from the business areas it serves. Within firms that adhere to the 2009 Walker Review on Corporate Governance, the risk management function is accountable to the board risk committee and is typically tasked with:

- Ensuring that the firm has a robust and consistent risk management and control framework.
- Providing support, oversight and challenge on the firm's risk appetite statements.
- Owning the top-level strategic risk assessment process.
- Monitoring the firm's risk profile against its risk appetites.
- Playing a leading role in defining and embedding the firm's risk culture.
- Providing risk training across the firm.
- Working with other oversight functions such as compliance and audit to provide a comprehensive, robust and efficient assurance framework.

In addition, for all risk-types, the risk management function would typically:

- Oversee and challenge the risk and control self-assessment programme to capture expected risks.
- Oversee and challenge the firm's scenario analysis to capture unexpected extreme risks.
- Help to define, and subsequently challenge, the KRIs used for risk monitoring.
- Ensure issues are properly escalated, assisting with root cause analysis for incidents and losses, and tracking any associated actions.
- Test risk models and key controls within the business, and recommend improvements.
- Advise on risk-based process mapping.
- Support the firm's risk IT system(s).
- Benchmark the firm's risk control framework against industry good practice.

2.5.7 Compliance

Compliance and risk management are not the same, although some of their duties overlap and certainly the compliance function is an important component of a firm's overall risk management.

It is crucial that regulatory rules are followed, and that exceptions are noted and corrected in a timely manner – to do otherwise would represent a significant risk to the firm. So, while there is clearly some overlap between compliance and risk management, each function nevertheless has a different agenda.

Compliance focuses primarily on ensuring that all rules and regulations are followed. Risk management focuses on ensuring that risks are understood, and that proactive decisions are made about which risks to take and which to manage or avoid.

Compliance risk is a significant factor in the overall risk framework of financial services firms. It is not limited to simple compliance with laws and regulations; it also encompasses sound fiduciary principles, prudent ethical standards, client documents, internal policies and procedures, and other contractual obligations.

Some examples of issues that could raise an institution's level of compliance risk are:

- substandard account acceptance and review processes
- shortcomings in the ethical culture and expertise of management and staff
- weak internal compliance systems and training programmes.

The compliance function has the same dilemma as the risk function – the need to be an adviser of the business on the one hand and the need to monitor relevant activities on the other. Compliance teams need to find a careful balance between the fundamentally different mindsets and approaches required by the proactive 'trusted adviser' versus the more reactive 'independent watchdog'. The independent watchdog will report deviations to an appropriate level of management or, if appropriate, to the board of directors.

Effective compliance risk management is a collaborative process that involves all the various control functions within the organisation, such as risk management, internal control, fraud detection, legal and human resources. For example, the risk management function could help to detect potential compliance risks by identifying visible lapses that might indicate a more pervasive pattern of non-compliant behaviour 'below the water line'. The human resources function would be involved in its role as the expert in managing people, communicating expected behaviours, designing appropriate appraisal and reward structures and determining disciplinary measures.

2.5.8 How Compliance and Risk Management Protect and Add Value

When firms embark on new areas of business or launch new products, they very often justify the strategy with a cost/benefit analysis. Such analysis compares the estimated likely revenues with the projected costs. If the former outweighs the latter, then the project is given the green light. Firms recognise that the value of such analysis is dependent upon accurate projections of both the costs and benefits and will strive to improve the accuracy of these numbers.

However, aside from the risk of poor projections, establishing new areas of business exposes a firm to additional risks – with the potential risk that the business sponsor within the firm may overlook the significance or scale of some risks. Certain risks, such as client litigation, can vastly overshadow the operational costs of supporting the venture. The same is true for compliance risks; it can be costly to use up a great deal of resource on a new business project and then find the product design is not compliant or the launch has to be delayed because authorisations are required.

If risk and compliance management staff are involved in the development process from the start, they will be able to advise on the likelihood and impact of any risks, including compliance risks. Ideally, this would take place at an early enough stage that mitigation can be built into the solution. Over time, this approach will protect and add value to the firm.

3. Compliance Risks

Learning Objectives

5.2.7 Know the BIS definition of 'compliance risk'

5.2.8 Know who BIS deem responsible for the management of compliance risk

5.2.9 Know what measures BIS state should be undertaken to manage compliance risk: formalised document establishing the compliance function; board approval; annual review

The expression 'compliance risk' is defined by the BIS as:

> *'the risk of legal or regulatory sanctions, material financial loss, or loss to reputation a firm may suffer as a result of its failure to comply with laws, regulations, rules, related self-regulatory organisation standards, and codes of conduct applicable to its banking activities (together, compliance laws, rules and standards)'.*

Compliance laws, rules and standards generally cover matters such as observing proper standards of market conduct, managing conflicts of interest, treating customers fairly, and ensuring the suitability of customer advice. They typically include specific areas such as the prevention of money laundering and terrorist financing and may extend to tax laws that are relevant to the structuring of banking products or customer advice. A firm that knowingly participates in transactions intended to be used by customers to avoid regulatory or financial reporting requirements, evade tax liabilities, or facilitate illegal conduct will be exposing itself to significant compliance risk.

Compliance laws, rules and standards have various sources. These include primary legislation, rules and standards issued by legislators and supervisors, market conventions, codes of practice promoted by industry associations, and internal codes of conduct applicable to the staff members of the firm. For the reasons mentioned above, these are likely to go beyond what is legally binding and embrace broader standards of integrity and ethical conduct.

While the board of directors is responsible for overseeing the management of the firm's compliance risk, the BIS deems the firm's senior management as responsible for the effective management of that risk, for establishing and communicating a compliance policy, for ensuring that it is observed, and for reporting to the board of directors on the management of the firm's compliance risk. Further details can be found in chapter 2, section 1.1.

3.1 Using Technology to Aid the Management of Compliance Risks

Learning Objective

5.2.10 Understand how technology can be utilised to enhance compliance risk assessment

A framework of technology tools can be used to aid the compliance function in the assessment of risks. Here are some examples of the ways in which technology can help the compliance function:

1. Prevention – ensuring that compliance requirements are built into line-of-business applications, such as workflow and image systems. An example would be to include prompts relating to anti-money laundering checks when new business applications are being processed.
2. Detection systems and reports which identify exceptions and specific types of transactions. These could aid the oversight of high-risk trades or enable the identification of politically exposed persons or sanctions list matches.
3. Recording incidents, control failures, breaches and complaints to meet record-keeping requirements; and the production of management information (MI) to identify trends in error rates. This will help to identify at an early stage any systemic problems that may arise.
4. Online regulatory information systems, providing up-to-date information on regulatory changes and industry developments, including regulator and supervisory actions. This will include information on any systemic risks identified.
5. Effective online training and refresher courses on key aspects, including financial crime prevention, treating customers fairly and handling complaints. The results of online testing can demonstrate any gaps in knowledge which may give rise to a compliance risk.

3.2 The Impact of Technology on Regulatory Risk

Learning Objective

5.2.11 Understand how technology changes impact regulatory risk: cyber crime; FinTech; RegTech; Cloud data housing

The advance of technology significantly alters the way in which financial services operate, and has provided opportunities for new entrants to the market. It does, however, also have an impact on regulatory risk, specifically in the areas of cybercrime, Fintech and Regtech.

3.2.1 Cyber Crime

Cyber crime is defined as a crime in which a computer is the object of the crime (hacking, phishing or spamming) or is used as a tool to commit an offence (child pornography or hate crimes). Criminals may use computer technology to access personal information, business trade secrets or use the internet for exploitive or malicious purposes. Criminals can also use computers for communication and document or data storage. Criminals who perform these illegal activities are often referred to as hackers.

Some common cyber threats for individuals are phishing, file hijacking, key logging, screenshot manager, and ad-clicker. Common cyber threats for businesses are hacking, Distributed Denial of Service (DDoS) attacks, and invoice fraud.

The National Cyber Crime Unit (NCCU) is the part of the National Crime Agency (NCA) that helps fight cyber crime in the UK. See the websites below for more information about the NCCU:

https://nationalcrimeagency.gov.uk/what-we-do/crime-threats/cyber-crime

https://nationalcrimeagency.gov.uk/who-we-are/publications/178-the-cyber-threat-to-uk-business-2017-18/file

3.2.2 Fintech

Financial technology, or Fintech, refers to the use of new technology to advance or change the financial sector. Common examples of Fintech include:

- cryptocurrency and digital cash
- blockchain technology
- smart contracts
- open banking
- financial inclusion
- cyber security.

Regulatory sandboxes are typically run by a regulator to allow businesses to test innovative products, services, business models and delivery mechanisms in the real market, with real consumers.

Example – Financial Conduct Authority (FCA)

The FCA's sandbox is open to authorised firms, unauthorised firms that require authorisation and technology businesses. The sandbox seeks to provide firms with:

- the ability to test products and services in a controlled environment
- reduced time-to-market at potentially lower cost
- support in identifying appropriate consumer protection safeguards to build into new products and services
- better access to finance.

The sandbox also offers tools such as restricted authorisation, individual guidance, informal steers, waivers and no enforcement action letters.

Tests are closely overseen using a customised regulatory environment for each test – including safeguards for consumers.

Sandbox tests are expected to have a clear objective (eg, reducing costs to consumers) and to be conducted on a small scale, so firms will test their innovation for a limited duration with a limited number of customers.

Example – Hong Kong Monetary Authority (HKMA)

The FinTech Supervisory Sandbox (FSS), launched by the HKMA in September 2016, allows banks and their partnering technology firms (tech firms) to conduct pilot trials of their Fintech initiatives involving a limited number of participating customers without the need to achieve full compliance with the HKMA's supervisory requirements. This arrangement enables banks and tech firms to gather data and user feedback so that they can make refinements to their new initiatives, thereby expediting the launch of new technology products, and reducing the development cost.

3.2.3 Regtech

Regtech, short for regulatory technology, is the use of technology to facilitate the delivery of regulatory requirements. Although the link between regulation and technology is not new, it is becoming more important with the increased levels of regulation and a focus on data and reporting. In addition, Regtech addresses the changes in financial services associated with dynamic Fintech which has driven a different way of undertaking financial services which need to be addressed by regulations. The disruption caused by Fintech will require a different, potentially significantly more data-intensive approach from regulators. Regtech is expected to incorporate automated analysis and real-time data provision as well as enhanced AML checking. The use of biometrics and social media changes how due diligence may be undertaken.

3.2.4 Cloud Data Hosting

Cloud data hosting agreements allow the data owner (eg, a financial institution) to store their data on a network of connected virtual and physical servers known as a cloud. The advantages are that the institution does not require in-house servers, the resources can be scaled to meet the needs of the user and the institution only pays for what they use. Cloud data hosting may, however, raise security issues, particularly in relation to sensitive data. Regulators usually consider cloud data hosting to be a form of outsourcing, and apply the outsourcing regulations. Within the EU, the General Data Protection Regulation (GDPR) in relation to data processors and data controllers, applies to cloud data hosting.

End of Chapter Questions

Think of an answer for each question and refer to the appropriate section for confirmation.

1. What is corporate governance?
   Answer reference: Section 1.1

2. What can lead markets to lose confidence in the ability of a bank to properly manage its assets and liabilities?
   Answer reference: Section 1.1

3. What is the definition of corporate governance according to the Organisation for Economic Co-operation and Development (OECD) Principles?
   Answer reference: Section 1.1

4. Name the board structure typically found in Germany.
   Answer reference: Section 1.4

5. What board structure is categorised by one single board comprising both executive and non-executive directors?
   Answer reference: Section 1.4

6. What is the difference between unitary and dual boards?
   Answer reference: Section 1.4

7. Define a silo structure.
   Answer reference: Section 1.5.2

8. Name the four elements of the concept of independence for compliance functions.
   Answer reference: Section 1.5.3

9. How can senior management enhance the ability of internal audit to identify problems with a bank's risk management systems?
   Answer reference: Section 1.6

10. Name five examination areas used when conducting due diligence on a hedge fund.
    Answer reference: Section 1.7

11. Name three of the key areas where the Basel Committee on Banking Supervision (BCBS) believes the greatest focus is necessary.
    Answer reference: Section 1.9

12. Name three of the Bank for International Settlements (BIS) principles for enhancing corporate governance.
    Answer reference: Section 1.9

13. What is the difference between risk and uncertainty?
Answer reference: Section 2.1

14. Name two external risks.
Answer reference: Section 2.2

15. What are the three main ways in which political change can affect the financial services sector?
Answer reference: Section 2.2.2

16. Risks can arise from external stakeholders, such as a parent company. Name two other external stakeholders that can also be a source of risk for a business.
Answer reference: Section 2.2.6

17. What is the key to managing stakeholder risk?
Answer reference: Section 2.2.6

18. What is gearing and how does it increase risk?
Answer reference: Section 2.3.3

19. What are the aims of risk management?
Answer reference: Section 2.4

20. Explain PESTLE analysis.
Answer reference: Section 2.5.1

21. How do you calculate a risk score?
Answer reference: Section 2.5.1

22. When assessing and scoring a risk, two aspects are considered. One is its likelihood. What is the other?
Answer reference: Section 2.5.1

23. What is a SWOT analysis?
Answer reference: Section 2.5.2

24. What is meant by a firm's risk appetite?
Answer reference: Section 2.5.3

25. Name four risk register column headings.
Answer reference: Section 2.5.4

26. What is the difference between compliance and risk management?
Answer reference: Section 2.5.7

27. Give three examples of issues that could raise an institution's level of compliance risk.
Answer reference: Section 2.5.7

28. What is the definition of compliance risk?
Answer reference: Section 3

29. Name five ways in which technology can help the compliance function.
Answer reference: Section 3.1 Prevention, detection, effective online training

30. What is cybercrime?
Answer reference: Section 3.2.1 Hacking, Phishing, Spamming. Computer is tool in which to commit offence

31. Describe FinTech and RegTech.
Answer reference: Sections 3.2.2 and 3.2.3 Use of technology to aid a or change financial sector, Technology is use to facilitate the delivery of regulatory requirement

32. What are the issues with cloud data hosting?
Answer reference: Section 3.2.4 GDPR data breaches.

Appendices

Appendix 1 – Compliance Manual – An Example of the Contents

Table of Contents

Appendix 2 – Sample Checklist of Regulatory Requirements for Outsourcing

A firm must:

1. when relying on a third party for the performance of operational functions which are critical for the performance of regulated activities, on a continuous and satisfactory basis, ensure that it takes reasonable steps to avoid undue additional operational risk
2. not undertake the outsourcing of important operational functions in such a way as to impair materially:
   a. the quality of its internal control, and
   b. the ability of the Regulator to monitor the firm's compliance with all obligations under the regulatory system.

A firm should have effective processes to identify, manage, monitor and report risks and internal control mechanisms.

If a firm outsources critical or important operational functions or any relevant services and activities, it remains fully responsible for discharging all of its obligations under the regulatory system and must comply, in particular, with the following conditions:

1. the outsourcing must not result in the delegation by senior personnel of their responsibility
2. the relationship and obligations of the firm towards its clients under the regulatory system must not be altered
3. the conditions with which the firm must comply in order to be authorised, and to remain so, must not be undermined, and
4. none of the other conditions subject to which the firm's authorisation was granted must be removed or modified.

A firm must exercise due skill, care and diligence when entering into, managing or terminating any arrangement for the outsourcing to a service provider of critical or important operational functions or of any relevant services and activities.

A firm must in particular take the necessary steps to ensure that the following conditions are satisfied:

1. the service provider must have the ability, capacity, and any authorisation required by law to perform the outsourced functions, services or activities reliably and professionally
2. the service provider must carry out the outsourced services effectively, and to this end the firm must establish methods for assessing the standard of performance of the service provider
3. the service provider must properly supervise the carrying-out of the outsourced functions, and adequately manage the risks associated with the outsourcing
4. appropriate action must be taken if it appears that the service provider may not be carrying out the functions effectively and in compliance with applicable laws and regulatory requirements, and
5. the firm must retain the necessary expertise to supervise the outsourced functions effectively and to manage the risks associated with the outsourcing, and must supervise those functions and manage those risks

6. the service provider must disclose to the firm any development that may have a material impact on its ability to carry out the outsourced functions effectively and in compliance with applicable laws and regulatory requirements
7. the firm must be able to terminate the arrangement for the outsourcing where necessary without detriment to the continuity and quality of its provision of services to clients
8. the service provider must cooperate with the Regulator and any other relevant competent authority in connection with the outsourced activities
9. the firm, its auditors, the Regulator and any other relevant competent authority must have effective access to data related to the outsourced activities, as well as to the business premises of the service provider; and the Regulator and any other relevant competent authority must be able to exercise those rights of access
10. the service provider must protect any confidential information relating to the firm and its clients
11. the firm and the service provider must establish, implement and maintain a contingency plan for disaster recovery and periodic testing of back-up facilities where that is necessary having regard to the function, service or activity that has been outsourced.

A firm must ensure that the respective rights and obligations of the firm and of the service provider are clearly allocated and set out in a written agreement.

A firm must make available on request to the Regulator and any other relevant competent authority all information necessary to enable the Regulator and any other relevant competent authority to supervise the compliance of the performance of the outsourced activities with the requirements of the regulatory system.

A firm should notify the Regulator when it intends to rely on a third party for the performance of operational functions which are critical or important for the performance of relevant services and activities on a continuous and satisfactory basis. In some countries prior approval may be required, and permission may be limited geographically or for certain activities may be denied.

Appendix 3 – Proforma Monitoring Report

Evaluation of Compliance and Controls for:

Area/Process/Activity [eg, Charities Dealing]

Period Covered [Q1 2020]

Overall Report Rating Level:

G

The controls in place adequately address all significant risks identified and are operating effectively

Risk & Compliance Monitor: [Manager]

Report Addressed to: [The executive/senior manager of the area concerned]

Board Directors	Group Executives or Senior Management	Key UK Recipients	Internal Audit
[A. Brown]	[B. Jones]	[C Shah]	[D. Patel]

Risk & Compliance Reviewing Manager: [Team Leader]

Copies to:
File Reference: [File location online]

Version: [Final Draft]

Date Published: [29/3/20]

Contents

Part A – Executive Summary

Introduction

This report sets out the findings of the Monitoring Team review of Dealing. Xxxxxx, Compliance Manager carried out the Compliance Monitoring work in Q1 2021.

Compliance Monitoring Opinion

Red	Amber	Green
		G

Prior Compliance Monitoring Opinion

Charities Dealing was last reviewed in Q3 2020, Green rating.

Level One Recommendations

None.

Rationale Supporting the Compliance Opinion

To ensure RAG ratings are applied consistently across all business areas, each Level 1, 2 and 3 recommendation will have a numeric value applied. The total will determine the overall RAG rating.

Level 1 recommendation 25 points.

Level 2 recommendation 5 points.

Level 3 recommendation 2 points.

The total of the scores applied are added together to determine the overall review status.

0-19 will receive a Green review, 20-49 Amber and 50 or over will be Red.

These scoring rules will serve as a guide, which will be applied in the main, but the Compliance Monitoring Team reserve the right to modify a RAG rating where they are able to provide an overriding rationale.

The controls in place adequately address all significant risks identified and are operating effectively.

The review identified:

No Level 1 recommendations

One Level 2 recommendation

Two Level 3 recommendations

No Observations

Business Area Executive Summary

Evaluation of the Control Environment

Process Overview:

Sample Size:

A total of (xx) work items were reviewed during the sampling period 1st October – 31st December 2020 across four client companies.

Staffing Levels:

Charities Dealing operates under the Executive Management of (name of executive).

The team consists of (13) staff:

One Senior Manager (T&C Regulatory Supervisor)

Three Managers (one T&C Regulatory Supervisor and two T&C Overseers)

(x) Team Leaders

(x) Senior Administrators

(x) Two Administrators

(The experience within the team ranges from two months to ten years.

There are two T&C Regulatory Supervisors and two T&C Overseers within the team. One Overseer is classed as Competent and one classed as a Trainee. There are two T&C Successors, both classed as trainees. One T&C file was reviewed and no exceptions were identified.)

Controls:

Checklists across all companies were reviewed for one individual day per month over the three months of the sampling period. The Duplicate Deals Report, Non-End Report, Deal Timing Report, Large Deals Report, Exceptions Report, Cancelled/Rebooked Deals Report, Cancelled Deals Report, Failed Correspondence Misc Report & Backdated Deals Report were also reviewed for each of these days and no exceptions were identified.

Control Certification has been reviewed across all companies during the sampling period. Postal Dealing UK raised one high issue and 31 low issues. All controls were reviewed and no exceptions were identified.

Procedures were reviewed and some exceptions were identified.

The Risk Assessment was reviewed and no exceptions were identified.

The Knowledge Base was reviewed and no exceptions were identified.

Breaches/Complaints:

(x) Breaches were recorded against the process during the sampling period, affecting two companies. One Deal was booked late and one Deal booked the wrong amount.

100% of breaches were sampled to check that the resolution had been actioned. No exceptions were identified.

No Data Protection Breaches were recorded against the process during the sampling period.

No Complaints were recorded against the process during the sampling period.

(xxx) pieces of work were completed during the sampling period.

Breach rate/Complaints rate (xx) (xx)

Recommendations:

There were four recommendations and no observations identified within this review.

There are no Level 1 recommendations.

There are two Level 2 recommendations.

- Xxxxxxxx
- Xxxxxxxx

There are two Level 3 recommendations:

- X
- X

There were no observations made.

Acknowledgements

Compliance Monitoring would like to thank the Charities Dealing Department for their help in completing this report.

Part B – Recommendations

Level One Recommendations

There are no Level 1 recommendations

Level Two Recommendations

Rationale		**Recommendation**			
Charities Dealing: [issue] **[details of the issue found]** **This issue affected [xxxx] company:**		[eg, Breach to be recorded] **Management response and comment** Breach raised [comment re action taken and feedback]			
Monitoring Recommendation Number	[000]	Responsibility	[Exec Director]	Status/Deadline	Closed

Level Three Recommendations

Rationale		**Recommendation**			
		 Management response and comment 			
Monitoring Recommendation Number	1315	Responsibility	B Jones	Status/Deadline	30/06/21

Observations made.

- Xxxxx
- Xxxxx
- Xxxxx
- Xxxxx

Appendix 4 – Regulator Enforcement Procedure

The diagram below shows the typical course of regulatory enforcement proceedings in the UK, as instituted by the Financial Conduct Authority (FCA):

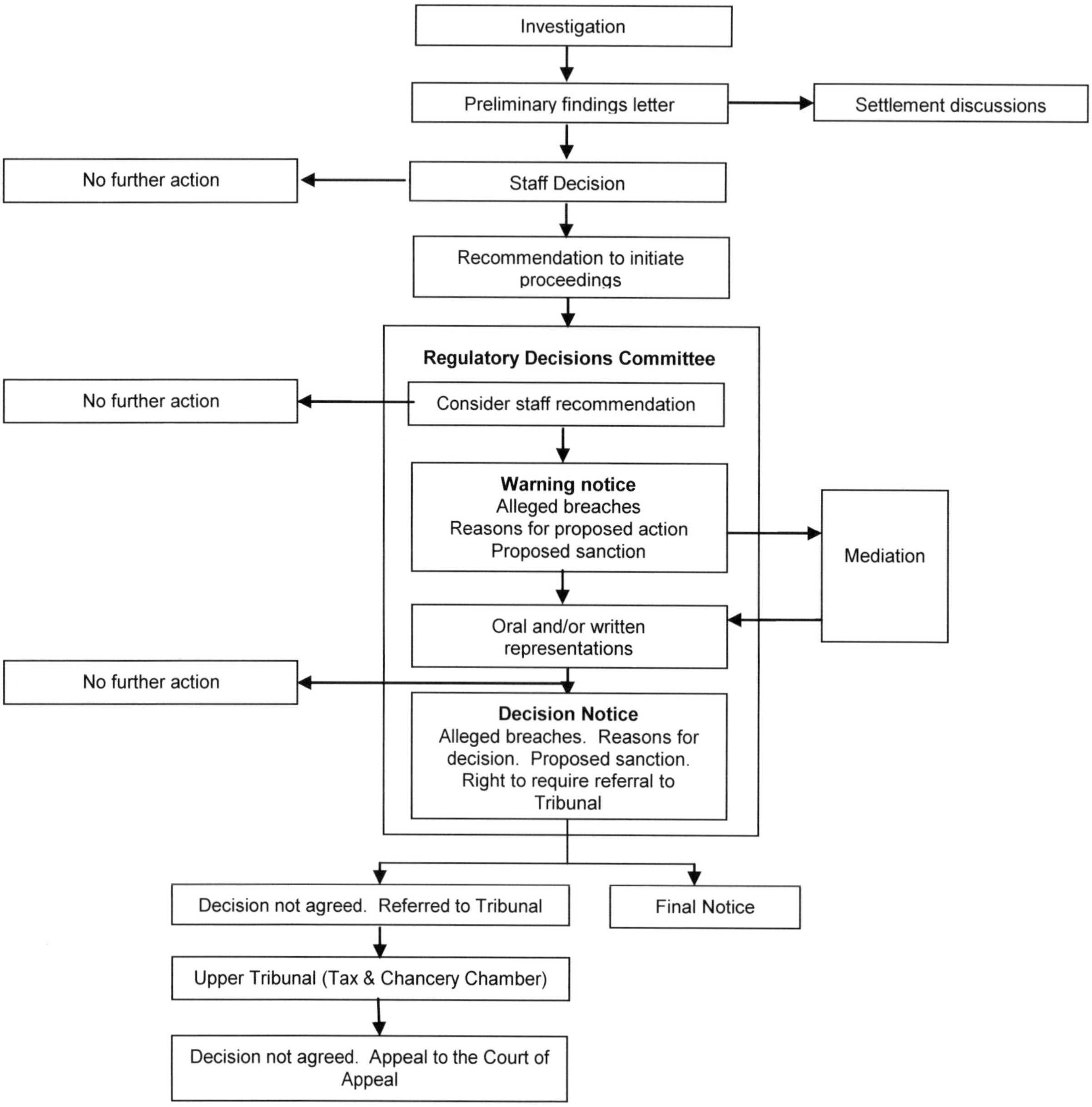

Appendix 5 – Case Study: Global Standards

Background

You are the Marketing Director of a UK-based international Fund Management Group which provides a range of collective funds sold mainly in the UK and Europe, where increasing competition has required ever greater marketing efforts and the development of innovative, new fund offerings.

One such new fund invests in high-tech companies located in and serving developing nations and uses some innovative derivative techniques to leverage performance, which has been very promising, although rather volatile.

As a result of UK regulatory requirements, detailed disclosure has been necessary in marketing and sales literature, to inform potential investors of the significant risks, including the volatility, to which the fund is subject. You consider that these explicit disclosures have constrained sales of what you are advised is, inherently, a sound fund.

The policy of your Group is that each group company must comply with the laws and regulations of the country in which they operate. There are no Group-wide standards.

The Situation

Faced with increasing competition and stringent regulatory requirements within the UK and European Union (EU), one of your team suggests that this high-tech fund be promoted, via your Asian subsidiaries, to potential investors in countries in that region where regulatory requirements are less demanding.

On researching this idea, you find that there are several countries in the region where there appears to be growing demand for similar investments and where the local regulatory requirements do not require specific disclosure of the degree of risk or of the likely volatility of the fund. Furthermore, you ascertain that in two of these particular countries there is no equivalent to the UK Financial Services Compensation Scheme (FSCS).

An additional attraction of the fund is that it invests in a number of high-tech companies which are located in the region where you are considering increasing your promotion.

Your research also reveals that one of your principal competitors has enjoyed recent success in promoting one of its funds in this region, without any apparent problems arising from regulators or investors. Their fund also seems to be relatively high-risk, but this factor is not prominent in their marketing literature. This seems to be an attractive marketing opportunity; what would you do?

Specific Factors to Consider

In favour of increased promotional and sales activity are:

- This is an inherently sound fund in a region where there is growing demand and where the fund invests directly.
- There are no legal or regulatory requirements for your subsidiary to make the detailed risk and volatility disclosures that may have hindered marketing in the UK.
- There are no investor compensation arrangements to worry about.
- A competitor is, apparently, enjoying success without any problems.

On the other hand:

- Benign regulatory requirements in the region might change.
- The volatile performance of the fund means that the possibility of loss, as well as profit, by investors is higher than is normally acceptable.
- Foreign investors would be treated less favourably than home investors.
- In the event of losses by unsophisticated investors in this unrestricted fund, there might be a significant public backlash.
- Such a situation might damage your Group's reputation.

Ethical Deliberations

Your first consideration might be whether it is actually ethical for your Group to selectively adopt weaker local legal/regulatory requirements rather than the higher standards required in your home country.

Should it be a matter for each subsidiary board as to the level at which it sets its ethical standards?

In the event that the fund loses money and your firm considers that it is in its interests to compensate UK investors, notwithstanding the risk warning given, would you be comfortable that a less generous approach is taken towards investors in a different regulatory environment?

How much should the fact that a competitor, possibly with less rigorous standards, is taking advantage of a particular situation, influence your recommendation?

Recommendation

For a group with international or global representation, the absence of a group standard can be corrosive of standards, which are likely to gravitate towards the acceptance of the lowest standard.

However, in devising group standards it should be recognised that the standards accepted in the 'home' state are not necessarily the 'best' and higher standards may apply elsewhere. Additionally, there may be a distinction between minimum acceptable commercial standards and regulatory requirements.

Accordingly, by adopting the positions first, that a minimum group standard should apply and, secondly, that this should require the adoption of the higher of local standards or minimum group standards, the answer in this case would be that investors overseas should be subject to the same protections as are offered to UK investors, notwithstanding that the opportunity exists to get away with lower standards.

CISI Principles Applicable

1. To act honestly and fairly at all times when dealing with clients.
2. To act with integrity in fulfilling your responsibilities.
3. To observe applicable law, regulations and professional conduct standards according to principles rooted in trust, honesty and integrity.
4. To strive to uphold the highest personal standards, including rejecting short-term profits which may jeopardise your reputation and that of your employer.

Appendix 6 – Principles of Good Practice for the Handling of Inside Information

1. **Policies and procedures**

Policies and procedures for the use and control of inside information should be established and reviewed from time to time. These should recognise the responsibility to control access to inside information and reduce risk of misuse. There should be clear responsibility within organisations for overseeing controls and procedures in relation to inside information.

2. **Awareness and training**

Appropriate measures should be taken, including training, to assist staff in understanding the importance of keeping information secret and the implications of improper disclosure – including the potential civil and criminal liabilities for the firm and the individual. Ensuring policies are capable of being readily understood by all relevant staff is an important part of this approach.

3. **'Need to know' and other information controls**

Reasonable steps should be taken to limit the number of those with access to inside information. Where practicable a 'need to know' policy should be applied.

4. **Passing price-sensitive information to third parties**

Reasonable care should be taken to ensure that where inside information is provided to a third party, the third party is aware of its obligations in relation to the use and control of the information.

5. **Information technology security**

Appropriate consideration should be given to the security of and access to inside information on IT systems, including the implementation of controls to limit access.

6. **Personal accounting policies**

Reasonable consideration should be given to establishing personal account (PA) dealing policies; those policies should be made clear to staff along with the civil and criminal penalties for dealing on the basis of inside information or for enabling such dealing.

The principles and the practice suggestions in the annex are not a substitute for the relevant laws and regulations nor are they intended to have any legal effect or to be used by the FCA or other regulators: their objective is simply to help raise standards generally in relation to the use and control of inside information.

Suggested Policies and Procedures for the Handling of Inside Information

1. **Policies and procedures**

A firm's policies and procedures for the use and control of inside information should be established and reviewed from time to time. These should recognise the responsibility to control access to inside information and reduce risk of misuse. There should be clear responsibility within organisations for overseeing controls and procedures in relation to inside information.

Good practice points to be considered include:

- Appoint a senior person with responsibility for maintaining good practice procedures; ensure they are trained and resourced and see that all members of staff know who this person is.
- Maintain documented policies on price-sensitive information handling that are regularly reviewed and updated.
- Conduct an internal review of the operation of policies, systems and procedures at least annually.
- Ensure that insider lists are complete, accurate and regularly updated.
- Have in place a policy on external contact enquiries, particularly with the media.
- Staff policies:
    - maintain procedures making it easy to report and discuss sensitive information being handled inappropriately
    - when staff who hold sensitive information leave a firm or change roles, conduct an 'exit interview' during which the leaver is reminded of the ongoing confidentiality of inside information
    - a policy on introducing temporary or contract staff to company policies regarding inside information
    - undertake staff vetting such as criminal record checks and references from previous employers
    - employment contracts to make staff aware of their duty of care regarding insider information together with the employer's right to access email, phone and other communication records as part of the employer's policy with regard to insider dealing.

2. **Awareness and training**

Appropriate measures should be taken, including training, to assist staff in understanding the importance of keeping information secret and the implications of improper disclosure – including the potential civil and criminal liabilities for the firm and the individual. Ensuring policies are capable of being readily understood by all relevant staff is an important part of this approach.

Good practice points for consideration include:

- Foster a culture that respects the sensitivity of inside information and establishes an awareness of the penalties for its abuse.
- Have a dedicated training responsibility.
- Hold induction training, as well as refresher training, for all staff regardless of position (including support staff).
- As new rules come into force, maintain an 'update' system.
- Test awareness and understanding from time to time.
- Maintain training records and review the process annually.

3. **'Need to know' and other information controls**

Reasonable steps should be taken to limit the number of individuals with access to inside information.

Where practicable, a 'need to know' policy should be applied.

Good practice points for consideration include:

- A policy for making someone an insider, including only passing inside information to colleagues if they are first alerted to their responsibilities regarding the information.
- Limit the number of insiders to a practical minimum and introduce a requirement to justify adding people to the insider list ('need to know' criteria).

- Communicate to other insiders when someone is removed from an insider list.
- Where practicable, separate deal teams from other parts of the business.
- Security of price-sensitive information:
  - have a policy on secure disposal of confidential documents/soft copy
  - monitor and enforce a clear desk policy to reduce the risk of non-insiders seeing papers left on desks (eg, contract cleaning companies)
  - maintain formal, written procedures for staff working off-site
  - use code names disguising the identities of relevant parties that are effective and not obvious
  - discourage staff reading or working on sensitive papers in public and discussing sensitive matters in public (eg, in taxis)
  - require staff working on deals only to discuss deals in meeting rooms
  - control the email distribution of sensitive information, ensuring the regular use of passwords on documents
  - control the hard copy distribution of papers (eg, numbered copies or bar codes on documents);
  - ensure hard copy sensitive information is stored in lockable cabinets and soft copy securely stored also,
  - use restricted access systems in work and IT systems areas where sensitive information is handled.

4. **Passing price-sensitive information to third parties**

Reasonable care should be taken to ensure that where inside information is provided to a third party, the third party is aware of its obligations in relation to the use and control of the information.

Good practice points for consideration include:

- Maintain formal, written procedures when adding third parties to the information chain, formally making them insiders and spelling out the responsibilities inherent in handling the information.
- Obtain comfort that third parties appreciate the importance of safeguarding inside information and have appropriate procedures in place.
- Consider the third party's suitability as a recipient.
- Include third parties in the information chain as late as practical in the process.
- Orally explain responsibilities rather than simply exchanging standard confidentiality letters.

5. **Information technology security**

Appropriate consideration should be given to the security and access to inside information on IT systems, including the implementation of controls to limit access.

IT configurations will differ significantly between service providers and some of the following may not be applicable; however good practice points for consideration include:

- Where practical, restrict IT access only to named individuals in preference to a company-wide, open IT access.
- The use of a secure 'data room' with a robust portal restricted to named individuals.
- IT and other management support considered as insiders to comply with appropriate policies.
- Once a member of staff leaves or changes roles, the individual's IT access is to be removed.
- Employ 'ethical hackers' to check the robustness of IT systems and keep abreast of any new methods of data theft.
- Use code names and passwords for IT files and folders, including email subject lines.

- Password-protect all electronic equipment.
- Laptops, smartphones and such devices to have automatic locking after brief periods.
- Technology to generate an audit trail of access to sensitive files.
- Restrict emails with sensitive information going to personal websites.
- Maintain procedures for 'fat finger' errors on emails, letters or faxes (recalling emails quickly and IT check showing if emails have been opened).
- Use virtual private networks for staff who need access to system when working off-site.

6. **Personal accounting policies**

Reasonable consideration should be given to establishing PA dealing policies; those policies should be made clear to staff along with the civil and criminal penalties for dealing on the basis of inside information or for enabling such dealing.

Good practice points for consideration include:

- Maintain a formal, written procedure regarding PA dealing for all members of staff, ensuring awareness of this (consider including it in employment contracts) and test compliance from time to time.
- Ensure that staff are aware that insider dealing is a criminal offence.
- Explicit reference in PA dealing policy to derivatives, related products, sector 'knock-on', etc.
- Policy covers dealings under power of attorney and by immediate family.
- Policy addresses approach to dealings through discretionary accounts or manager, having regard to the independence of discretionary manager dealings.
- Consider restricting staff or relevant staff members from dealing without permission from their immediate manager or compliance officer. Refusal may be given without further explanation.
- Restrict staff members of service providers from dealing in client companies. (This should not apply where assets are managed by others for a staff member on a discretionary basis without input from the person concerned.)
- Require staff to maintain updated declarations of their holdings.
- Keep a written log of permission requests and their outcomes, including risk-based records of staff trading against announcements.

Glossary

Anti-Money Laundering Directive (AMLD)

The European Union's (EU's) AMLD is aimed at preventing the use of the financial system for the purposes of money laundering or terrorist financing. Since the first directive was adopted in 1990, it has been updated a number of times to ensure it remains current. The AMLD is incorporated in the laws and regulations of all EU member states.

Appointed Representative

An appointed representative is an individual or an organisation that carries on certain regulated activities on behalf of an authorised firm under contract. The authorised person must have accepted in writing responsibility for the conduct of these regulated activities.

Authorisation

The requirement for firms to obtain authorisation from their regulator prior to conducting investment business.

Business Risk

The risk of loss due to an adverse external environment, such as high inflation affecting labour costs; an over-competitive market reducing margins or legal, tax or regulatory changes in the markets.

Central Bank

Central banks typically have responsibility for setting a country's or a region's short-term interest rate, controlling the money supply, acting as banker and lender of last resort to the banking system and managing the national debt.

Central Counterparty (CCP)

The guarantor of contracts normally, but not necessarily, for exchange-traded products. Usually the clearing house of an exchange.

Chinese Walls

Organisational barriers to the flow of information set up in large firms, to prevent the movement of confidential, sensitive information between departments and to manage any potential conflicts of interest.

Client

Individuals or firms that conduct business through an authorised person. Every client is either a customer (retail or professional) or an eligible counterparty.

Client Assets

Securities or other assets held by a firm on behalf of its clients. The assets have to be kept separate from the firm's own assets (segregated).

Compliance Risk

The risk to earnings or capital arising from violations; or non-conformance with laws, rules, regulations, prescribed practices or ethical standards.

Controlled Functions

Certain roles within authorised firms for which the Financial Conduct Authority (FCA) requires the role holder to be approved.

Credit Default Swap (CDS)

A bilateral financial contract in which one counterparty (the protection buyer) pays a periodic, or one-off fee (typically expressed in basis points on the notional amount), in return for a contingent payment by the other counterparty (the protection seller) following a credit event of a reference entity.

Credit Risk

The potential loss of earnings or capital due to an obligor's failure to meet the terms of a contract or otherwise failing to perform as agreed.

Dematerialised

The term used to describe stock which is held in electronic form rather than having ownership evidenced by way of paper certificates.

European Economic Area (EEA)

The 27 member states of the EU, plus Iceland, Liechtenstein and Norway.

European Securities and Markets Authority (ESMA)

The European body responsible for the regulation of investment firms and markets, and directly responsible for the regulation of credit rating agencies.

European Supervisory Authorities (ESAs)

Pan-European financial services regulatory bodies, each with responsibility for a different financial sector, introduced in early 2011. The three ESAs are the European Securities and Markets Authority (ESMA), the European Banking Authority (EBA) and the European Insurance and Occupational Pensions Authority (EIOPA).

European Union (EU) Directives

Legislation issued by the EU to its member states requiring them to enact and implement local legislation.

Financial Conduct Authority (FCA)

The FCA and the Prudential Regulation Authority (PRA) replaced the Financial Services Authority (FSA) in 2013. The FCA is the body responsible for regulating conduct in retail and wholesale markets, and supervising the trading infrastructure that supports those markets. The PRA provides prudential regulation and supervision of banks, building societies, insurers and major investment.

Future

A futures contract is a form of legally binding arrangement by which parties commit to buying/ selling a standard quantity and (if applicable) quality of an asset from/to another party on a specified date in the future, but at a price agreed today. Because the price is agreed at the outset, the seller is protected from a fall in the price of the underlying asset in the intervening time period (and vice versa).

Home State

The term used for the country where a financial services firm conducting cross-border business is based.

Host State

The term used for a country in which a financial services firm is doing business but is not based.

Inside Information

Information relating to a security, or an issuer, which is not publicly known and which would affect the price of the security if it were made public.

Insider Dealing

An offence which may be committed by an insider in possession of unpublished price-sensitive information if they attempt to deal in affected securities, encourage others to deal, or pass the information on.

Integration

The third stage of money laundering; integration is the stage at which the laundered funds appear to be of legitimate provenance.

Key Risk Indicators (KRIs)

Objective measurement criteria that measure a firm's ongoing risk status. **Know Your Client/ Customer (KYC)**

The Money Laundering Regulations and the FCA rules require firms to take sufficient steps, before taking on a client, to satisfy themselves as to the identity of that client.

Layering

The second stage of money laundering, in which money or assets are typically passed through a series of transactions to obscure their true origin.

Liquidity Risk

The risk that an institution will not be able to meet its liabilities as they become due because of an inability to liquidate assets or obtain enough funding, or because it cannot easily unwind or offset specific exposures without significantly lowering market prices because of inadequate market depth or market disruptions.

Market Abuse

Offences judged on what a regular user would view as a failure to observe required market standards. The offences include abuse of information, misleading the market, and distortion of the market.

Market Maker

A firm which quotes bid and offer prices for a named list of securities in the market. Such a firm is normally under an obligation to make a price in any security for which it is a market maker at all times.

Market Risk

The potential loss of earnings or capital arising from changes in the value of portfolios of financial instruments.

Markets in Financial Instruments Directive (MiFID)

An EU directive which replaced the Investment Services Directive (ISD) on 1 November 2007. It allows firms authorised in one member state to provide/offer financial services to customers in another member state, subject to some restrictions. The second MiFID Directive (MiFID II) was implemented in 2018.

Misleading Statement

The term used for false, misleading or incomplete information given about an investment, in order to (or with the effect of) affecting its value.

Money Laundering

The process whereby criminals attempt to conceal the true origins of the proceeds of their criminal activities, and to give them the appearance of legitimacy by introducing them into the mainstream financial system.

Money Laundering Regulations

The regulations under which authorised firms, and some other businesses, are required to comply with certain administrative obligations in order to prevent money laundering. The obligations include record-keeping, identification of clients, appointment of a nominated officer to receive suspicion reports, and staff training. Failure to comply may result in a fine and/or imprisonment.

Money Laundering Reporting Officer (MLRO)

A senior employee who is responsible for assessing internal suspicion reports, and if these appear justified, reporting those suspicions to a law enforcement agency.

Multilateral Trading Facilities (MTFs)

A system operated by authorised firms which brings together multiple buyers and sellers of securities, but which is not an exchange.

Nominated Officer

A term for the officer who is required to receive a firm's internal suspicion reports under the Proceeds of Crime Act (POCA) 2002, the Terrorism Act and the Money Laundering Regulations; in practice, this is usually the same individual as the MLRO.

Nominee

The party which, under a legal arrangement, holds assets in its own name on behalf of the true beneficial owner.

Operational Resilience

The ability to prevent, adapt, respond to, recover and learn from, operational disruptions.

Option

An option gives the holder the right (but not the obligation) to buy or sell a fixed quantity of an underlying asset on, or before, a specified date in the future. There are two basic types of option – puts and calls. The holder of a call option has the right to buy the underlying asset at a given price. The holder of a put option has the right to sell the underlying asset at a given price.

Permissions

Permissions are the specific activities which an authorised firm is permitted to carry on.

Placement

The first stage of money laundering in which money is introduced into the financial system.

Politically Exposed Person (PEP)

An individual who is or has, at any time, been entrusted with a prominent public function, or an individual who is closely related to such a person. May also be referred to as a senior foreign political figure.

Prudential Regulation Authority (PRA) Handbook

The document that contains the PRA rules, guidance and other provisions, with which PRA-authorised firms must comply. The Handbook is divided into a number of separate sourcebooks and manuals covering different subjects.

Quran

The central religious text of Islam and the primary source for jurists. The Book of Divine Revelation that was delivered to humankind by the Prophet Mohammed (PBUH).

Regulated Activities

Activities for which authorisation from a regulator is needed unless it is exempt from the need for authorisation. Regulated activities are often defined in relation both to the activities themselves, and to the investments to which they relate.

Robo-Advice

Digital platforms that provide automated financial planning services with little, or no, human intervention.

Securities and Exchange Commission (SEC)

The US SEC is an independent agency of the US federal government whose main responsibility is to enforce federal securities laws, proposing securities rules, and to regulate the securities industry.

Senior Manager and Certification Regime (SM&CR)

The SM&CR was introduced to the UK in 2015 with the aim of reducing damage to consumers and to strengthen market integrity. As part of the SM&CR, each senior manager must have a statement of responsibilities (SoR), setting out their roles and responsibilities. Senior managers and members of the board can be held directly and personally accountable if they did not take reasonable steps to prevent or stop a breach in regulatory requirements.

Stabilisation

The activity of supporting the price of a new issue of securities or bonds in order to minimise the volatility that can sometimes arise with new issues.

Strategic Risk

The risk of loss due to a suboptimal strategy being employed and associated with the way the institution is managed. For instance, a competitor or product strategy may be employed that fails to maximise the return on the investment made.

Stress Testing

A means of testing the accuracy of value at risk (VaR) models against 'extreme' market event scenarios.

Tipping Off

An offence established under various pieces of anti-money laundering and terrorist financing legislation. It involves disclosing the fact that an investigation is, or is likely to be, underway, if that disclosure may imperil any such investigation.

Trustee

A person or organisation who is the legal owner of assets held in trust for someone else. The trustee is responsible for safeguarding the assets, complying with the trust deed and (if the trust is a unit trust) overseeing the activities of the unit trust's manager.

UK Bribery Act 2010

Law applicable to all commercial organisations, making it an offence to offer or take bribes or negligently prevent bribery. It will be a defence for a firm if it can demonstrate that it has 'adequate procedures' to prevent such conduct by persons associated with it.

Value at Risk (VaR)

The maximum loss that can occur with a specified confidence over a specified period of days.

Whistleblowing

The term used when an individual raises concerns over potential wrongdoing. In some countries, legislation provides some statutory protections for whistleblowers.

Multiple Choice Questions

The following questions reflect the standard that you will experience in your examination. Please note, however, they are not the actual CISI examination questions.

1. Who is responsible for setting international standards to combat money laundering and terrorist financing?

   A. The Financial Action Task Force (FATF)

   B. The United Nations Office on Drugs and Crime (UNODC)

   C. The International Development Association (IDA)

   D. The International Bank for Reconstruction and Development (IBRD)

2. How are corporate governance standards usually monitored in financial firms?

   A. At an individual level according to individual ethical standards

   B. Through the compliance function

   C. Through the board

   D. Through the use of external vendors

3. Which of the following BEST describes the purpose of a compliance manual?

   A. It provides potential clients with an understanding of which regulations affect them

   B. It demonstrates that the company knows which regulations are relevant to its work

   C. It formally documents the standards to be followed by all employees

   D. It enables the compliance function to define how the business is performed

4. When regulators look at the culture of the firms they regulate, what are they looking for?

   A. Evidence that good behaviour is rewarded with higher bonuses

   B. Evidence of a compliance culture

   C. A high level of regulatory awareness

   D. Underlying values and ethics

5. Which of the following is not an International Organisation of Securities Commissions (IOSCO) objective of securities regulation?

   A. The protection of investors

   B: Ensuring that markets are fair, efficient, and transparent

   C: Ensuring engagement by firms in the development of regulations

   D: The reduction of systemic risk

6. Which of the following categorises a matrix structure of management?

   A. Each board director defines responsibility between the departments of their own function
   B. Different offices/locations will adopt different structures in performing equivalent functions
   C. The non-executive directors are specialised and oversee the work of a specific executive
   D. Some individuals are accountable to multiple executive managers

7. If a trader deliberately gives the misleading impression that demand for a particular share is greater than it really is, this type of behaviour is likely to be classed as:

   A. a conflict of interest
   B. whistleblowing
   C. money laundering
   D. market abuse

8. Which of the following statements is TRUE regarding a two-tier board?

   A. Such boards are common within the UK
   B. The management board appoints the members of the supervisory board
   C. The supervisory board oversees the work of the management board
   D. The management board includes three non-executive directors

9. To whom should an individual first report suspicion of money laundering?

   A. The regulator
   B. The police
   C. The nominated officer
   D. The customer

10. The European Systemic Risk Board (ESRB) is responsible for the:

   A. supervision of the European Central Bank (ECB)
   B. creation of a single EU rule book
   C. oversight of the financial system within the EU
   D. supervision of the European Banking Authority (EBA)

11. The Bank for International Settlements (BIS) Principle 4 for enhancing corporate governance places what obligation on the board of the parent company in a group structure?

    A. Appoint a chief compliance officer at group level, to ensure consistency of interpretation across different group companies

    B. Implement a conflicts of interest policy that prevents any director serving on the boards of more than two group companies

    C. Ensure that there are governance policies and mechanisms appropriate to the structure, business and risks of the group

    D. Ensure that the non-executive directors of the parent company have rights to attend the board meetings of all subsidiary companies

12. Which of the following BEST describes the difference between principles-based and rules-based approaches to financial regulation?

    A. A principles-based approach is more prescriptive than a rules-based approach

    B. A rules-based approach is more prescriptive than a principles-based approach

    C. A principles-based approach is less flexible than a rules-based approach

    D. A rules-based approach is less flexible than a principles-based approach

13. What does the Bank for International Settlements (BIS) define as 'the risk of loss arising from processes, people, systems, or external events'?

    A. Regulatory influence

    B. Operational risk

    C. Market risk

    D. Political risk

14. For which of the following activities is a firm subject to the Markets in Financial Instruments Directive (MiFID)?

    A. Providing investment advice without executing any trades

    B. Performing foreign exchange transactions

    C. Operating a collective investment scheme

    D. Owning shares listed in a different EU country

15. Which ONE of the following statements relating to best practice in compliance is TRUE?

    A. Compliance is the responsibility of specialist compliance staff alone

    B. Compliance is the sole concern of the board of directors

    C. Compliance is the sole concern of the senior management team

    D. Compliance is a concern of everyone in an organisation

16. If a firm has a new products committee, which of the following is considered best practice in terms of the relationship between that committee and the compliance department?

    A. The compliance department should be told of any issues that are relevant to them
    B. Compliance department staff should be asked to attend meetings when necessary
    C. Compliance department staff should be represented on the committee
    D. The committee should report directly to the head of compliance

17. Which one of the following is NOT an objective of self-regulation?

    A. Preservation of market integrity
    B. Reduction of systemic risk
    C. Investor protection
    D. Reduced government involvement

18. A Chinese wall is an arrangement made by a firm to:

    A. segregate duties between any controlled functions roles
    B. help manage conflicts of interest
    C. ensure bonus allocations between different departments are fair
    D. create a firewall that stops computer hackers from China

19. Which of the following instances of non-compliance with laws and regulations by an individual should the firm report to the regulator?

    A. Partaking in market abuse
    B. Regularly failing to pass annual refresher training
    C. Theft from colleagues
    D. Failure to pass appropriate external examinations

20. In respect of the Foreign Account Tax Compliance Act (FATCA) under the UK-US intergovernmental agreement, which of the following are UK foreign financial institutions required to do?

    A. Report monthly to the Internal Revenue Service (IRS) on account holders who are US persons or foreign entities
    B. Report annually to the IRS on account holders who are UK domiciled
    C. Report to Her Majesty's Revenue and Customs (HMRC) on account holders who are US persons or foreign entities
    D. Report monthly to HMRC on account holders who are UK domiciled

21. Which of the following aspects of risk is not applicable to uncertainty?

   A. Potential to occur

   B. Measurable

   C. Impact

   D. Consequences for decision-making

22. In the last few years, regulators have encouraged firms to adopt which ONE of the following types of culture in order to ensure they embody the values which underlie the whole regulatory structure?

   A. A pragmatic culture

   B. A compliance culture

   C. An ethical culture

   D. A charitable culture

23. What information should be provided to a client at point of sale?

   A. Terms and features of a product

   B. Details of how to make a complaint

   C. Details of the Financial Ombudsman Service (FOS)

   D. Expected and actual product performance

24. How often should a money laundering reporting officer (MLRO) or other responsible senior executive provide information to its governing body and senior management on the effectiveness of the anti-money laundering systems and controls?

   A. Every quarter

   B. Every six months

   C. At least annually

   D. Each time an incident occurs

25. Who does the Bank for International Settlements (BIS) deem responsible for overseeing the effective management of compliance risk?

   A. The board of directors

   B. The chief executive officer

   C. The compliance director

   D. The risk manager

(4)

26. Which of the following is TRUE in relation to continuing professional development (CPD)?

    A. The compliance function is not permitted to review CPD records of individuals because they concern personal development
    B. The individual responsible for compliance oversight must complete 50 hours each year
    C. Regulation requires that the compliance function approves all internal CPD material developed by the firm
    D. It can include reading industry update materials as well as attending seminars and conferences

27. What is the most damaging effect of poor corporate governance in the financial sector?

    A. Inappropriate bonus payments and rogue trader risk
    B. Loss of confidence in an institution's ability to properly manage its assets and liabilities
    C. Promotion and reward of unsuitable managers and directors
    D. Failure of the bank itself, creating job losses and loss of shareholder wealth

28. The Bank for International Settlements (BIS) defines what form of risk as 'the risk of loss arising from processes, people, systems, or external events'?

    A. Counterparty risk
    B. Financial risk
    C. Operational risk
    D. Technology risk

29. Irrespective of a firm's organisational structure, the compliance structure needs to be:

    A. operating independently
    B. sparsely resourced
    C. subject to Basel Committee on Banking Supervision (BCBS) monitoring
    D. an audit responsibility

30. What Act of Parliament defines UK-permitted business?

    A. Data Protection Act
    B. Regulation of Investigative Powers Act
    C. Proceeds of Crime Act
    D. Financial Services and Markets Act

31. Which of the following BEST describes the Islamic concept of *Riba*?

    A. Prohibition on giving/receiving interest

    B. Fairness

    C. Care for the environment at all times

    D. Profitability

32. Under the Sarbanes-Oxley Act (SOX), which two officials must ensure that internal controls and procedures can provide accurate financial disclosures?

    A. The compliance officer and the money laundering reporting officer (MLRO)

    B. The compliance officer and chief financial officer

    C. The chief executive officer and the chief financial officer

    D. The chief operating officer and the chief financial officer

33. Which of the following enables the board to enhance the ability of internal audit to identify problems with risk management systems?

    A. By setting internal examinations for internal audit staff

    B. By ensuring that the internal audit function reports to, or has access to, the board or the board's audit committee

    C. By requiring executive managers to respond to internal audit findings within one month of identification

    D. By requiring internal audit managers to spend three months performing operational tasks every three years

34. Under the Sarbanes-Oxley Act (SOX), what is the maximum punishment for defrauding securities investors?

    A. A fine of up to $1 million, plus gross business income for three years

    B. Up to seven years in prison

    C. Up to 25 years in prison

    D. There is no limit

35. Which of the following is a Markets in Financial Instruments Directive (MiFID) investment service?

    A. Running a pension scheme

    B. Being the depositary of an open-ended investment company (OEIC)

    C. Printing and distribution of product sales literature

    D. Operating a multilateral trading facility (MTF)

36. What action does the Foreign Account Tax Compliance Act (FATCA) require of US taxpayers holding financial assets outside the US?

A. They should report to the Inland Revenue Service (IRS) that the assets are held

B. They should advise the IRS when interest/savings income is received on assets held outside the US

C. They should sell the assets if/when instructed by the IRS

D. FATCA imposes no obligations on the US taxpayer

37. Which European Supervisory Authority (ESA) has direct supervisory responsibility for credit rating agencies?

A. European Banking Authority (EBA)

B. European Securities and Markets Authority (ESMA)

C. European Banking Committee (EBC)

D. European Insurance and Occupational Pensions Authority (EIOPA)

38. The effect of house price movements on a firm's mortgage business is an example of what type of risk?

A. Economic risk

B. Political risk

C. Technology risk

D. Operational risk

39. One purpose of capital adequacy standards is to:

A. prevent a regulated firm from having an overdrawn bank account

B. prevent a bank from supporting excessive overdrawn accounts

C. ensure market liquidity for trading purposes

D. provide time for supervisors to intervene if a firm experiences difficulties

40. In many countries, if a firm wishes to change the authorised business it can perform, which of the following should it submit?

A. Change of designation

B. Part III submission

C. CRD IV notice

D. Variation of permission

41. Which ONE of the following is a key difference between terrorist financing and other money laundering activities?

    A. Only the layering of funds is required
    B. Only quite small sums of money are often required to commit terrorist acts
    C. Terrorist funding rarely involves the transfer of funds between jurisdictions
    D. Terrorist groups do not tend to have links with other criminal activities

42. What stipulation is included in the Bank for International Settlements (BIS) Principle 5?

    A. The compliance function should be independent
    B. Staff should be vetted prior to hiring
    C. Continuing professional development (CPD) should be performed and evidenced
    D. Firms should not retain any benefit arising from regulatory breaches

43. If your firm is subject to a dawn raid, which of the following best describes the officials you should allow to enter the premises?

    A. Any member of the regulator's staff, providing that they have proof of identity and you verify it with the regulator concerned
    B. Any member of the regulator's staff (who will normally be accompanied by a police officer) named in the search warrant
    C. Any person named in the search warrant
    D. Only police officers

44. Which statement BEST describes the confidentiality surrounding suspicious activity reports (SARs)?

    A. The relevant client should be notified of the SAR
    B. Confidentiality is subject to the obligations to report a valid SAR
    C. General staff can be briefed regarding the control failure and resolution steps taken once the SAR has been submitted
    D. The money laundering reporting officer (MLRO) should advise the company's board about the SAR

45. Which of the following was a primary point of the Basel Committee's 2006 principles for enhancing corporate governance?

    A. Compensation policies should be consistent with the bank's long-term objectives
    B. Thematic complaints against the bank should be subject to board reporting each quarter
    C. The finance director should not have responsibility for the internal audit function
    D. All operational data input should be subject to review for accuracy

4

CISI
CHARTERED INSTITUTE FOR SECURITIES & INVESTMENT

46. Which of the following is a stage in a successful money laundering operation?

  A. Segregation
  B. Differentiation
  C. Integration
  D. Aggregation

47. Which of the following is the BEST description of 'layering'?

  A. The process of defining a Chinese wall
  B. Aggregating a firm's capital adequacy across a range of financial asset groupings
  C. The process of obtaining regulatory permissions
  D. Moving money around through a series of transactions to disguise the ultimate owner

48. Which of the following BEST describes a 'Ponzi' scheme?

  A. A loan to a client made on terms favourable to the client rather than the firm
  B. A fraudulent investment that uses a new investor's money to pay old investors a profit
  C. A type of scam in which investors are subjected to high-pressure selling tactics
  D. An investment vehicle featuring a high initial charge (known as a haircut)

49. Which of the following outcomes could arise for a regulated firm exposed to counterparty risk?

  A. The firm may be subject to regulatory penalty
  B. The firm may need to submit a suspicious activity report (SAR)
  C. The firm may need to replace its chief financial officer (CFO)
  D. The firm may suffer financial loss due to default

50. In which circumstances will a firm freeze the funds/assets it holds for a client?

  A. When a suspicious activity report (SAR) is raised regarding the client's account
  B. When a SAR is reported to a law enforcement agency (LEA) regarding the client's account
  C. When the client is identified as a politically exposed person (PEP)
  D. When the client is identified as a sanctioned individual

51. To what do the Lord George Principles relate?

  A. Financial accounting
  B. Integrity
  C. Prevention of financial crime
  D. Becoming an authorised firm

5

52. Which of the following is a document issued by the Organisation for Economic Co-operation and Development (OECD) that is of relevance to corporate social responsibility (CSR)?

    A. The Model Code of Ethics
    B. Convention on Combating Bribery
    C. Embedding Integrity
    D. Defence against Financial Crime

53. The Bank for International Settlements (BIS) definition of 'compliance risk' notes that a firm may suffer as a result of failure to comply with relevant laws, highlighting the risk of legal or regulatory sanctions, material financial loss, and what other consideration?

    A. Loss of reputation
    B. Loss of senior staff
    C. Loss of clients through regulatory action
    D. Loss of opportunity

54. Which of the following documents is most likely to give rise to concerns about misuse of inside information?

    A. A magazine article about recruitment highlighting staffing issues at a company
    B. Confidential government papers regarding a change to capital gains tax
    C. A paper listing possible implications of Greece leaving the euro currency
    D. Unpublished draft reports and accounts of a listed company

55. Which of the following does NOT need to be recorded on an insider list?

    A. The name of the person who identified the individual as being an insider
    B. The identity of each person who has access to inside information
    C. The reason why the person is on the insider list
    D. The date on which the insider list was created and updated

56. What can be described as a typical self-regulatory model?

    A. Industry to decide how best to regulate itself, no government intervention
    B. Combination of industry rules with government oversight
    C. Industry regulates itself, but the government decides appropriate qualifications for participants
    D. Industry takes responsibility for the implementation of government policy

57. Which of the following BEST describes due diligence?

A. A contractual obligation to provide monitoring reports to a client
B. The care a reasonable person should take before entering into an agreement or transaction
C. A financial payment to pay for second line of defence functions
D. The process by which a principles-based regulator oversees a firm

58. What actions should a firm take in respect of personal account (PA) dealing?

A. Ensure all staff use the firm's client money bank account to effect dealing
B. Ensure that all staff are invited to refresher training every 24 months
C. Install system-based controls to prevent individuals dealing in their own name
D. Ensure any outsourced service provider maintains records of transactions by relevant persons

59. Which of the following is a feature of a multilateral trading facility (MTF)?

A. It must deliver transparency pre-trade, though not post-trade
B. Firms use such facilities to execute trades for their clients against their own book or other clients
C. They must meet the standards required by the Accounting and Auditing Organization for Islamic Financial Institutions (AAOIF) and the Islamic Financial Services Board (IFSB)
D. Prices/charges are public and applied consistently across all members

60. Which of the following is an effect of the two-tier board structures?

A. The chairman needs to accept the views of the executive management
B. The firm must appoint three non-executive directors to ensure executive accountability
C. There is clear separation between the functions of supervision and management
D. The finance function is independent of the operational executives

61. Where is the Committee on Banking Supervision based?

A. The Hague
B. Brussels
C. Basel
D. Luxembourg

62. Why should a firm perform breach analysis?

A. It is a monthly regulatory requirement
B. The firm must ensure the logging process is working correctly
C. The third line of defence will raise a recommendation if the second line of defence has not performed this review
D. Such analysis can indicate trends and so help control the business

4

63. Which of the following is a partnership between the World Bank Group and United Nations Office on Drugs and Crime (UNODC) to end safe havens for corrupt funds?

    A. Stolen Asset Recovery Initiative (StAR)
    B. Politically exposed person (PEP)
    C. Financial Action Task Force (FATF)
    D. International Monetary Fund (IMF)

64. Which of the following would NOT satisfy the definition of a politically exposed person (PEP)?

    A. Tony Blair (former UK Prime Minister)
    B. Piers Corbyn (brother of Jeremy Corbyn MP)
    C. Lady Hale (Deputy President of the UK Supreme Court)
    D. Air Chief Marshall Sir Stephen Hillier (Chief of the Air Force)

65. Which of the following is key to managing stakeholder risk?

    A. Appoint non-executive directors
    B. Establish a remuneration committee
    C. Reduce the firm's risk appetite
    D. Build relationships at senior levels

66. What is the key objective of corporate governance in banks?

    A. To ensure that a company is well managed for the benefit of shareholders
    B. To ensure that employees are able to work in an ethical workplace
    C. To give clarity to non-executive directors on their roles
    D. To achieve and maintain the confidence and trust of the public

67. Which of the following BEST describes an outsourcing relationship?

    A. Firm A retains the services of Firm B, which assumes regulatory and practical responsibility for completing the tasks
    B. The outsourcing firm performs all the work
    C. The outsourcing firm retains regulatory responsibility for those tasks outsourced
    D. The service provider and outsourcing firm must have equivalent regulatory authorisation

68. Which of the following roles has specific statutory responsibilities?

    A. Group compliance officer
    B. Money laundering reporting officer (MLRO)
    C. Head of IT
    D. All employees of an authorised financial services firm

4

69. In what way should a risk-based approach to combating money laundering produce better results?

A. Firms should think about the underlying issues, rather than adopting a 'tick-box' approach to compliance

B. If the risk is sufficient, a nominated officer must be appointed

C. The risk priority will ensure discussion of money laundering at board meetings

D. It ensures that the firm's risk management function collaborates with the money laundering reporting officer (MLRO)

70. Tax avoidance is best described as which one of the following:

A. Falsely claiming to live in another country to receive payments without paying tax

B. Use of legally permissible methods to reduce the amount of tax owed

C. Intentionally avoiding paying part of all tax liability by illegal means

D. Performing a large number of transactions to disguise the origins of an asset

71. Under the 'three lines of defence' model, which is generally viewed as the third line?

A. Risk management

B. Internal audit

C. The regulator

D. The board

72. Which of the following is NOT an action that an investor could take to protect themselves from becoming a victim of financial crime?

A. Shred sensitive material, such as financial statements, before disposal

B. Keep passwords and personal identification number (PIN) numbers secure

C. Carefully read the terms and conditions of a product

D. Consider whether the investment sounds too good to be true

73. Industry specialised knowledge is a key element of an effective self-regulatory model because:

A. the complexity of markets and products increases

B. the government must levy fines where firms do not abide by the code

C. a standard approach to compliance monitoring activity must be agreed

D. International Organization of Securities Commissions (IOSCO) Principle 4 requires firms to demonstrate their engagement in establishing the framework

(2)

74. Which of the following is NOT an aspect of the compliance role in the development of new business?

A. Performing a risk assessment
B. Determining the scope of regulation
C. Signing off from the operating model
D. Highlighting material changes to existing relationships

75. Which of the following methods would NOT enable a criminal to steal the personal data held by a financial services firm?

A. Theft of computers or data files
B. Social engineering
C. Using logger tools
D. Obtaining a copy of the money laundering reporting officer's (MLRO's) report

76. What concept might be described as 'the level of loss that the firm is willing to accept in its different businesses over a specified time horizon at a given level of confidence'?

A. Stress testing
B. Return on capital employed
C. Profitability coefficient
D. Risk appetite

77. Which of the following describes a key element of a 'dawn raid'?

A. It is performed by regulatory staff in isolation, acting under their statutory powers
B. The team can only interview personnel present at the point the raid began
C. All persons participating in the raid should be named on a warrant
D. IT equipment must not be touched if the data is encrypted

78. Which of the following is a non-Organisation for Economic Co-operation and Development (non-OECD) member country that has adopted the OECD Convention on Combating Bribery of Foreign Public Officials in International Business Transactions?

A. Bulgaria
B. Dominican Republic
C. Lithuania
D. St. Kitts & Nevis

79. Which of the following is NOT an element of the independence of the compliance function?

A. Their responsibilities should not lead to conflicts of interest

B. They should have access to information and personnel

C. Compliance should have a formal status within the firm

D. The group compliance officer or head of compliance should not have responsibility for other functions (such as legal, risk management, or finance)

80. What is the mandate of the United Nations Office on Drugs and Crime (UNODC)?

A. It sets principles for self-regulatory models

B. It publishes lists of politically exposed persons (PEPs)

C. It assists member states in the struggle against illicit drugs, crime, and terrorism

D. It supports corporate governance in developing countries

81. Which of the following is a predicate offence in respect of money laundering?

A. Depositing stolen money in a bank account

B. Performing multiple investment transactions to disguise the audit trail of stolen goods

C. Bribing a public official

D. Tipping off a money launderer

82. The Committee of European Banking Supervisors (CEBS) defines what form of risk as 'the current or prospective risk to earnings and capital arising from changes in the business environment and from adverse business decisions, improper implementation of decisions or lack of responsiveness to changes in the business environment'?

A. Economic risk

B. Political risk

C. Company risk

D. Strategic risk

83. Which of the following is an EU policy goal supported by the Markets in Financial Instruments Directive (MiFID)?

A. The free movement of people

B. Strengthening the euro

C. Extending the range of services that can be 'passported'

D. Ensuring that asset managers are subject to appropriate supervision

(3)

84. Which of the following BEST describes the three stages used to create a model to drive a compliance monitoring programme?

    A. Research, review, repeat
    B. Information gathering, scoring, weighting
    C. Placement, layering, integration
    D. Accuracy, completeness, existence

85. Which of the following is NOT an example of money laundering?

    A. Handling the proceeds of crime
    B. Handling stolen goods
    C. Assisting a known criminal to buy a house
    D. A client of the firm requesting the proceeds of a share sale in cash

86. Which of the following is an example of tax evasion?

    A. Falsely claiming to live outside the UK in order to receive payments without paying tax
    B. Investing using an individual savings account (ISA)
    C. Investing using an offshore trust
    D. Performing a large number of transactions to disguise the origins of an asset

87. Which of the following is an element of compliance independence?

    A. The internal audit function should report to the chief finance officer
    B. The head of compliance has overall responsibility for coordinating the management of the firm's compliance risk
    C. The compliance department should only have restricted access to operational material
    D. The compliance director's budget should increase according to pre-tax profits

88. Which of the following is NOT said to have extraterritorial reach?

    A. UK Bribery Act
    B. Sarbanes-Oxley Act
    C. Foreign Corrupt Practices Act
    D. Independent Commission on Banking

89. Robo-advice is best described as a digital platform that provides:

    A. a tool for financial advisors when assessing risk appetite
    B. automated financial advice with limited human intervention
    C. call centre activities for wealth management advice
    D. tailored financial advice alongside the financial advisor

5

90. Why might an 'orphan structure' offshore trust be appealing to criminals?

A. No checks are required when depositing money

B. Offshore jurisdictions have no suspicious activity reporting controls

C. It enables mortgage fraud through misrepresentation

D. The trust's beneficiary is not identified

91. What variable is commonly combined with 'likelihood' to determine risk for business continuity planning (BCP) purposes?

A. Impact

B. Distance

C. Cost

D. Probability

92. In what areas of the firm should the compliance function be able to exercise oversight?

A. All departments where compliance risk exists

B. Operational processing areas

C. All areas aside from corporate finance (which is subject to financial audit)

D. Corporate services departments, such as legal and human resources

93. In what way does a rules-based approach to regulation put strain on the regulator?

A. It must hold an increased range of public hearings

B. It must find an increased number of firms to penalise for poor behaviour

C. The rules must always provide a reliable distinction between right and wrong

D. More firms must receive individual guidance

94. What mechanism should deliver an independent review of the operational work performed by the firm?

A. Capital adequacy calculation

B. Regulatory returns

C. Compliance monitoring programme

D. Money laundering reporting officer (MLRO) report

95. In respect of the firm's systems and controls for financial crime prevention, which of the following is a responsibility of the firm's directors and senior management?

A. Internal audit must review the controls every two years

B. Ownership of financial crime prevention must be allocated to the chief risk officer or chief compliance officer

C. To understand their personal liability if legal obligations are not met

D. Publish the money laundering reporting officer (MLRO) report for review by all shareholders

(5)

96. The misappropriation of assets is a typical objective of financial misstatement. Which of the following is an example of misappropriation of assets?

   A. Pressure to meet market expectations, minimise tax or inflate earnings to secure bank finance
   B. Embezzling receipts through collections accounts
   C. Effecting payments to fictitious vendors
   D. Opening a custody account in a false name

97. Which ONE of the following statements BEST describes principles-based regulation?

   A. It is based on very detailed statements of what firms and individuals should do in order to comply
   B. Firms and individuals decide how, and to what extent, they must meet the principles
   C. Regulation based on principles was discredited after the financial crisis of 2008
   D. In the event of conflict, rules override principles

98. What ensures an effective compliance function?

   A. The compliance function must be able to accommodate the needs of both management and 'front desk'
   B. Compliance must be able to demonstrate that it has systems and controls in place to accommodate the regulators needs
   C. Compliance must be able to maintain up-to-date records for the board and the regulators
   D. Compliance must be able to advise and assist the relevant persons responsible for carrying out regulated activities to comply with the firm's obligations

99. In the context of money laundering, layering is BEST described as:

   A. introducing money into the financial system
   B. moving money around the financial system
   C. legitimately maintaining the funds in the financial system
   D. taking the funds out of the financial system

100. What is the purpose of setting standards and principles for firms and key individuals?

   A. To provide non-binding guidance
   B. To provide binding guidance
   C. To ensure that firms abide by both standards and regulations
   D. To ensure that the spirit as well as the letter of the regulations are met

(4)

101. The maximum penalty for a breach of the General Data Protection Regulation (GDPR) is the higher of:

A. up to 2% of annual turnover or €50 million
B. up to 4% of annual turnover or €20 million
C. up to 10% of annual turnover or €5 million
D. up to 12% of annual turnover or €15 million

102. Under the Second Payment Services Directive (PSD2), a payment service is defined as a service enabling:

A. cash to be deposited or withdrawn
B. transfers to be made
C. paper transactions
D. Society for Worldwide Interbank Financial Telecommunication (SWIFT) transactions

103. The Office of Foreign Asset Control is part of the:

A. UN Security Council
B. European Central Bank
C. US department of Treasury
D. Financial Action Task Force (FATF)

104. Cyber crime is BEST defined as a crime in which:

A. a computer is the object of the crime
B. the crime is committed using the internet
C. the government is restricting internet access
D. a call centre defrauds the customers

105. The Taskforce on Climate-Related Financial Disclosures has identified recommendations along which of the following four themes?

A. Governance, strategy, risk management, metrics and targets
B. Compliance, operational risk, statistics, profitability
C. Governance, operational risk, compliance, climate returns
D. Board of directors, compliance, governance, climate effort

Answers to Multiple Choice Questions

1. A Chapter 3, Section 1.3.4

The Financial Action Task Force (FATF) sets standards to combat money laundering and terrorist financing.

2. B Chapter 5, Section 1.3

The firm should maintain sound control functions, including an effective compliance function that, among other things, routinely monitors compliance with laws, corporate governance rules, regulations, codes and policies to which the bank is subject; and ensures that deviations are reported to an appropriate level of management and, in case of material deviations, to the board.

3. C Chapter 2, Section 1.3.1

The purpose of the compliance manual is to formally document the standards to be followed by all employees.

4. D Chapter 4, Section 1

Regulators are looking for an ethical culture that embodies the values that underlies the whole regulatory structure, giving proper protection to consumers of financial services. This goes deeper than regulatory awareness, which is taken as a given, or a compliance culture which risks a 'tick-box' mentality. Bonuses may be reduced for poor behaviour but are ultimately revenue-related.

5. C Chapter 1, Section 2.2.3

The three International Organisation of Securities Commissions (IOSCO) objectives of securities regulation are protection of investors, ensuring that markets are fair, efficient, and transparent, and the reduction of systemic risk.

6. D Chapter 5, Section 1.5.1

The principle of matrix management is that an individual may serve two or three managers rather than just one.

7. D Chapter 4, Section 2

Any behaviour that is likely to distort the market is classed as market abuse.

8. C Chapter 5, Section 1.4

The management board is accountable to the supervisory board, elected by shareholders.

9. C Chapter 3, Section 3.4

A nominated officer in practice is usually the money laundering reporting officer (MLRO). The MLRO is responsible for reviewing and reporting cases onwards.

10. C Chapter 1, Section 2.2.4

The European Systemic Risk Board (ESRB) was established on 1 January 2011 with responsibility for the macro prudential oversight of the financial systems within the EU.

11. C Chapter 5, Section 1.9

Principle 4 states: *'In a group structure, the board of the parent company has the overall responsibility for adequate corporate governance across the group and ensuring that there are governance policies and mechanisms appropriate to the structure, business and risks of the group and its entities'*.

12. B Chapter 1, Section 1.3

A principles-based approach to financial regulation is one where principles are set at a high level and it is left to the firm or individual to decide how, and to what extent, they must meet these principles. In contrast a rules-based approach is much more prescriptive, often provides very detailed rules and is much less flexible.

13. B Chapter 5, Section 2.3.2

This is the Bank for International Settlements' (BISs') definition of operational risk.

14. A Chapter 1, Section 1.5.3

Providing investment advice is the only option here that is a Markets in Financial Instruments Directive (MiFID) activity. While deals involving collective investment scheme units are subject to MiFID, the operators of such schemes are exempt.

15. D Chapter 2, Section 1.1.1

It is vital that compliance is a concern of everyone in an organisation and should be viewed as an integral part of the firm's everyday activities. Compliance is not the responsibility of specialist compliance staff alone.

16. C Chapter 2, Section 1.4.1

The compliance function should, on a proactive basis, identify, document and assess the compliance risks associated with the firm's business activities, including the development of new products. If the firm has a new products committee, compliance function staff should be represented on that committee.

17. D Chapter 1, Section 1.4.1

The broad objectives of self-regulation are the same as those identified for government regulation of financial markets in the International Organisation of Securities Commissions (IOSCO) Objectives and Principles of Securities Regulation, namely to preserve market integrity (fair, efficient and transparent markets), to preserve financial integrity (reduce systemic risk) and to protect investors.

18. B Chapter 4, Section 2.4.1

There is no requirement for a firm to have Chinese walls in place; they are just one example of how to manage conflicts of interest.

19. A Chapter 2, Section 2.1.5

It is possible that an individual may be subject to external regulatory sanction, particularly if the breach amounted to serious market abuse.

20. C Chapter 1, Section 1.5.4

Under the Foreign Account Tax Compliance Act (FATCA) and the US-UK intergovernmental agreement, a UK foreign financial institution must report to Her Majesty's Revenue and Customs (HMRC) on its account holders who are US persons or foreign entities with substantial US ownership.

21. B Chapter 5, Section 2.1

Uncertain matters are not measurable; where we can apply data and probability theory to analyse potential outcomes we talk of 'risk'.

22. C Chapter 4, Section 1.1

Regulators are increasingly taking the view that they have an obligation to consider and make judgments in relation to the ethics and culture of the firms they regulate; having a compliance culture is simply not enough. What is needed is an ethical culture in the firm which embodies the values which underlie the whole regulatory structure.

23. A Chapter 4, Section 4.7

Terms and features of a product are pre-sales requirements; the others are all post-sales.

24. C Chapter 3, Section 2.5

To prove corporate governance, a firm should ensure that any review includes the effectiveness of the anti-money laundering (AML) systems and controls and is conducted at least annually.

25. A Chapter 5, Section 3

The board of directors is responsible for overseeing the management of the firm's compliance risk.

26. D Chapter 2, Section 1.6

Only D is true. Continuing professional development (CPD) may include appropriate professional examinations, access to regulatory updates and bulletins and industry updates.

27. B Chapter 5, Section 1.1

The single most widespread and damaging effect of poor corporate governance in the financial sector is loss of confidence by the public in an institution and in the financial sector as a whole. The damage is inflicted contagiously onto well-run institutions too. Inappropriate bonus payments, rogue trader risk, promotion of unsuitable or incompetent managers and bank failure are symptoms of poor corporate governance – these symptoms can act as a bellwether or early warning that something is amiss in an institution.

28. **C** **Chapter 5, Section 2.3.2**

This is the Bank for International Settlements (BIS) definition of operational risk.

29. **A** **Chapter 2, Section 1.1.1**

Irrespective of the organisational structure, an effective compliance function should operate independently and be sufficiently resourced.

30. **D** **Chapter 1, Section 1.2**

The Financial Services and Markets Act (FSMA) sets out UK-permitted business.

31. **A** **Chapter 1, Section 1.4.2**

Riba is a prohibition on the giving and earning of interest.

32. **C** **Chapter 1, Section 1.5.3**

The chief executive officer and chief finance officer are responsible for ensuring that internal controls and procedures can provide accurate financial disclosures.

33. **B** **Chapter 5, Section 1.6**

Promoting the independence of the internal auditor, for example by ensuring that the internal audit function reports to, or has direct access to, the board or the board's audit committee.

34. **C** **Chapter 1, Section 1.5.3**

The maximum punishment for defrauding securities investors is up to 25 years in prison.

35. **D** **Chapter 1, Section 1.5.3**

Markets in financial instruments directive (MiFID) investment services include investment advice, some underwriting activities, and operating a multilateral trading facility (MTF).

36. **A** **Chapter 1, Section 1.5.4**

Under the Foreign Account Tax Compliance Act (FATCA), US taxpayers holding financial assets outside the US will report those assets to the Inland Revenue Service (IRS).

37. **B** **Chapter 1, Section 2.2.4**

The European Securities and Markets Authority (ESMA) has direct supervisory responsibility for credit rating agencies.

38. **A** **Chapter 5, Section 2.2.1**

This risk arises in the wider economy, rather than within the firm's activity or political sphere.

39. D Chapter 1, Section 2.7.2

Capital standards are designed to provide supervisory authorities with time to intervene to accomplish the objective of orderly wind-down.

40. D Chapter 2, Section 1.8.3

The process by which a firm amends its authorisation is known in many countries as a 'variation of permission'.

41. B Chapter 3, Section 1.1

One of the major differences between terrorist financing and other money laundering activities is that, often, only quite small sums of money are required to commit terrorist acts. Terrorist organisations can, however, require significant funding and will employ modern techniques to manage and transfer the funds between jurisdictions, hence the similarities with money laundering. Terrorist groups also tend to have links with other criminal activities.

42. A Chapter 2, Section 2.1.3

The Banking Committee on Banking Supervision (BCBS) states in Principle 5 that the compliance function should be independent.

43. C Chapter 2, Section 3.1.5

Regulatory staff will normally be accompanied by a police officer and have a warrant (in which they are named) to search the premises. This includes any technical staff named on the warrant. The investigators are entitled to use reasonable force to enter the premises but they are obliged to show the warrant.

44. D Chapter 2, Section 3.1.7

Staff may refer concerns about specific transactions or other activity to their line manager to obtain advice or guidance. However, the suspicion should still be logged and referred to the money laundering reporting officer (MLRO).

45. A Chapter 5, Section 1.9

A primary point of the 2006 principles was that compensation policies should be consistent with the bank's long-term objectives.

46. C Chapter 3, Section 1.2

The three stages of a successful money laundering operation are placement, layering, and integration.

47. D Chapter 3, Section 1.2

Layering involves moving money around in order to make it difficult for the authorities to link the placed funds with the ultimate beneficiary of the money.

48. B Chapter 3, Section 1.3.6

A 'Ponzi scheme' is a fraudulent investment operation that pays returns to separate investors, not from any actual profit earned by the organisation, but from their own money or money paid by subsequent investors.

49. D Chapter 3, Section 2.1

The potential that a firm may be unable to deliver on its promises to another is termed 'counterparty risk' (or sometimes 'default risk').

50. D Chapter 3, Section 3.4

The firm must freeze funds if a customer is identified as being on the sanctions list on the government website of suspected terrorists or sanctioned individuals and entities.

51. B Chapter 4, Section 1.3.2

The CISI principles are also known as the Lord George Principles in recognition of the contribution made to standards of integrity by the late Lord George FSI(Hon).

52. B Chapter 4, Section 5.2

The Organisation for Economic Co-operation and Development (OECD) has issued a number of documents, including the Convention on Combating Bribery.

53. A Chapter 5, Section 3

Compliance risk is defined by the Bank for International Settlements (BIS) as 'the risk of legal or regulatory sanctions, material financial loss, or loss to reputation a firm may suffer as a result of its failure to comply with laws, regulations, rules, related self-regulatory organisation standards, and codes of conduct applicable to its banking activities.'

54. D Chapter 4, Section 2.2

Such a document contains specific and price-sensitive information and has not yet been made public.

55. A Chapter 4, Section 2.4.2

Every insider list must contain: the identity of each person having access to inside information; the reason why such person is on the insider list; and the date on which the insider list was created and updated.

56. B Chapter 1, Section 1.4

In the financial services sector, self-regulation (typically involving a unique combination of private interests with government oversight) has delivered an effective and efficient form of regulation for a complex and dynamic environment.

57. B Chapter 5, Section 1.7

Generally, due diligence refers to the care a reasonable person should take before entering into an agreement or a transaction with another party.

58. D Chapter 4, Section 2.4.3

When outsourcing takes place, arrangements must be such that the outsource service provider maintains a record of personal transactions undertaken by relevant persons and provides it to the firm promptly on request.

59. D Chapter 1, Section 1.6.2

For a multilateral trading facility (MTF), prices/charges are public and applied consistently across all members.

60. C Chapter 5, Section 1.4

Dual boards consist of a supervisory board and an executive board, where there is clear separation between the functions of supervision and management.

61. C Chapter 2, Section 1.1.1

It is the Basel Committee on Banking Supervision (BCBS).

62. D Chapter 2, Section 3.1.6

Analysis of breaches will be helpful to indicate trends and provide managers and senior managers with information to help control the business.

63. A Chapter 3, Section 1.3.3

The Stolen Asset Recovery Initiative (StAR) is a partnership between the World Bank Group and the United Nations Office on Drugs and Crime (UNODC) that supports international efforts to end safe havens for corrupt funds.

64. A Chapter 3, Section 2.7.3

A politically exposed person (PEP) is defined as an individual who has, at any time in the preceding year, been entrusted with prominent public functions and an immediate family member or known close associate of such a person. This includes Members of Parliament, members of Supreme Courts, and high-ranking officers in the armed forces.

65. D Chapter 5, Section 2.2.6

The key to managing stakeholder risk is to:

- build relationships at senior levels
- understand their agenda and how it may differ from the firm's
- manage expectations with any new developments.

66. **D** **Chapter 5, Section 1.1**

Effective corporate governance practices are essential to achieving and maintaining public trust and confidence in the banking system, which are critical to the proper functioning of the financial sector and economy as a whole.

67. **C** **Chapter 2, Section 1.8.1**

The outsourcing firm retains regulatory responsibility for the tasks outsourced.

68. **B** **Chapter 2, Section 1.4**

The compliance function may contain specific statutory responsibilities – such as an officer fulfilling the role of money laundering reporting officer (MLRO).

69. **A** **Chapter 3, Section 2.4**

Without the flexibility of a risk-based approach, firms may inadvertently implement a 'tick box' approach to compliance, with the focus on meeting those regulatory needs rather than combatting money laundering or terrorist financing.

70. **B** **Chapter 3, Section 1.3.8**

Tax avoidance is the use of legally permissible methods to reduce the amount of tax owed. This is generally achieved by claiming permissible deductions, credits and allowances

71. **B** **Chapter 2, Section 2.1.3**

The third line of defence is generally delivered by the firm's internal audit function.

72. **C** **Chapter 3, Section 2.6**

Investors can do a number of things to reduce the likelihood of becoming a victim of financial crime: use a shredder to shred statements before disposal; keep passwords and PIN numbers secure; and remember that if an investment sounds too good to be true, it probably is.

73. **A** **Chapter 1, Section 1.4.1**

Industry specialised knowledge is important given the increasing complexity of markets and products.

74. **C** **Chapter 2, Section 2.1.6**

The five aspects of compliance's role in the development of new business are:

- due diligence
- risk assessment
- scope of regulation
- highlighting material changes in the nature of existing relationships
- assessing and reporting potential reputational risks.

75. D Chapter 3, Section 2.2

There are many ways that criminals can target financial firms with a view to stealing data, including the theft of computers and data files, using logger tools to gather data, and social engineering. The MLRO report gives comment on the firm's controls and would not contain personal data.

76. D Chapter 5, Section 2.5.3

This is a description of risk appetite, also expressed as the level of expected loss that the firm will not (or cannot) mitigate.

77. C Chapter 2, Section 3.1.5

Regulatory staff will normally be accompanied by a police officer and have a warrant (in which they are named) to search the premises.

78. A Chapter 1, Section 1.5.4

The 34 Organisation for Economic Co-operation and Development (OECD) member countries and four non-member countries (Argentina, Brazil, Bulgaria, and South Africa) have adopted the Convention.

79. D Chapter 2, Section 2.1.3

The four elements are:

1. compliance should have a formal status within the firm
2. there should be a group compliance officer or head of compliance
3. their responsibilities within the firm should not lead to conflicts of interest
4. they should have access to information and personnel.

80. C Chapter 3, Section 1.3.1

The United Nations Office on Drugs and Crime (UNODC) is mandated to assist member states in their struggle against illicit drugs, crime and terrorism.

81. C Chapter 3, Section 1.3.5

A predicate offence is the underlying criminal offence that gives rise to criminal proceeds, which is then the subject of a money laundering charge.

82. D Chapter 5, Section 2.3.1

This is the Committee of European Banking Supervisors (CEBS) definition of strategic risk.

83. C Chapter 1, Section 1.5.3

The Markets in Financial Instruments Directive (MiFID) supports two key policy goals of the EU, one of which is extending the range of investment services for which a firm can obtain an EU passport.

84. B Chapter 2, Section 1.5

There are essentially three key stages in establishing a programme: information gathering, scoring, and weighting.

85. D Chapter 3, Section 1.1

Requesting share proceeds in cash is unusual, and may even be suspicious, but does not constitute money laundering. A money launderer is more likely to want the proceeds of a sale to remain within the banking system as 'clean money'. Handling proceeds of a crime is clearly money laundering. Handling stolen goods is money laundering as this is also the proceeds of a crime. Assisting a known criminal to buy a house is likely to be with laundered money unless the criminal can prove beyond doubt that the money was obtained legitimately. Ethically, you would not even consider this account.

86. A Chapter 3, Section 1.3.8

Tax evasion is the illegal act of not paying taxes due – such as by claiming tax reliefs to which the individual was not entitled.

87. B Chapter 5, Section 1.8.2

An element of independence is that there should be a group compliance officer or head of compliance with overall responsibility for coordinating the management of the firm's compliance risk.

88. D Chapter 1, Section 1.5

The UK Bribery Act, the Sarbanes-Oxley Act, and the Foreign Corrupt Practices Act are examples of legislation that have an effect beyond national borders.

89. B Chapter 1, Section 1.8.1

Robo-advice or robo-advisors are digital platforms that provide automated financial planning services with little, or no, human intervention. A robo-advisor collects information from customers concerning their financial situation, future goals, and risk appetite by means of online surveys. This information is then used as input into an algorithm to provide investment advice.

90. D Chapter 3, Section 1.3.6

The use of orphan models might be used to disguise the chain of ownership for certain assets, and the identity of the beneficiaries is not stated.

91. A Chapter 5, Section 2.5.1

A simple risk assessment is derived by multiplying the likelihood rating scores with the impact rating scores.

92. A Chapter 2, Section 1.8.5

The compliance function should be able to carry out its responsibilities on its own initiative in all departments of the firm in which compliance risk exists.

93. C Chapter 1, Section 1.3

A rules-based approach must be sufficiently detailed to always provide a reliable distinction between right and wrong.

94. **C** **Chapter 2, Section 1.5**

The purpose of the compliance monitoring programme is to provide an independent review of the operational work performed by the firm.

95. **C** **Chapter 3, Section 2.3**

The directors and senior management of an authorised financial firm are expected to understand the potential personal liability if legal obligations are not met.

96. **B** **Chapter 3, Section 1.3.7**

Embezzling receipts through collections accounts is an example of misappropriation of assets.

97. **B** **Chapter 1, Section 1.3**

The success of a principles-based approach will depend upon firms and individuals making the right choices and doing the right thing because that is what they ought to do. Having strong ethical standards, often set by professional bodies like the CISI, plays a key role.

98. **D** **Chapter 2, Section 1.1**

An effective compliance function needs to be independent of both the front desk and management. At the same time, a compliance culture must be embedded throughout the firm itself and not simply a departmental function. Maintenance of records forms part of the compliance duties, but does not necessarily show that the function is effective.

99. **B** **Chapter 3, Section 1.2**

Layering involves moving money around in order to make it difficult for the authorities to link the placed funds with the ultimate beneficiary of the money. This might involve buying and selling foreign currencies, shares or bonds in rapid succession, investing in collective investment schemes or insurance-based investment products, or moving the money from one country to another.

100. **D** **Chapter 4, Section 1.2**

By setting such standards and principles for firms and key individuals the regulator aims to ensure that the culture and operation of a firm meets the spirit, as well as the letter, of the regulations.

101. **B** **Chapter 1, Section 1.5.1**

Under the General Data Protection Regulation (GDPR), organisations in breach of GDPR can be fined up to 4% of annual global turnover or €20 million (whichever is greater).

102. **A** **Chapter 1, Section 1.5.3**

Payment services are defined as services enabling cash to be deposited in or withdrawn from, for example, a bank account, as well as all the operations required to operate the account. This can include transfers of funds, direct debits, credit transfers and card payments. Paper transactions are not covered by the directive.

103. **C** **Chapter 3, Section 2.7.2**

The Office of Foreign Asset Control (OFAC) is part of the US Department of the Treasury and acts under presidential national emergency powers, as well as the authority granted to it by specific legislation.

104. **A** **Chapter 5, Section 3.2.1**

Cybercrime is defined as a crime in which a computer is the object of the crime (hacking, phishing or spamming) or is used as a tool to commit an offence (child pornography or hate crimes).

105. **A** **Chapter 4, Section 5.1**

The Taskforce on Climate-Related Financial Disclosures has identified recommendations around governance, strategy, risk management, metrics and targets.

Syllabus Learning Map

Syllabus Unit/ Element		Chapter/ Section
Element 1	**The International Regulatory Environment**	**Chapter 1**
1.1	**Models of regulation** On completion, the candidate should:	
1.1.1	Understand the objectives and benefits of regulation	1.1
1.1.2	Know the interaction between law and regulation	1.2
1.1.3	Understand the main differences between rule-based and principles-based approaches to financial regulation	1.3
1.1.4	Understand models of self-regulation	1.4
1.1.5	Understand the regulation of faith- and ethical-based finance and the attendant regulatory implications	1.4
1.1.6	Understand the purpose of the following: • Data Protection, eg, GDPR • Tax Reporting, eg, CRS, FATCA • Banking Reform, eg, ICB, Dodd-Frank • Market Integrity, eg, MiFID II, MiFIR, MAR, EMIR, PSD2, Sarbanes Oxley Act (2002) • Financial Crime, eg, UK Bribery Act (2010), FCPA, AMLD	1.5
1.1.7	Understand how regulation operates in an exchange-traded environment	1.6
1.1.8	Understand the key benefits of regulated market structures • exchanges • trading venues (multilateral trading facilities and organised trading facilities) • systematic internalisers	1.6
1.1.9	Understand how regulation applies to OTC derivatives transactions	1.7
1.1.10	Understand how regulators approach Fintech products • distributed ledger technology (DLT) and cryptoassets • robo-advice	
1.2	**The International Approach to Regulation** On completion, the candidate should:	
1.2.1	Know the jurisdiction of different types of regulator	2.1

Syllabus Unit/ Element		Chapter/ Section

1.2.2	Understand the role of International regulatory organisations:
	• Bank for International Settlements (BIS)
	• Financial Stability Board (FSB)
	• The International Organization of Securities Commissions (IOSCO)
	• European regulatory bodies
	  ◦ The European System of Financial Supervision (ESFS)
	  ◦ European Supervisory Authorities (ESAs)
	  ◦ The European Systemic Risk Board (ESRB)
	  ◦ Securities and Exchange Commission (SEC)
		2.2

1.2.3	Know the role that professional bodies play in relation to regulatory requirements	2.2
1.2.4	Understand how international regulatory organisations aid the implementation of regulation in developing countries	2.2
1.2.5	Know the three objectives of securities regulation as defined by IOSCO	2.2
1.2.6	Understand how regulators implement their regulatory objectives	2.3
1.2.7	Understand different regulatory approaches to supervision • risk-based • rules-based • thematic • relationship-based • principles-based	2.3
1.2.8	Know IOSCO's Principles 1 to 8 relating to the Regulator	2.4
1.2.9	Know regulators' enforcement powers	2.5
1.2.10	Understand what types of activities and investment products are generally required to be regulated	2.6
1.2.11	Understand the requirements regulation places on firms: • minimum entry standards • initial and ongoing capital and other prudential requirements • requirement to establish an internal compliance function • conduct of business	2.7
1.2.12	Understand how regulators facilitate and regulate cross-border business • specific legislation • memoranda of understanding between individual regulators • supervisory colleges • recognition of third countries	2.8
1.2.13	Understand what regulations apply to a firm with international branches and subsidiaries: • contractual agreements between regulators • home/host	2.8

Syllabus Unit/ Element		Chapter/ Section
1.2.14	Understand the challenge of conducting business whilst meeting the regulatory expectations and approach of multiple regulatory bodies • international • domestic	2.8

Element 2	**The Compliance Function**	Chapter 2
2.1	**International Best Practice** On completion, the candidate should:	
2.1.1	Understand the fundamental systems and controls a firm should implement in order to conduct its business in line with international regulatory standards	1.1
2.1.2	Understand BIS Principle 6 and the requirement for adequate resources	1.2
2.1.3	Understand the practical applications of a formalised document of compliance policies and procedures: • compliance manual	1.3
2.1.4	Understand how an effective compliance function can add value to a business	1.4
2.1.5	Know how to produce and implement an effective compliance programme	1.4
2.1.6	Understand how regulatory requirements should be integrated into operating systems, policies and procedures	1.6
2.1.7	Know the difference between regulations and internal policies and procedures	1.7
2.1.8	Understand the potential regulatory implications of business strategies: • outsourcing and oversight • capital requirements • variation of permissions • control framework	1.8
2.1.9	Know how to prepare an effective compliance report for management	1.8.5
2.1.10	Know what basic information compliance officers should have access to	1.8.5
2.2	**The Role of the Compliance Function within a Firm** On completion, the candidate should:	
2.2.1	Understand the responsibilities and accountabilities of management and staff for compliance with regulations	2.1
2.2.2	Understand how to monitor whether a business is in compliance with regulations and internal policies and procedures	2.1.1
2.2.3	Understand the risks associated with non-compliance for firms and the financial services sector	2.1.2

Syllabus Unit/ Element		Chapter/ Section
2.2.4	Understand BIS Principle 5 relating to the independence of the compliance function and senior management accountability	2.1.3
2.2.5	Understand the relationship between compliance and other departments including the 'three lines of defence'	2.1.3
2.2.6	Understand the role compliance has in training and maintaining competence and awareness: • educating staff on compliance issues • acting as a contact point for compliance queries from staff members • providing written guidance to staff	2.1.4
2.2.7	Understand how to monitor an individual's compliance with regulations and internal policies and procedures	2.1.5
2.2.8	Understand the range of potential outcomes to remedy non-compliance by an individual within a firm • training and development activities • internal disciplinary measures • external regulatory sanction • legal avenues	2.1.5
2.2.9	Understand the role compliance plays in new business development: • due diligence • risk assessment • scope of regulation and approval • highlighting material changes in the nature of existing relationships • assessing and reporting potential reputational risks	2.1.6
2.2.10	Understand the purpose of a compliance monitoring programme: • risk-based • reporting • planned	1.5
2.2.11	Understand the key considerations in developing a compliance monitoring programme	1.5
2.2.12	Understand how to conduct an effective compliance monitoring programme: • working papers • minutes of meetings with senior management • management responses • risk mitigation plans	1.5
2.3	**Managing Regulatory Relationships** On completion, the candidate should:	
2.3.1	Understand the relationship between the firm and regulator	3.1

Syllabus Unit/ Element		Chapter/ Section
2.3.2	Understand how an effective regulatory relationship can be of strategic importance to a firm: • advocating opinion • involvement in consultation • drafting regulatory responses • making representations and applications • obtaining effective guidance	3.1
2.3.3	Understand what to do if your firm is the subject of a regulatory or law enforcement visit: • scheduled • unscheduled ('dawn raid')	3.1.5
2.3.4	Understand what to do if a regulatory breach occurs	3.1.6
2.3.5	Know what types of information must be disseminated to whom in the event of a regulatory breach	3.1.6
2.3.6	Know what information may be disseminated and what should remain confidential if financial crime is suspected or detected	3.1.7
2.3.7	Know what types of information should remain confidential in the normal course of business	3.1.7

Element 3	Managing the Risk of Financial Crime	Chapter 3
3.1	**Money Laundering, Terrorist Financing and the Standards Required of Firms** On completion, the candidate should:	
3.1.1	Understand the concept of money laundering and terrorist financing	1.1
3.1.2	Know the stages of the money laundering process: • placement • layering • integration	1.2
3.1.3	Know the role of international agencies in combating money laundering and the financing of terrorism: • United Nations Office on Drugs and Crime (UNODC) • International Monetary Fund (IMF) • World Bank	1.3
3.1.4	Know the role of the Financial Action Task Force (FATF) in combating money laundering and terrorist financing: • jurisdictions with strategic deficiencies • the challenge of jurisdictional differences	1.3

Syllabus Unit/ Element		Chapter/ Section
3.1.5	Understand the role of predicate offences in financial crime: • fraud • embezzlement • bribery • corruption	1.3.5
3.1.6	Understand how financial services firms may be utilised for financial crime: • Ponzi schemes • boiler rooms • money laundering • offshore trusts • beneficial ownership • cyber crime	1.3.6
3.1.7	Understand how a firm or its representatives may collude in the propagation of financial crime: • misstatement of financial circumstances • corporate fraud	1.3.7
3.1.8	Know the concepts of facilitation of tax evasion and tax avoidance	1.3.8
3.1.9	Know the concepts of dual criminality, extradition and mutual legal assistance	1.3.9
3.2	**Practical Implications** On completion, the candidate should:	
3.2.1	Understand how external financial crime issues may impact on a firm: • reputational • systemically • counterparty risk • unreliable market valuations	2
3.2.2	Understand how financial crime may directly impact a firm: • theft of data • theft of assets	2
3.2.3	Understand the responsibilities of directors and senior management in relation to anti-money laundering (AML), combating financial crime (CFC) and anti-corruption (AC) initiatives	2.3
3.2.4	Understand the role of the Money Laundering Reporting Officer (or equivalent) in relation to financial crime	2.5
3.2.5	Understand the implications of using a risk-based approach to identifying money laundering	2.4
3.2.6	Know the measures firms can adopt to inhibit the likelihood of financial crime	2.5

Syllabus Unit/ Element		Chapter/ Section
3.2.7	Know the measures individuals can adopt to inhibit the likelihood of financial crime	2.6
3.2.8	Understand the rationale behind sanctions screening	2.7.1 & 2.7.2
3.2.9	Understand the purpose behind screening individuals: • risk-based approach • politically exposed persons (PEPs)	2.7.3
3.3	**Policies, procedures and controls required of firms** On completion, the candidate should:	
3.3.1	Understand the risks to a firm posed by its clients, products and delivery systems	3
3.3.2	Understand the controls a firm should have in place to minimise its risk to fraud, money laundering and terrorist financing including a training programme	3.2 & 3.3
3.3.3	Know the criteria for an effective suspicious transaction reporting system	3.4

Element 4	Ethics, Integrity and Fairness	Chapter 4
4.1	**Ethics** On completion, the candidate should:	
4.1.1	Understand how ethical principles relate to the financial services sector: • regulatory standards • professional codes of conduct • internal codes of conduct	1
4.1.2	Understand the impact of the following when applying an ethical approach within an organisational or team environment: • self-interest • fiduciary responsibilities • the role of the agent • the role of stakeholders • the role of the group or team	1.5
4.1.3	Understand the advantage of ethical behaviours and decision-making over rule-based compliance	1.5
4.1.4	Understand the importance of senior management leadership in developing and maintaining ethical standards	1.5.6
4.1.5	Know how training programmes can be used to promote ethical decision-making	1.5.7
4.2	**Market Integrity** On completion, the candidate should:	
4.2.1	Understand the benefits of a fair and orderly market	2.1

Syllabus Unit/ Element		Chapter/ Section
4.2.2	Understand the implications of false and misleading statements, behaviours and practices	2.1
4.2.3	Understand what type of information may be deemed to be price-sensitive non-public information	2.2
4.2.4	Understand how individuals may legally possess price-sensitive non-public information	2.3
4.2.5	Know what activities can constitute 'insider dealing'	2.2
4.2.6	Understand how systems and controls can minimise exposure to strategies and behaviours that might impair market integrity: • information barriers/'Chinese walls' • insider lists (including watch and restricted lists) • personal account dealing • gifts and entertainment • conflicts of interest policies • whistleblowing	2.4
4.3	**Fair Conduct** On completion, the candidate should:	
4.3.1	Understand expected compliant standards of behaviour for firms and individuals: • honesty & fair trade • acting in best interest	3
4.3.2	Understand how the concept of fairness impacts on financial services firms	3.3
4.3.3	Understand legal concepts and considerations relevant to financial advice	3.4
4.3.4	Understand the role senior management play in maintaining fair conduct: • senior management responsibilities • management information • corporate culture	3.5
4.4	**Client Vulnerability** On completion, the candidate should:	
4.4.1	Understand how associated but non-transactional activities impact on the firm: • product design and marketing • financial promotions/advertising • client documentation • fair contracts	4

Syllabus Unit/ Element		Chapter/ Section
4.4.2	Understand the factors to consider prior to entering into a transaction: • client/counterparty objectives • client/counterparty risk profile • affordability • suitability of the investment	4.5
4.4.3	Understand factors that should be considered at the point of sale: • clear information • suitability of advice	4.5
4.4.4	Understand post-sale factors that may impact on the firm: • handling complaints in line with international standards • avenues of redress • expected and actual product performance • safeguarding customer money and assets • reporting requirements	4.8
4.5	**Environmental, Social and Governance (ESG)** On completion, the candidate should:	
4.5.1	Know what is meant by environmental, social and governance (ESG)	5
4.5.2	Know the main ESG initiatives: • Task Force on Climate-Related Financial Disclosures (TCFD) • United Nations supported Principals for Responsible Investment (PRI)	5.1
4.5.3	Understand the importance of initiatives on environmental and corporate social responsibility	5.2

Element 5	Governance, Risk Management and Compliance	Chapter 5
5.1	**Corporate Governance** On completion, the candidate should:	
5.1.1	Understand the objectives of corporate governance	1.1
5.1.2	Understand the importance of senior management leadership, accountability and personal responsibility	1.2
5.1.3	Understand the role of the compliance function in implementing and monitoring corporate governance standards	1.3
5.1.4	Know the main corporate governance structures in UK/US and Europe: • unitary board • two-tier structure	1.4

Syllabus Unit/ Element		Chapter/ Section
5.1.5	Understand the impact of business and or management structures on the effective management of the compliance function: • matrix structures • silo structures • maintaining independence	1.5
5.1.6	Understand how auditing contributes to prudential corporate governance, accounting and reporting requirements: • audit committees • internal audit • external auditors	1.6
5.1.7	Know the purpose and key elements of due diligence: • identification • selection • fitness & propriety	1.7
5.1.8	Understand how an effective training programme can contribute to good corporate governance	1.8
5.1.9	Understand the factors behind the formulation of the BIS Principles for enhancing corporate governance	1.9
5.1.10	Know the BIS Principles for enhancing corporate governance	1.9
5.2	**Key Risk Types, their Application and Impact on the Compliance Function** On completion, the candidate should:	
5.2.1	Understand the difference between risk and uncertainty	2.1
5.2.2	Know the key external sources of business risk and their potential impact	2.2
5.2.3	Know the key internal sources of business risk and their potential impact	2.3
5.2.4	Know the components and practical application of an effective risk management process	2.4
5.2.5	Understand how the impact of risks on a firm's business activities are assessed and managed including operational resilience	2.5
5.2.6	Understand the key aims of the risk management function, the risk committee and their relationship with the compliance department	2.5.5
5.2.7	Know the BIS definition of 'compliance risk'	3
5.2.8	Know who BIS deem responsible for the management of compliance risk	3

Syllabus Unit/ Element		Chapter/ Section
5.2.9	Know what measures BIS state should be undertaken to manage compliance risk: • formalised document establishing the compliance function • board approval • annual review	3
5.2.10	Understand how technology can be utilised to enhance compliance risk assessment	3.1
5.2.11	Understand how technological changes impact regulatory risk: • cyber crime • Fintech • Regtech • cloud data hosting	3.2

Examination Specification

Each examination paper is constructed from a specification that determines the weightings that will be given to each element. The specification is given below.

It is important to note that the numbers quoted may vary slightly from examination to examination as there is some flexibility to ensure that each examination has a consistent level of difficulty. However, the number of questions tested in each element should not change by more than plus or minus 2.

Element number	Element	Questions
1	The International Regulatory Environment	20
2	The Compliance Function	24
3	Managing the Risk of Financial Crime	20
4	Ethics, Integrity and Fairness	19
5	Governance, Risk Management and Compliance	17
Total		100

Assessment Structure

A two-hour examination of 100 multiple choice questions.

Candidates sitting the exam by Computer Based Testing will have, in addition, up to 10% of additional questions as trial questions that will not be separately identified and do not contribute to the result. Candidates will be given proportionately more time to complete the test.

CISI Associate (ACSI) Membership can work for you...

Studying for a CISI qualification is hard work and we're sure you're putting in plenty of hours, but don't lose sight of your goal!

This is just the first step in your career; there is much more to achieve!

The securities and investments sector attracts ambitious and driven individuals. You're probably one yourself and that's great, but on the other hand you're almost certainly surrounded by lots of other people with similar ambitions.

So how can you stay one step ahead during these uncertain times?

Entry Criteria:
Pass in either:

- Investment Operations Certificate (IOC), IFQ, ICWIM, Capital Markets in, eg, Securities, Derivatives, Advanced Certificates; or
- one CISI Diploma/Masters in Wealth Management paper

Joining Fee: £25 or free if applying via prefilled application form **Annual Subscription (pro rata):** £125

Using your new CISI qualification* to become an Associate (ACSI) member of the Chartered Institute for Securities & Investment could well be the next important career move you make this year, and help you maintain your competence.

Join our global network of over 40,000 financial services professionals and start enjoying both the professional and personal benefits that CISI membership offers. Once you become a member you can use the prestigious ACSI designation after your name and even work towards becoming personally chartered.

* ie, Investment Operations Certificate (IOC), IFQ, ICWIM, Capital Markets

Benefits in Summary...

- Use of the CISI CPD Scheme
- Unlimited free CPD seminars, webcasts, podcasts and online training tools
- Highly recognised designatory letters
- Unlimited free attendance at CISI Professional Forums
- CISI publications including *The Review* and *Change – The Regulatory Update*
- 20% discount on all CISI conferences and training courses
- Invitation to the CISI Annual Lecture
- Select benefits – our exclusive personal benefits portfolio

The ACSI designation will provide you with access to a range of member benefits, including Professional Refresher where there are currently over 100 modules available on subjects including Anti-Money Laundering, Information Security & Data Protection, Integrity & Ethics, and the UK Bribery Act. CISI TV is also available to members, allowing you to catch up on the latest CISI events, whilst earning valuable CPD.

Plus many other networking opportunities which could be invaluable for your career.

Revision Express

You've bought the workbook... now test your knowledge before your exam.

Revision Express is an engaging online study tool to be used in conjunction with most CISI workbooks.

Key Features of Revision Express:

- Questions throughout to reaffirm understanding of the subject
- Special end-of-module practice exam to reflect as closely as possible the standard you will experience in your exam (please note, however, they are not the CISI exam questions themselves)
- Extensive glossary of terms
- Allows you to study whenever you like, and on any device

IMPORTANT: The questions contained in Revision Express products are designed as aids to revision, and should not be seen in any way as mock exams.

Price per Revision Express module: £35
Price when purchased with the corresponding CISI workbook: £108 (normal price: £119)

To purchase Revision Express:

call our Customer Support Centre on:
+44 20 7645 0777

or visit the CISI's online bookshop at:
cisi.org/bookshop

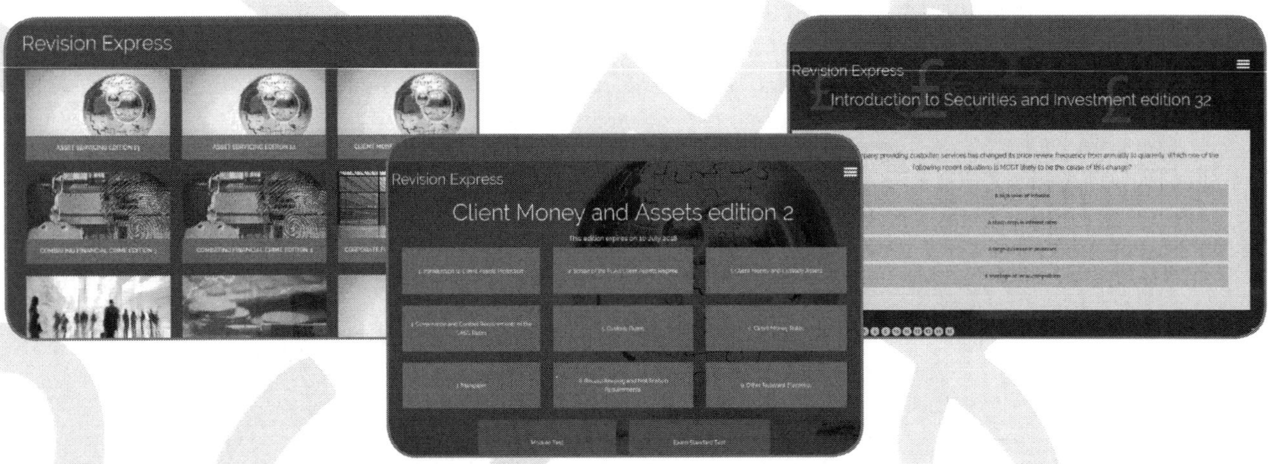

For more information on our elearning products, contact our Customer Support Centre on +44 20 7645 0777, or visit our website at cisi.org/elearning

Professional Refresher

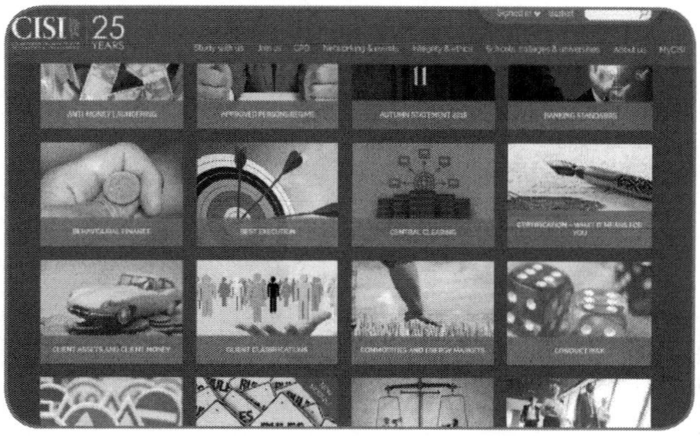

Self-testing elearning modules to refresh your knowledge, meet regulatory and firm requirements, and earn CPD.

Professional Refresher is a training solution to help you remain up-to-date with industry developments, maintain regulatory compliance and demonstrate continuing learning.

This popular online learning tool allows self-administered refresher testing on a variety of topics, including the latest regulatory changes.

There are over 120 modules available which address UK and international issues. Modules are reviewed by practitioners frequently and new ones are added to the suite on a regular basis.

Benefits to firms:

- Learning and testing can form part of business T&C programme
- Learning and testing kept up-to-date and accurate by the CISI
- Relevant and useful – devised by industry practitioners
- Access to individual results available as part of management overview facility, 'Super User'
- Records of staff training can be produced for internal use and external audits
- Cost-effective – no additional charge for CISI members
- Available for non-members to purchase

Benefits to individuals:

- Comprehensive selection of topics across sectors
- Modules are regularly refreshed and updated by industry experts
- New modules added regularly
- Free for members
- Successfully passed modules are recorded in your CPD log as active learning
- Counts as structured learning for RDR purposes
- On completion of a module, a certificate can be printed out for your own records

The full suite of Professional Refresher modules is free to CISI members, or £250 for non-members. Modules are also available individually. To view a full list of Professional Refresher modules visit:

cisi.org/refresher

If you or your firm would like to find out more, contact our Client Relationship Management team:

+ 44 20 7645 0670
crm@cisi.org

For more information on our elearning products, contact our Customer Support Centre on +44 20 7645 0777, or visit our website at cisi.org/refresher

Feedback to the CISI

Have you found this workbook to be a valuable aid to your studies? We would like your views, so please email us at learningresources@cisi.org with any thoughts, ideas or comments.

Accredited Training Partners

Support for exam students studying for the Chartered Institute for Securities & Investment (CISI) qualifications is provided by several Accredited Training Partners (ATPs), including Fitch Learning and BPP. The CISI's ATPs offer a range of face-to-face training courses, distance learning programmes, their own learning resources and study packs which have been accredited by the CISI. The CISI works in close collaboration with its ATPs to ensure they are kept informed of changes to CISI exams so they can build them into their own courses and study packs.

CISI Workbook Specialists Wanted

Workbook Authors

Experienced freelance authors with finance experience, and who have published work in their area of specialism, are sought. Responsibilities include:

- Updating workbooks in line with new syllabuses and any industry developments
- Ensuring that the syllabus is fully covered

Workbook Reviewers

Individuals with a high-level knowledge of the subject area are sought. Responsibilities include:

- Highlighting any inconsistencies against the syllabus
- Assessing the author's interpretation of the workbook

Workbook Technical Reviewers

Technical reviewers to provide a detailed review of the workbook and bring the review comments to the panel. Responsibilities include:

- Cross-checking the workbook against the syllabus
- Ensuring sufficient coverage of each learning objective

Workbook Proofreaders

Proofreaders are needed to proof workbooks both grammatically and also in terms of the format and layout. Responsibilities include:

- Checking for spelling and grammar mistakes
- Checking for formatting inconsistencies

If you are interested in becoming a CISI external specialist call:

+44 20 7645 0609

or email:

externalspecialists@cisi.org

For bookings, orders, membership and general enquiries please contact our Customer Support Centre on +44 20 7645 0777, or visit our website at cisi.org

CISI
CHARTERED INSTITUTE FOR SECURITIES & INVESTMENT
Well done for finishing your studies...
But what's next?
Book your CISI exam!
Our exams can be sat at a test centre near you or via remote invigilation from your home or a meeting room.
To find your nearest test centre venue, visit cisi.org/cbt
To learn more about remote invigilation, visit cisi.org/ri
To book your exam, visit cisi.org/exam-booker or contact our Customer Support Centre on +44 20 7645 0777